# Instant
# HTML

**Steve Wright**

**Wrox Press Ltd.®**

# Instant HTML

© 1996 Wrox Press

Published by Wrox Press Ltd. 30 Lincoln Road, Olton,
Birmingham, B27 6PA.

Printed in Canada
Library of Congress Catalog no. 96-61408

ISBN 1-861000-76-6

## *Trademark Acknowledgements*

Wrox has endeavored to provide trademark information about all the companies and products mentioned in this book by the appropriate use of capitals. However, Wrox cannot guarantee the accuracy of this information.

## *Credits*

**Author**
Steve Wright

**Additional Material**
Rick Stones
Robert Barker

**Editors**
Gina Mance
Chris Ullman
Martin Anderson

**Technical Reviewers**
Rick Stones
Jack Stefani
Kevin Roche

**Design/Layout**
Neil Gallagher
Andrew Guillaume

**Proof Reader**
Pam Brand

**Index**
Simon Gilks
Dominic Shakeshaft

**Cover Design**
Third Wave

For more information on Third Wave, contact Ross Alderson on 44-121 236 6616

# About the Author

Steve Wright is proprietor of Business Machine Services, a supplier of office machines specializing in photocopiers and facsimiles. As well as office machines, he and his company also develop leading edge web sites for local as well as national and international companies.

Steve can be contacted by email on **steve@stevewri.demon.co.uk**

# Thank You

It seems that every book has a 'Thank You' section in it somewhere, and this one is no exception. It isn't until you sit down and start writing that you realize what a mammoth task you've undertaken. The next realization is that you're going to need a lot of help and support!

Many people have contributed either directly, or indirectly, in the writing of this book. Some offered advice, opinions, and ideas. Others offered enthusiasm, inspiration, and a sympathetic ear when things weren't going to plan. Still more managed to unglue my fingers from the keyboard when they knew I needed to 'take a break' before I disappeared up my own monitor.

Firstly, I'd like to thank Wrox Press, the publishers. Particularly Gina Mance who was brave enough to let me attempt this in the first place! Secondly, the people behind the scenes for making it look like I know what I'm writing about, as well as how to spell and punctuate.

Also, everyone who participates in the Usenet newsgroups devoted to the Web. A lot of help and support was freely given by this important resource.

Thanks also to my friends and family including (in no particular order, honest):

Bear, Dave, Melv, Alan, Heather, Becky, Mel, and the rest of the crew at the Lord Nelson.

Finally, a special thank you to Shirley Cartney, who will always be a constant reminder to me that there is more to life than computers!

Steve Wright

# Table of Contents

## Introduction                                                                1

How the World Wide Web Works                                                    2
  Some Terminology                                                    3
    An Introduction to SGML and the HTML DTD                4
    SGML                                                     4
    DTD                                                      5
  HTML Standards and Specifications                                   5
What You Need to Use this Book                                                  6

## Chapter 1: Creating an HTML Document                                        7

The Different Components of HTML                                                7
  Tags                                                               7
    Nesting Tags                                            9
  Attributes                                                         9
Creating an HTML Document                                                     10
  Creating the Skeleton of the Document                             11
    <!DOCTYPE>                                            11
    <HTML>                                                12
    <HEAD>                                                12
    <TITLE>                                               13
    <BASE>                                                13
    <ISINDEX>                                             13
    <LINK>                                                14
    <STYLE>                                               15
    <SCRIPT>                                              15
    <META>                                                15
    Using <META>                                          16

About Ratings 17
The Body Section 18
    <BODY> 18
    Colors 20
    An Example 21
Adding Comments 23
Revision Numbers 23
Universal Attributes 24
  CLASS 24
  ID 24
Summary 25

# Chgapter 2: Formatting Text    27

Text Layout 27
  Headings 27
  Breaking up Text 28
    Paragraphs 29
    Line Breaks 29
  Lists 30
    Unordered Lists 31
    Using <UL> 32
    Ordered Lists 33
    Definition Lists 34
  Horizontal Rules 36
    Using Horizontal Rules 38
Text Emphasis and Style 39
  Fonts 39
    <FONT> 39
    <BASEFONT> 41
  Using Physical and Logical Style Tags 43
    Physical Tags 44
    Logical Tags 45
    <MARQUEE> 46
Summary 49

# Chapter 3: Graphics    51

Images 51
    <IMG> 51
Formats 55

GIF Image Format                                           55
JPEG Image Format                                          57
PNG Format                                                 57
   The Single Pixel GIF Trick              57
Audio                                                      60
  Using Plug-ins                                 60
  Using the Anchor Tag                           61
  <BGSOUND>                                      61
Summary                                                    62

# Chapter 4: Linking to Other Files    63

Hypertext Links                                            63
  Creating Hypertext Links                       63
    URLs                               63
    <A> - The Anchor Tag               64
  Using Text as a Hyperlink                      67
  Using an Image as a Hyperlink                  68
  Using the NAME Attribute                       69
Imagemaps                                                  73
  Server-side Imagemaps                          73
    Creating a Server-side Imagemap    74
  Client-side Imagemaps                          77
    Creating a Client-side Imagemap    77
    <MAP>                              78
    <AREA>                             78
    A Simple Client Map                79
Summary                                                    80

# Chapter 5: Tables    81

Creating a Table                                           81
  A Basic Table                                  81
  More Complex Tables                            83
    <TABLE>                            83
    IE Extensions to <TABLE>           86
    <TR>                               87
    Microsoft Extensions to <TR>       88
    <TD>                               89
    Microsoft Extensions to <TD>       90
  Adding Row and Column Headings                 91
  Adding a Caption                               91

| | |
|---|---|
| Using Tables | 91 |
| Overriding Settings | 93 |
| <COL> | 93 |
| <COLGROUP> | 94 |
| Using Column Groups | 94 |
| Table Head, Foot, and Body Elements. | 95 |
| Other Elements Inside Tables | 96 |
| Summary | 100 |

# Chapter 6: Frames — 101

| | |
|---|---|
| Creating Frames | 101 |
| An Example Frame | 102 |
| Examining the Code | 102 |
| <NOFRAMES> | 103 |
| Frameset and Frame Attributes | 104 |
| <FRAMESET> | 105 |
| <FRAME> | 106 |
| Targets for Hyperlinks | 109 |
| Named Frames | 109 |
| Frame Layout | 112 |
| Nested Frames | 113 |
| Floating Frames using <IFRAME> | 115 |
| Summary | 118 |

# Chapter 7: Forms — 119

| | |
|---|---|
| Creating a Form | 119 |
| <FORM> | 120 |
| Name/Value Pairs | 121 |
| An Example Form | 121 |
| Entering Data | 124 |
| <INPUT> | 124 |
| <TEXTAREA> | 127 |
| <SELECT> | 128 |
| Examples | 129 |
| Testing Your Forms | 134 |
| Processing Forms | 135 |
| The Common Gateway Interface | 135 |
| Summary | 136 |

# Chapter 8: Animation and Other Media <OBJECTS>    137

Getting Animated!                                              137
  Animated GIF Images                                          137
  Creating a Simple GIF Animation                              138
    Incorporating an Animated GIF into HTML                    139
Vendor-specific Tags for Other Media                           139
  Netscape's <EMBED> Tag                                       139
    Attributes of the Netscape <EMBED> Tag                     140
    Using Netscape's <EMBED>                                   141
  Microsoft's <EMBED> Tag                                      141
    Attributes of the Microsoft <EMBED> Tag                    141
    Using Microsoft's <EMBED>                                  142
  Netscape's LOWSRC Attribute                                  143
  Microsoft's DYNSRC Attribute                                 143
    Controlling the DYNSRC Attribute                           144
    The DYNSRC Attribute in Action                             145
Other Ways of Incorporating Animation                          146
  Client Pull                                                  146
  Server Push                                                  147
<OBJECT >                                                      148
    The <OBJECT> Tag's Attributes                              149
    An Introduction to ActiveX Controls                        153
    Showing an ActiveX Movie                                   154
Java Animation and Graphics Applets                            155
  <APPLET>                                                     155
    The <APPLET> Tag's Attributes                              155
    Incorporating the <APPLET> Tag into HTML                   157
    Using the Animator Applet                                  157
    Using the Animator Applet                                  158
Summary                                                        159

# Chapter 9: Scripting    161

<SCRIPT>                                                       161
    <SCRIPT> Tag Attributes                                    162
    IE Extensions for <SCRIPT>                                 163
JavaScript                                                     164
  Alert Example                                                164
  SRC Example                                                  166

Form Validation Example 167

VBScript 169

Dialog Box Example 169

Control of Flow Example 171

Forms Validation Example 173

Other Concerns 175

Compatibility 175

Security 175

Additional Sources of Information 175

Summary 176

# Chapter 10: Style Sheets 177

Using Style Sheets 177

The Advantages of Using Style Sheets 178

An Example 178

Implementing Style Sheets 180

Using <LINK> 180

Using <STYLE> 180

Using @import 181

Using STYLE with Individual Tags 182

Creating Style Sheets 182

Syntax 182

Inheritance 183

Contextual Selectors 184

Classes 184

Pseudo-classes and Pseudo-elements 185

Cascading Style Sheets 186

CSS1 Properties 188

Font Properties 188

Color and Background Properties 190

Text Properties 191

Box Properties 193

Classification Properties 195

Units of Measurement 197

Summary 198

## Appendix A: Alphabetical List of Tags 199

## Appendix B: Commonly Used Tags by Category 227

| | |
|---|---|
| Document Structure | 227 |
| Titles and Headings | 228 |
| Paragraphs and Lines | 228 |
| Text Styles | 228 |
| Lists | 229 |
| Tables | 230 |
| Links | 230 |
| Graphics and Multimedia | 231 |
| Forms | 231 |

## Appendix C: Special Characters 233

## Appendix D: Color Names 237

## Appendix E: VBScript Reference 239

| | |
|---|---|
| Array Handling | 239 |
| Assignments | 240 |
| Constants | 240 |
| Control Flow | 240 |
| Functions | 242 |
| Variable Declarations | 243 |
| Error Handling | 243 |
| Input/Output | 244 |
| MsgBox | 244 |
| InputBox | 246 |
| Procedures | 247 |
| Other Keywords | 247 |
| Visual Basic Run-time Error Codes | 247 |

## Appendix F: JavaScript Reference     **251**

General Information    251
Values    252
Variables    252
Arrays    253
Assignment Operators    253
Equality Operators    254
Other Operators    254
Comments    255
Control Flow    255
   Conditional Statements    255
   Loop Statements    256
Input/Output    257
   Alert    257
   Confirm    258
   Prompt    258
   JavaScript Events    259
Built-in Objects    259
   Date Object    259
   Math Object    261
   Navigator Object    261
   String object    262
   Window Object    263
Other Objects    264
Reserved Words    265
Additional Information    265

## Index     **267**

# Introduction

HTML stands for **Hyper Text Markup Language** and is the publishing language of the World Wide Web.

The concept of the World Wide Web, or simply the Web, was born in 1983 at the CERN laboratory in Geneva, when Tim Berners-Lee was looking for a way of disseminating information in a friendly, but platform-independent, manner. The scheme he devised was placed in the public domain in 1992, and the World Wide Web was born.

Most of the activity in developing the many standards and technologies that go into making the World Wide Web function have now been transferred from CERN to the World Wide Web Consortium (W3C). Their web site at **http://www.w3.org/** is always a good starting place for discovering more about the Web. Here is the home page of the World Wide Web Consortium:

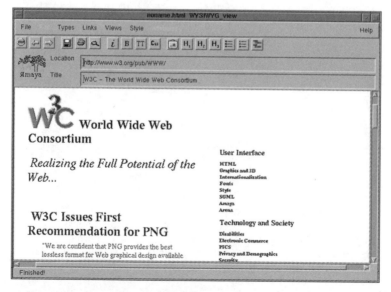

# How the World Wide Web Works

In this book, we don't intend to spend a lot of time examining how the World Wide Web works, but it is important to understand the basics of the technology that make it possible.

There are three parts to this technology:

- The server that holds the information
- The client that is viewing the information
- The protocol that connects the two

Documents, including text, images, sounds, and other types of information are held on a server computer, viewed on a client computer, and transferred between the two using the HTTP (Hyper Text Transfer Protocol).

When a client (the computer or workstation being used by the person that wishes to view the document) makes a request to the server, it uses the HTTP protocol across a network to request the information—in the form of a URL—from the server. The server processes the request and, again, uses HTTP to transfer the information back to the client. As well as transferring the actual document, the server must tell the client the type of document being returned. This is usually defined as a MIME type. The client must then process the information before it presents it to the human viewer.

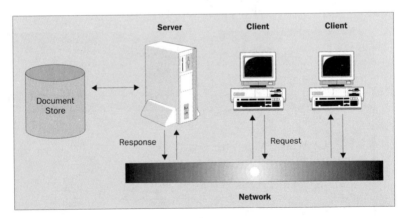

In this simplified diagram, we have shown the documents as fixed; however, in some cases, they can be dynamic documents, created 'on the fly' by the server as the client requests them. Perhaps the simplest example of a dynamic document is the ubiquitous 'hit counter' that appears on many pages.

# Some Terminology

Before we go any further, it's perhaps a good idea to get some terminology defined.

**RFC** (Request For Comments)—this is something of a misnomer, as almost all of the protocols and conventions that make the Internet function are defined in documents called RFCs. For example, RFC1725 defines POP3, the protocol often used for retrieving Internet mail, and HTML 2.0 can be found in RFC1866. All RFC documents can be found on the Internet.

**URL** (Uniform Resource Locator)—this is a way of specifying a resource. It consists of a protocol name, a colon (**:**), two forward slash characters (**//**), a machine name, and a path to a resource (using **/** as a separator). For example, the Wrox Press home page can be found at **http://www.wrox.com/**. URLs are the way that all resources are specified on the web. Note that URLs can specify more than just web pages. For example, to retrieve RFC1866 using FTP, we could specify **ftp://ds.internic.net/rfc/rfc1866.txt**. URLs are often embedded inside web pages, to provide links to other pages, as we shall see later.

**SGML** (Standard Generalized Markup Language)—a standard for defining markup languages. More about this in a moment.

**DTD** (Document Type Definition)—a set of rules on how to apply SGML to a particular markup language. Again, more in a moment.

**HTML** (Hyper Text Markup Language)—the subject of this book!

**MIME** (Multimedia Internet Mail Extensions)—this was originally intended as a way of embedding complex binary documents in mail messages, but is now used much more widely. When a server serves web information to a client browser, it first tells the client the type of information it is going to send using a MIME type and a subtype. The browser can then decide how it wishes to handle that document type. It may choose to process it internally, or invoke an external program to handle the information. MIME types consist of a main type and subtype. For example, plain text is 'text/plain', but 'image/mpeg' specifies an image stored in mpeg format.

**HTTP** (Hyper Text Transfer Protocol)—this is the protocol used to transfer information between the client and server computer. Although vital for the operation of the Web, it is not generally necessary to know any details of HTPP to provide information across the Web, so we will not consider it further here.

Now we have some terminology defined, we can look in more detail at how HTML is defined.

# An Introduction to SGML and the HTML DTD

The original documents that were used in the World Wide Web were in a new format called HTML—Hyper Text Markup Language. Perhaps the two most important features of this were that a basic HTML document was simple to create, and that HTML was almost totally platform and viewer independent.

HTML is a markup language that tells the client, in general terms, how the information should be presented. For example, to define a heading in an HTML document, you might write:

```
<H2>This is a heading</H2>
```

This tells the client that the text 'This is a heading' should be displayed as a level 2 heading, but leaves it up to the client to decide the most appropriate way of displaying it. As HTML develops, this original scheme is being diluted, and more and more specific information can be defined to the client, such as fonts, point size, and colors.

> An interesting side-effect of this way of defining documents is that it allows people with visual disabilities to use special browsers that render the document in a form which they are better able to comprehend.

The first version of HTML was a fairly loosely-defined standard. Not until version 2 of HTML was it more rigorously defined in terms of another standard, known as SGML.

## SGML

SGML is the abbreviation for 'Standard Generalized Markup Language'. This language, or meta-language as it should be called, was defined by International Standards in 1986 as ISO 8879:1986.

The purpose of SGML is very simple. At the time it was developed, there were several 'markup languages', none of which were particularly portable between platforms or even software packages. The purpose of SGML is to allow a formal definition of markup languages that can then be used to give complete flexibility and portability of information display between applications and platforms.

It is tempting for the newcomer to SGML to view it as a markup language in its own right—defining a set of tags, etc., and providing meanings for those tags. This is not the case. What SGML *does* do is describe the relation of components within a document. As such, SGML is not a competitor with the likes of TeX or Postscript which define such things as layout, but a way of describing what the document 'is' rather than how it should be 'rendered'.

A markup language consists of a set of conventions that can be used together to provide a way to encode text. A markup language must also specify what markup is allowed, what markup is required and how the markup is distinguished from the text of the document. SGML does all this—what it doesn't do is specify what the markups are, or what they mean.

## DTD

DTD stands for Document Type Definition. Its purpose is to define the legal productions of a particular markup language. A simple DTD would do nothing more than, say, define a set of tags that can be used by a particular markup language.

The HTML 3.2 standard is a formally defined SGML DTD. In other words, the definition of HTML 3.2 is itself specified using the SGML meta-language. This allows HTML specifications to be rigorously defined.

To fully define HTML 3.2, two different specifications are required. The first is the relatively small SGML definition that defines general features, such as the character set and size limits. The main information is contained in the DTD, which defines the detail, such as the tags and attributes, which we will learn more about later.

The HTML 3.2 DTD can be found at the following address:

```
http://www.w3.org/pub/WWW/TR/WD-html32
```

# HTML Standards and Specifications

The latest standard is HTML 3.2. This has led to some confusion over what is now standard and what isn't. HTML 3.0 was never an official standard, it was always only a working draft. The Web developed so rapidly, with vendors implementing proprietary tags all the time, that the draft HTML 3.0 specification was left looking dated before it could even be issued. The consortium decided, probably wisely, that rather than continue work on HTML 3.0, they would move immediately to HTML 3.2. The HTML 3.2 standard incorporates all of HTML 2.0 (with some very minor changes) plus many of the proposals that were in the HTML 3.0 draft, and additional features such as tables and applets.

Hopefully, HTML 3.2 will become a standard that many information providers on the Web will adhere to, allowing the viewing of platform-independent information from across the planet on many different varieties of computer.

# What You Need to Use this Book

To create an HTML document, all you need is a text editor that is capable of saving files in ASCII format, and a browser such as Netscape's Navigator or Microsoft's Internet Explorer. The latest version of both these browsers can be downloaded to your system via the Internet from the following sites:

 Netscape Navigator

`http://home.netscape.com/comprod/mirror/`
`index.html`

 Internet Explorer

`http://www.microsoft.com/ie/ie.htm`

The examples and screenshots in this book were all taken from a PC running Windows 95 and using Windows Notepad as the text editor. However, HTML is a platform-independent language, so you can just as easily use a Macintosh or other operating system with the same results.

The past several months have seen many HTML editors come onto the market. Some of these do a very good job of adding tags, in-line images, etc., and presenting the page in a WYSIWYG format. By all means, try these editors out, they certainly make the sometimes laborious task of adding tags much easier and quicker. For the purposes of this book, however, it is suggested that you stay with a plain text editor as there are some tricks and techniques that even the most powerful HTML editor can't handle.

So, let's get started....

# Creating an HTML Document

HTML is incredibly easy to learn, and if you have done any surfing at all, you will have seen just how much can be achieved with this simple language. In this chapter, we will look at what you need to create the basis of an HTML document.

## The Different Components of HTML

HTML is a markup language and so consists of a set of predefined tags that are typed along with the text. These tags tell the browser whether the text is to be a paragraph, a heading, an image, an address, etc. At the same time, the tags also allow a certain amount of formatting information to be included, such as alignment of images with respect to text.

## Tags

There are two basic parts to any web page: the **head** and the **body**. Both parts use **tags** to achieve their respective purposes. Tags are normally typed in capitals, but browsers are case-insensitive—you can use lowercase or mixed case if you prefer. I recommend you use capitals, though, since this makes the tags stand out and therefore makes your life a lot easier when you come to alter the code in several months time.

There are two types of tag: **start tags** and **end tags**. Both are placed inside angled brackets, e.g. **<H1>**. End tags are the same as start tags, except that they are preceded by a forward slash, e.g. **</H1>**. They are used to indicate where the special effect started by the start tag should be 'turned off'.

For example, if you type the following code into a text editor:

```
<HTML>
<HEAD>
<TITLE>Instant HTML</TITLE>
</HEAD>

<BODY>
<H1>An Introduction to Tags</H1>
In HTML tags are used to add special effects to plain text.
</BODY>
</HTML>
```

and save it as a file with an **htm** extension (or **html** if your system isn't constrained by the 8.3 naming convention), and then view it in a browser via the File, Open menu options, you will see:

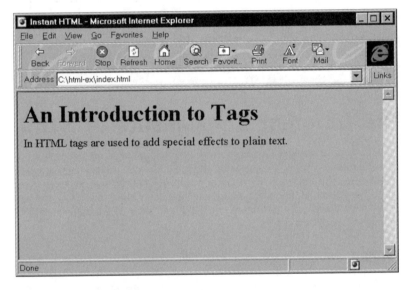

Most tags have a start and end tag, but not all. If you think of the end tag as 'switching off' the start tag, it will seem logical. For example, the **<P>** tag (new paragraph) does not require a corresponding end tag, although you can use one if you wish. Other tags simply don't have an end tag at all, for example, the **<IMG>** tag (insert an image). Tags with both start and end versions are often referred to as 'enclosures'.

> Each structural part of the document is referred to as an element. So, the following are all examples of elements: paragraphs, tables, forms, images, and lists.

## Nesting Tags

Most tags can be nested. In other words, you can have tags inside other tags. The order of nesting is important. For instance, this is legal:

```
<B>This word is <I>emphasized</I></B>
```

but this isn't:

```
<B>This word is <I>emphasized</B></I>
```

Although the above line of code is illegal, most browsers will still render the text as you would expect—it just makes your code harder to understand!

# Attributes

**Attributes** allow you to extend the capabilities of tags. You can use attributes to control fonts, border spacing, text alignment, etc. For example, the **<H1>** tag, which prints text on a separate line and in a larger font (as a level 1 heading), has an **ALIGN** attribute as defined by HTML 3.2, which affects the positioning of the heading on the screen.

So, as you might expect,

```
<H1 ALIGN=CENTER>An Introduction to Tags</H1>
In HTML tags are used to add special effects to plain text.
```

will result in:

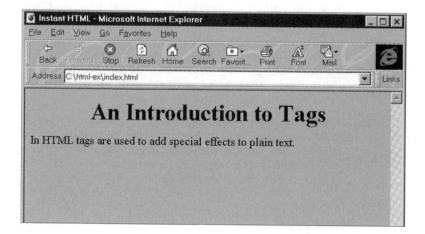

The syntax for attributes is as follows:

```
<TAGNAME ATTRIBUTE=VALUE>
```

> Note that if the **VALUE** contains anything other than letters, numbers, hyphens, or periods, it must be contained within quotes.

# Creating an HTML Document

When writing HTML, the first thing you need to understand is that it is almost impossible to format a page so that it will look exactly the same, no matter who is looking at it. Indeed, the original idea of HTML was specifically based on not telling the client exactly how the page should look.

There are several good reasons for this:

- Different people use different systems and even different operating systems. You can't guarantee that the font you have chosen for the page is present on another computer, nor can you guarantee the resolution—your system may be set to a resolution of 800 x 600, and the page may be viewed by someone with a computer set to 640 x 480, etc.

- The user of the browser has complete control over aspects such as default font type, link colors, whether or not to display inline images, etc. Bearing this in mind, it is worth setting your browser to its default settings. At least that way, the majority of people will see your page as you intended.

- There are some tags that will have different effects on text, depending on which browser they are viewed with. For example, one browser may use italics for emphasis, another may use bold type. Check your HTML documents on as many different browsers as possible.

- Different browsers support different extensions to the HTML standard. We'll talk more about this in later chapters, but what it means is that if you want your pages to be readable to as wide an audience as possible, you should stick to the standard syntax. Compromise is the order of the day! Staying with the standard tags, etc., will mean that as many people as possible will be able to view your pages.

Having said all this, HTML's great strength lies in its flexibility. For instance, if a browser is incapable of displaying an image, then providing the HTML has been properly written, text describing the image can be shown instead; likewise, still images can be shown in place of video, etc.

When an HTML viewer is presented with a tag it doesn't understand, it usually just skips past that tag. This means that it's possible to use vendor extensions to HTML, providing you ensure that your document still looks reasonable with other browsers. Naturally, though, the best approach to ensure the widest possible audience for your HTML is to stick to the standard.

# Creating the Skeleton of the Document

There are several elements that should be included in all HTML documents. These define the structure of the document and allow browsers to correctly interpret the content. Have a look at this code:

```
<!DOCTYPE>

<HTML>

<HEAD>
<TITLE> A description of the page </TITLE>
Other head elements
</HEAD>

<BODY>
Body elements go here
</BODY>

</HTML>
```

This is the basic form that every HTML document should take. Let's have a look at each of the elements.

## <!DOCTYPE>

The `<!DOCTYPE>` tag is used to declare the type of document in which it appears. This is most useful for parsers, as it declares what version of HTML the document is written in, and thereby allows the parser to interpret the coding correctly. A rigorous HTML-checking program will reject any document which does not include this tag. However most browsers are not so fussy, and most of the documents on the web do not include this tag, even though it is required by the HTML 3.2 standard. This tag should be the first item in any proper HTML document.

`<!DOCTYPE>` has the following syntax for documents adhering to the W3C HTML 2.0 DTD (Document Type Definition):

```
<!DOCTYPE HTML PUBLIC "//IETF//DTD HTML 2.0//EN">
```

For documents that conform to the HTML 3.2 standard, the declaration should be as follows:

```
<!DOCTYPE HTML PUBLIC "-//W3C//DTD HTML 3.2 Draft//
EN">
```

Note the word **Draft** in the declaration above. This is present because HTML 3.2 is still a draft standard. When the standard has been fully ratified, the word **Draft** will be replaced with **Final**.

> **Remember, this tag is required by the HTML 3.2 standard. However, if your document includes vendor specific extensions or deviates from the standard in any other way, it should be left out. Otherwise, you may get unpredictable results.**

## <HTML>

This tag signals the beginning of the HTML document. Although `<!DOCTYPE>` appears first, this is the tag that defines the beginning and end of the HTML document, and encapsulates everything that is supposed to be parsed as HTML. Closing this tag with `</HTML>` ends the document—anything appearing afterwards is supposed to be ignored by browsers.

With HTML 3.2, this tag is no longer required, but it is strongly recommended; browsers that do not understand the `<!DOCTYPE>` declaration will act strangely if you don't include `<HTML>`.

## <HEAD>

This tag signals the document header, which is used to contain generic information about the document, such as: the title, the base URL of the document, what the style of the document is, and so on. With the advent of the HTML 3.2 standard, it's no longer strictly necessary to include a `<HEAD>` tag, but most browsers will behave oddly if you omit it—so we recommend using it at all times.

The `<HEAD>` tag can enclose a number of tags:

  TITLE

<HEAD>

- BASE
- ISINDEX
- LINK
- SCRIPT
- STYLE
- META

We'll look at these now.

## <TITLE>

Every valid HTML 3.2 document must have a **<TITLE>** statement. The title is usually (but not always) displayed by the browser in the title bar. Note, however, that you can't apply any other HTML tag inside the **<TITLE>** tag. If you do, the tags will be rendered on-screen, rather than applied. The title should be a meaningful description of the page, since it is usually the title that gets used as a bookmark by browsers.

## <BASE>

This tag defines the base URL, or original location, of the document. Without **<BASE>**, if the document were moved somewhere, relative links (links that do not include the entire server and directory path) would no longer work. This is because the base URL would be defined as the new, current URL for the document. However, if **<BASE>** is included, the base URL is always the original URL, specified by **<BASE>**. The syntax is:

```
<BASE HREF="http://this-server.org/inthisdir/
filename.html">
```

Note that some older browsers do not support the use of **<BASE>** though others will use it as the URL to 'bookmark'.

> Browsers use bookmarks (or as they are known in the Internet Explorer, favorites) to build up a list of sites and pages that you visit often. You can normally add a bookmark to any page that you are currently viewing.

## <ISINDEX>

This tag means that the document creates a search string which will be sent to the server. This means that you can send keywords back to the server via the document you are reading. It does not mean that the document you are reading is searchable. If you include `<ISINDEX>`, your document will automatically display the following text:

You can search this index. Type the keyword(s) you want to search for:

and this will be followed by a text box for user input.

Submitting a search in this way appends the keywords you enter to the document's URL. They are then sent to the server for processing, provided that the server has been set up to do so. This is a somewhat clumsy way of performing a search, since it involves some server-side processing and the search will only apply to the current document. Forms are now the preferred way to instigate a search.

# <LINK>

This defines the current document's relationship with other documents. `<LINK>` is rarely used because it requires properly defined values which, as yet, haven't been fully determined. In principle, `<LINK>` can be used for document specific navigation, and for controlling the rendering of collections of HTML nodes into printed documents.

Allowable attributes for `<LINK>` are:

### HREF

Specifies a URL which designates the linked resource.

### REL

The forward relationship, also known as the 'link type'. Values for **REL** are yet to be confirmed, but some proposed values are:

| | |
|---|---|
| **CONTENTS** | References a document serving as a table of contents. |
| **INDEX** | References a document providing an index for the current document. |
| **GLOSSARY** | References a document providing a glossary of terms for the current document. |
| **COPYRIGHT** | References a copyright statement for the current document. |
| **NEXT** | References the next document to visit in a guided tour. |
| **PREVIOUS** | References the previous document in a guided tour. |

| HELP | References a document offering help. This is aimed at helping users who have lost their way. |
| BOOKMARK | Provides a means for orienting users in an extended document. Several bookmarks may be defined in each document. |

### *REV*

Defines a reverse relationship.

### *TITLE*

An advisory title for the linked resource.

## <STYLE>

At the time of writing, this element is described as 'reserved for future use with style sheets'. We'll discuss style sheets in detail in Chapter 10.

## <SCRIPT>

The **<SCRIPT>** element is also 'reserved for future use with scripting languages'. We'll look at scripting in Chapter 9.

## <META>

The **<META>** tag is used to add additional information about the HTML document. This meta-information can be extracted by web servers to identify, index, or perform other specialized functions. For example, you can add keywords which can be used by search engines to find your page, or use **<META>** to force browsers to automatically load a new page at a specified interval.

There are several attributes for the **META** tag:

 **NAME**

 **CONTENT**

 **HTTP-EQUIV**

### *NAME*

Used to specify the name of a property for your web page, such as author, date, company, etc.

```
NAME="metaname"
```

### CONTENT

Specifies the value for the **NAME** property.

```
CONTENT="metacontent"
```

### HTTP-EQUIV

Maps the tags and their respective names to an HTTP response header for processing.

# Using <META>

The **<META>** element must include the **CONTENT** attribute. It should also contain either the **NAME** or **HTTP-EQUIV** attribute. **<META>** tags with the **NAME** attribute are usually intended for interpretation by the browser, while those with the **HTTP-EQUIV** attribute are intended for the server. This can sometimes be a bit confusing when the browser attributes are intended to be read by web search robots.

So that you understand the tag, we'll take a look at a few examples of how it is used.

A search engine that is indexing a page with:

```
<META NAME="keywords" CONTENT="Cars, motorbikes, trucks,
lorries, coaches">
```

would use the words contained within the content to index the page. Using this means that your site will be categorized more effectively, which means more 'hits' or people visiting your site. Remember that a web site's effectiveness is measured mainly by the number of people it attracts.

Some search engines will describe your site from the first few sentences on the index page. If you prefer, you can use the **CONTENT** attribute to specify the description instead:

```
<META NAME="description" CONTENT="This site is devoted to
all those people that love anything to do with coffee and
coffee beans">
```

Alternatively, if the element was:

```
<META HTTP-EQUIV="REFRESH" CONTENT="5; URL=http://
www.server.org/next.html">
```

then after five seconds the browser will load the next page. Very useful, should you move the location of the page, because the new location will be loaded automatically.

If you include:

```
<META HTTP-EQUIV="Expires" CONTENT="Tue, 24 Oct 1996
17:45:00 GMT">
```

it ensures that if the page is reloaded after the expiry date, it is reloaded from the server rather than from a cached copy. This is useful if you want your readers to get the latest version of your documents.

## About Ratings

The **&lt;META&gt;** tag can also be used to declare a rating for your page. If you don't include a rating, certain browsers will lock themselves out of your site.

The method of associating labels with the content of a web page is known as PICS or Platform for Internet Content Selection. Originally PICS was designed for use by parents and teachers to effectively control what could be viewed on the Web by minors, whilst protecting everyone's rights of free speech. New uses for PICS are, however, being developed all the time; these include privacy and code signing. PICS does not provide a rating system itself, it merely provides the ability to apply ratings to content. Comprehensive information on the PICS specification can be viewed at:

**http://www.w3.org/pub/WWW/PICS/**

The actual rating information is known as the rating label. The label appears in a Web document as part of the HTML code and each part of the content that is rated has its own label.

To include ratings within your code, you specify the rating as part of the **&lt;META&gt;** tag in this general form:

```
<HTML>
<HEAD>
<META http-equiv="PICS-Label" content='(PICS-1.0 "http://
www.rsac.org"
labels on "1996.11.05T08:15-0500"
until "1996.12.31T23:59-0000"
for "http://www.rsac.org/index.html"
by "RSAC "
rating (language 2 nudity 0 violence 1))'>
</HEAD>
```

For more information on how to rate your own content, go to:

**http://www.rsac.org/labels.html**

**17**

# The Body Section

The body section is where the meat of your HTML goes. Here, you add the text you want displayed in the main browser window, add tags and attributes to modify that text, create hyperlinks to other documents, etc. You can also affect the color of the text, background, etc., of your document.

## <BODY>

This tag marks the beginning of the body section. There are several attributes that can be used with the **<BODY>** tag:

- BACKGROUND
- BGCOLOR
- ALINK
- LINK
- VLINK
- TEXT

There are also three Microsoft extensions for this tag which are supported by Internet Explorer:

- BGPROPERTIES
- LEFTMARGIN
- TOPMARGIN

### BACKGROUND

Specifies a background picture. The syntax is:

```
<BODY BACKGROUND=url>
```

where **url** is the name (and directory path) of the picture to display. The picture is tiled behind all images and text.

### BGCOLOR

Sets the background color of the page. The syntax is:

```
<BODY BGCOLOR="#rrggbb">
```

where **rrggbb** are hexadecimal numbers for red, green, and blue, respectively (for example, FFFFFF would be white, and 000000 would be black; we'll discuss this further a bit later). **BGCOLOR** can be used in conjunction with **BACKGROUND**. If the background is a large image, you can first set the color, so that this color will be rendered by the browser while the image is loading. This is useful if, for example, you are using white text: set a dark background color, so that the text is visible even before the image loads.

## ALINK

Sets the color of an active hypertext link. A hypertext link is active only while the mouse is clicked on the link. The syntax is:

```
<BODY ALINK="#rrggbb">
```

where **rrggbb** are hexadecimal values for red, green, and blue.

## LINK

Sets the color of hypertext links that have not been visited. The syntax is:

```
<BODY LINK="#rrggbb">
```

where **rrggbb** are hexadecimal numbers relating to red, green, and blue.

## VLINK

Sets the color of visited hypertext links. The syntax is

```
<BODY VLINK="#rrggbb">
```

where **rrggbb** are hexadecimal numbers relating to red, green, and blue.

## TEXT

Sets the color of normal text on the page. The syntax is:

```
<BODY TEXT="#rrggbb">
```

where **rrggbb** are hexadecimal numbers relating to red, green, and blue.

### BGPROPERTIES

Sets a watermark. The watermark is the background picture, previously set with the **BACKGROUND** attribute. It remains 'fixed' in place and doesn't scroll with the rest of the page. The syntax is simply:

```
<BODY BGPROPERTIES=FIXED>
```

### LEFTMARGIN

Specifies the left margin for the entire page. The syntax is:

```
<BODY LEFTMARGIN=n>
```

where **n** is a numeric value expressed in pixels. If **n** is set to 0, the left margin will be exactly aligned with the left edge of the page.

### TOPMARGIN

Specifies the top margin for the page. The syntax is:

```
<BODY TOPMARGIN=n>
```

where **n** is a numeric value expressed in pixels. If **n** is set to 0, the top margin will be on the top edge of the page.

## Colors

When creating web pages, you will find yourself wanting to use colors to make the page attractive, and to draw the user's eye to certain parts. With HTML, you express the color you want to be displayed as a six digit hexadecimal value that represents red, green, and blue. The first two digits are the red component, the second two are the green component, and the last two are the blue component. Setting a value to **00** means the component is off. A value of **FF** means the component is fully on. Different colors are achieved by 'mixing' different levels of the three components. White is all three components fully on, represented as **FFFFFF**; black is all components fully off, represented as **000000**.

> Note that hex rgb colors are exactly the same as the rgb colors used in most graphics editing programs—the only difference is that they are expressed in hex, not decimal.

As an example, to display normal text in red, you would use the **TEXT** attribute of the **<BODY>** element:

```
<BODY TEXT="#FF0000">
```

If you're confused by hexadecimal notation, don't worry. There's a much easier way of defining the color you want. Both Netscape and Internet Explorer support the use of color names: you can replace the hexadecimal value with a name—which is somewhat easier to remember.

The sixteen color names that are understood by Netscape and Internet Explorer are:

| | | | |
|---|---|---|---|
| AQUA | BLACK | BLUE | FUCHSIA |
| GRAY | GREEN | LIME | MAROON |
| NAVY | OLIVE | PURPLE | RED |
| SILVER | TEAL | WHITE | YELLOW |

Netscape actually supports several dozen other color names in addition to the ones shown here; a full list is supplied in Appendix D.

## An Example

Let's put some of this into practice. Type the following, exactly as shown:

```
<!DOCTYPE HTML PUBLIC "-//W3C//DTD HTML 3.2 Draft//EN">
<HTML>
<HEAD>
<TITLE>Welcome to The Global Coffee Club</TITLE>
</HEAD>

<BODY BGCOLOR="#FFFFEA" TEXT="#0000A0" LINK="#FF0000"
VLINK="#808080" ALINK="#008040">
<H1>The Global Coffee Club welcomes you to its
Web-Site!</H1>
<H2>We hope you enjoy your visit</H2>
<P>News flash! You can now<A HREF="taste.html" > taste our
range of beans on-line</A>
</BODY>
</HTML>
```

> The <A HREF> tag defines a hypertext link. We'll be looking at this in more detail in Chapter 4.

Save the file as **index.html** and view it. It should look like this:

If your page doesn't look exactly as above, don't worry. There are many reasons why your browser may be rendering the page differently. What you should see, though, is that all the text is in blue—with the exception of the hypertext link, which should be red, and the background is an off-white. At the moment, of course, the hypertext link doesn't lead anywhere, because we have yet to create the **taste.html** document. Clicking on the link may result in an error message, or maybe nothing at all; it depends on your browser. Let's look at this example more closely:

The first line:

```
<!DOCTYPE HTML PUBLIC "-//W3C//DTD HTML 3.2 Draft//EN">
```

is where we define the standard that this particular document conforms to.

Next, we have:

```
<HTML>
<HEAD>
<TITLE>Welcome to The Global Coffee Club</TITLE>
</HEAD>
```

The **<HTML>** tag indicates the beginning of the HTML document, and within the **<HEAD>** section, we have just one element: the **<TITLE>**.

Now we come to the document body. The `<BODY>` tag is where we set the color attributes for the rest of the document.

```
<BODY BGCOLOR="#FFFFEA" TEXT="#0000A0" LINK="#FF0000"
VLINK="#808080" ALINK="#008040">
```

Note that we could just as easily (in fact, more easily) have used color names instead of the hexadecimal numbers.

The rest of the code looks like this:

```
<H1>The Global Coffee Club welcomes you to its
Web-Site!</H1>
<H2>We hope you enjoy your visit</H2>
<P>News flash! You can now<A HREF="taste.html"> taste our
range of beans on-line</A>
</BODY>
</HTML>
```

The first two lines format the text to be rendered as different sized headings. Then comes a new paragraph, in which we specify a hypertext link. The code ends by closing the body section of the document and then the HTML document itself.

# Adding Comments

Adding comments to your documents is as good an idea in HTML as it is in other languages. Comments allow you to re-acquaint yourself with the code when you come to alter it two months later. Anything between the `<!--` and `-->` tags will be ignored by the browser, and forms a comment:

```
<!-- This text will be visible only to someone viewing the
source code -->
```

Note that this comment spans two lines—comments can be multi- or single-line; they will still be ignored by the browser.

# Revision Numbers

In keeping with general programming practice, it's a good idea to add revision numbers to all your documents. The majority of visitors to your site will want to know when the last revision was made, and it's common to add the current date to the bottom of a document. Many authors just put the following:

```
<P ALIGN=RIGHT>Last Revision : Oct 23 1996 by Steve Wright
```

> Remember that the World Wide Web is a global entity. Avoid using country or regional-specific syntax, such as 15/09/96.

# Universal Attributes

The draft HTML 3.2 standard suggests that the next version of HTML after 3.2 will support the use of 2 new universal attributes—attributes that can be used with most, if not all elements and tags. These two attributes are **CLASS** and **ID**.

# CLASS

**CLASS** will be used to **subclass** an element. For example, you could subclass paragraphs into quotes and normal text and then apply a particular style to each type of subclass, so that all quotes are rendered in the same style.

The syntax for **CLASS** will probably be:

```
CLASS=class.subclass
```

For example `<P CLASS=para.quote>`.

The actual formatting information for the subclasses will be defined by a stylesheet: either an external file to the HTML document, or else included within the **HEAD** section of the HTML document itself. (See Chapter 10 for more details on style sheets.) Each time you wish to apply the style to an element, e.g. a paragraph, you need only include the **CLASS** attribute with the element's tag.

**CLASS** can also provide information about the characteristics of a particular element or subclass of element that may be useful in the future. At the moment, the Arena browser and Microsoft's Internet Explorer 3.0 are the only browsers that recognize the **CLASS** attribute.

# ID

The **ID** attribute defines a unique identifier or label for an element. The syntax is:

```
ID=identifier
```

where **identifier** is a unique name or label for the element.

For instance:

```
<P ID=#top>
This is the top of the page
```

defines that the `<P>` element has a unique name, **top**. This name can then be used as a reference and you can jump to the position it marks from anywhere in the document or from another document. You will see in Chapter 4 that the attribute **NAME** is used in this way at the present time. For example:

```
<A NAME=top>Go to the top of the page</A>
```

means that if you click on the text Go to the top of the page, it will take you to the label named **top**. ID can be used in exactly the same way:

```
<A ID=top>Go to the top of the page</A>
```

> At the present time, most browsers do not recognize the ID attribute but it is possible to use both **NAME** and **ID** at the same time to allow for backward compatibility.

# Summary

This chapter has introduced you to the basics of HTML. We talked about the difference between tags and attributes, and how these together create the effects you see on all web pages. We looked at the tags that you must include in a valid HTML document, and we looked at other tags that you can include to enhance its appearance. Remember that your documents will not necessarily appear the same to all users; you should get into the habit of testing your pages on different machines and using different browsers.

In the next chapter, we'll go on to look at creating text documents— using different formatting and styles.

# Formatting Text

The basis of any HTML document is the information you are trying to get across. More often than not, this comes in the form of text. In this chapter, we will look at how you can manipulate the text of your document to use styles, alter layout, and add special effects.

## Text Layout

One way of enhancing the text on your page is to lay it out well, so that the user can easily follow what's written. You can do this by breaking the text up into paragraphs and sections, by grouping related information together in lists, and by using rules. Tables are another popular means of laying out information, but we'll leave these until Chapter 5.

## Headings

There are six levels of headings. Level 1 is the largest and level 6 is the smallest. Most browsers allow the user to alter the relative sizes of headings, so don't be surprised if you find that checking your site on another system shows a level 1 heading at the same size as a level 3 heading on your system.

Under HTML 2.0, headings have no associated attributes. HTML 3.2, however, allows the use of the **ALIGN** attribute. The syntax is:

```
<Hn ALIGN=alignment>
```

where **n** is a number 1 through 6, and **alignment** is one of **LEFT**, **RIGHT**, or **CENTER**. The default here is **LEFT**. The corresponding end tag **</Hn>** must be used.

It's possible to create different size headings using the <FONT> tag, but be warned—not all browsers will display the attributes of <FONT>, so you risk your headings not appearing as you want them to for some users. Also, some search engines use words that appear in higher level headings as items to index.

# Breaking up Text

You can't use carriage returns to create new paragraphs or to break lines in HTML, since they are ignored by browsers. Have a look at the following code:

```
<HTML>
<HEAD>
<TITLE>Examples of line breaks</TITLE>

<BODY>
This line has a carriage return here,
but it is ignored by the browser.
</BODY>
</HTML>
```

The carriage return after the word **here** is ignored by the browser. It's the width of the window that determines where lines break, not the carriage returns you put in your code.

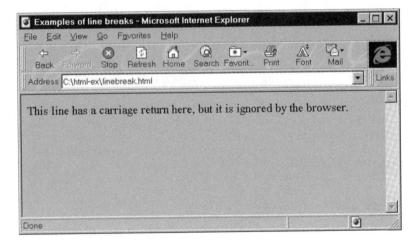

To break text up, you must use special tags.

## Paragraphs

Paragraphs are defined with the **<P>** tag. HTML 3.2 defines one attribute for this tag: **ALIGN**. The syntax is:

```
<P ALIGN=alignment>
```

where **alignment** is **LEFT**, **RIGHT**, or **CENTER**.

The use of the end tag **</P>** is optional. The rule for paragraphs is that the next **<P>** tag ends the previous paragraph.

Note that the **ALIGN** attribute is new in HTML 3.2. Previously, you had to use the following code to center a paragraph:

```
<CENTER>
<P>
Anything between the start and end CENTER tags will be
centered
</CENTER>
```

Until browser vendors catch up with the HTML 3.2, it's valid to use both the **ALIGN** attribute and the **<CENTER></CENTER>** tags.

## Line Breaks

Line breaks are achieved by using the **<BR>** tag.

In some browsers, including Internet Explorer and Netscape, you can use consecutive **<BR>** elements if you want to space out blocks of text:

```
<BR><BR><BR>
```

> It is not valid HTML to use consecutive **<P>** elements.
> By definition, a paragraph can't be empty. If you do use
> consecutive **<P>** elements, some browsers will add the
> space, some will ignore all but the first **<P>**, and some
> will complain about the use of invalid HTML.

The **CLEAR** attribute, which is new in HTML 3.2, can be used with the **<BR>** tag to extend the wrapping options of text around images. When **CLEAR** is used in text that's wrapped round an image, it ensures that any subsequent text begins below the image:

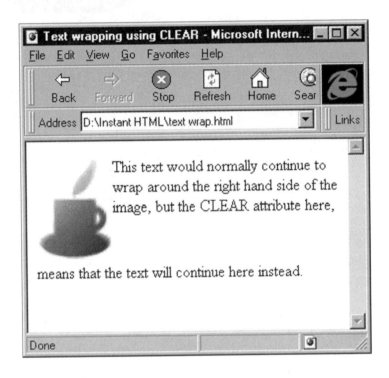

The syntax is:

```
<BR CLEAR=value>
```

where **value** is **LEFT**, **RIGHT**, or **ALL**. **LEFT** means that the text will appear at the first clear left margin position. **RIGHT** means the text will appear at the first clear right margin position. **ALL** means that both margins have to be clear before text will appear. If, on the other hand, you don't want a line of text to be broken, you can use the Netscape extension **<NOBR>**, like this:

```
<NOBR>Here's a line of text I don't want broken … here's
the end</NOBR>
```

## Lists

Lists are used to organize information in a clear and easily understood format. There are three main types of list that you can set up in a document:

- Unordered, or bulleted lists (using **<UL>**)
- Ordered, or numbered lists (using **<OL>**)

Definition lists (using **<DL>**)

**<UL>**, **<OL>**, and **<DL>** are the tags that define the type of list. They are all container tags—in other words, they must have a corresponding end tag. The list entries themselves are defined by **<LI>** in bulleted and numbered lists, and by **<DT>** and **<DD>** in a definition list.

You can add a list header to any type of list using **<LH>**, although you should note that not all browsers will start a new line after the closing **</LH>**. Netscape will give you the results you would expect, but many other browsers won't.

## Unordered Lists

The purpose of **<UL>** is to produce an unordered list, which is the same as a bulleted list that you would type in a word processor. The syntax for unordered lists is:

```
<UL>
<LI>first list item
<LI>second list item
<LI>third list item
<LI>etc... .
</UL>
```

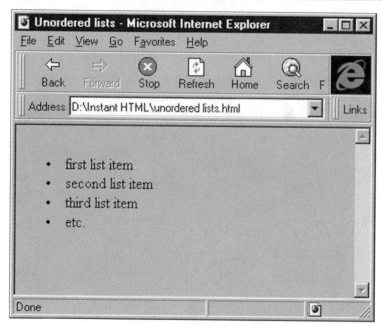

The **<UL>** tag has two attributes: **COMPACT** and **TYPE**.

### COMPACT

**COMPACT** tells the browser to fit the list into a smaller space. This is usually achieved by removing white space from between each list item. However, not all browsers support the use of **COMPACT**; some will just ignore it.

### TYPE

The **TYPE** attribute allows you to change the appearance of the bullets. You can set it equal to **disc**, **circle**, or **square**, to display the appropriate shape.

> Note that these attributes are not supported by Internet Explorer.

## Using <UL>

The following example displays a compact, unordered list with square bullets:

```
<LH> Using different bullets </LH>
<UL COMPACT TYPE=SQUARE>
<LI>First list item
<LI>Second list item
<LI>Third list item
</UL>
```

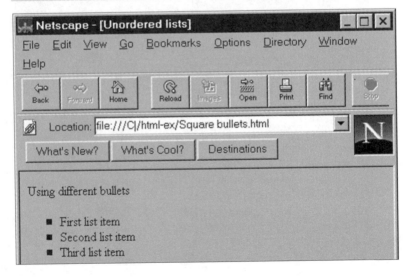

## Ordered Lists

<OL> will produce an ordered list numbered in a style of your choice. The default style is 1, 2, 3, but you can choose various other styles such as a, b, c, or i, ii, iii, etc. The syntax is:

```
<OL>
<LI>This is the first item
<LI>This is the second item
<LI>This is the third item
<LI>And so on …
<OL>
```

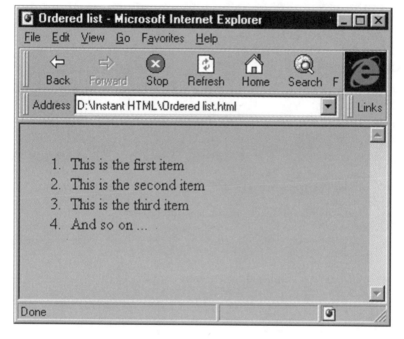

Note how the numbers have been inserted for you by the browser. Allowable attributes for <OL> are TYPE and START.

### *TYPE*

The TYPE attribute specifies the type of numbering used. The syntax is:

```
<OL TYPE=n>
```

where **n** is one of the following:

| | |
|---|---|
| 1 | Arabic numerals (default) |
| A | Capital letters |
| a | Small letters |
| I | Large roman numerals (I, II, III) |
| I | Small roman numerals (i, ii, iii) |

### START

Alters the number that the list starts with. The syntax is:

`START=n`

where **n** specifies the new start number, e.g. 3, C, c, III, or iii.

# Definition Lists

Definition lists are used when you want to include a description for each list item. You could use a definition list to produce, for example, a glossary of terms. Use **<DT>** for the definition term, and **<DD>** for the description:

```
<DL>
<DT>HTML
  <DD>HyperText Markup Language
<DT>HEAD
  <DD>The first part of an HTML document
<DT>BODY
  <DD>The main part of an HTML document
</DL>
```

This would be displayed as follows:

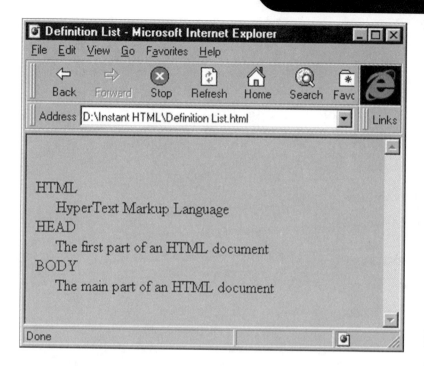

> Note that there is no need to use closing tags for `<LI>`, `<DL>`, and `<DD>`.

### Nesting Lists

Lists can be **nested,** as can most elements within HTML. Nesting means placing a set of tags or elements inside another set. The nested list is independent of the outer list, so if it is numbered, it will start again from 1 (unless you explicitly change this).

```
<OL TYPE=i>
<LI>first list item
<LI>second list item
<LI>third list item
      <OL TYPE=i>
            <LI>fourth list item
            <LI>fifth list item
            <LI>sixth list item
      </OL>
</OL>
```

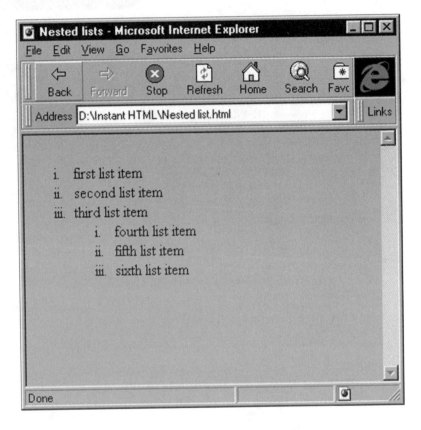

Don't forget to close each start tag when nesting lists.

### Other Types of List

As well as the types of list discussed above, you can also use
**<MENU>** and **<DIR>** for lists. You can use **<LI>** with both, and each
will indent the items in the list. These tags are likely to become
obsolete in the future.

# Horizontal Rules

Horizontal rules are used to break up sections of a document from
each other. You place a horizontal rule using the **<HR>** element. As
this isn't a container element, no end tag is required or allowed.
Allowable attributes for **<HR>** are:

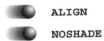 **ALIGN**

**NOSHADE**

- SIZE
- WIDTH
- COLOR

## ALIGN

Specifies the position of the rule. The syntax is:

**ALIGN=alignment**

where **alignment** is **LEFT**, **RIGHT**, or **CENTER**. The default value is **CENTER**.

## NOSHADE

**NOSHADE** means the rule is displayed without any 3D shading effects.

## SIZE

Sets the height of the rule. The syntax is:

**SIZE=n**

where **n** is the height in pixels. The default value is 2.

## WIDTH

Sets the width of the rule across the browser window. The syntax is:

**WIDTH=n**

where **n** is the width in pixels. To express the width as a percentage of the window's width, add **%**, e.g. **WIDTH=50%**.

## COLOR

Specifies the color that the rule is displayed in. The syntax is:

**COLOR="#rrggbb"**

where **"#rrggbb"** is a hexadecimal number defining the amount of red, green, and blue that make up the color, or a color name. The default color is based on the background. This attribute is not part of the draft standard, but both Netscape and IE support it.

## Using Horizontal Rules

Have a look at the following example:

```
<!DOCTYPE HTML PUBLIC "-//W3C//DTD HTML 3.2 Draft//EN">
<HTML>
<HEAD>
<TITLE>An example of a horizontal rule</TITLE>
</HEAD>
<BODY>

<HR ALIGN=CENTER SIZE=5 WIDTH=70%>
<HR ALIGN=CENTER SIZE=10 WIDTH=80%>
<HR ALIGN=CENTER SIZE=2 WIDTH=50% NOSHADE>

</BODY>
</HTML>
```

This gives:

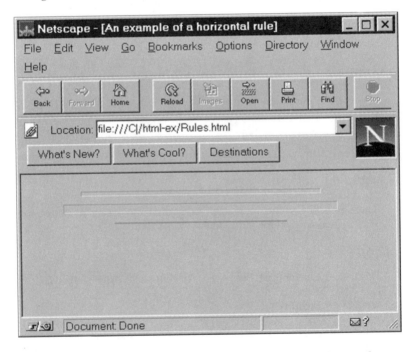

Note that the first two horizontal rules appear in 3D, whereas the last example is flat, because we've used the **NOSHADE** attribute. This is particularly useful when the background color is very light, as the 3D shading won't show up very well.

# Text Emphasis and Style

There are many different tags for emphasizing and styling text. You can change the font of a piece of text or you can use tags to affect appearance in other ways. These tags can broadly be split into two categories:

- Physical tags
- Logical style tags

We'll look at using fonts first.

# Fonts

Most documents on the web are in the default font, which can be set by the user of the browser. Until recently, it hasn't been possible to define the font in a web document. The main reason for this is that it can't be guaranteed that the font you define for the text is installed on the user's system.

At the time of writing, Microsoft (among others) is working on the possibility of embedding fonts into web documents. This means that the font would be transferred to the user's system at the same time as the rest of the page downloads. Although the technology does exist now to achieve this, the problem is one of bandwidth. It would take considerably longer to download a page with embedded fonts than a page without.

In the meantime, there are several compromises. You could, of course, place an image containing text in the desired font—but again the problem is one of speed. The most efficient method is to use the `<FONT>` tag.

## <FONT>

This tag defines the appearance of the text it encloses. Allowable attributes are:

- SIZE
- FACE
- COLOR

## SIZE

Specifies the size of the lettering. The syntax is:

`SIZE=n`

where n is a number 1 through 7; 1 is the smallest, 7 the largest. The actual size of the font is relative to the `<BASEFONT>` element (see next section). The `SIZE` attribute can be used on its own with the `<FONT>` element. This will result in the default system font being displayed, but at the size you've specified.

## FACE

Specifies the font you want to use. The syntax is:

`FACE="fontname1, fontname2, fontname3"`

At present, this attribute is an extension to HTML 3.2, but it's supported by both Netscape Navigator 3.0 and Internet Explorer 3.0.

When `FACE` is used to specify a list of fonts, if the first font in the list isn't present on the user's system, the second will be tried, and so on. If none of the specified fonts exist on the user's system, the default font will be used.

Microsoft has recently announced a list of special TrueType web fonts, that anyone can download from their web site. The idea is that you code your pages with the relevant fonts, and then put a link to Microsoft's site so that the user can download the fonts for use on their system. To check the latest details on this, go to:

`http://www.microsoft.com/truetype/fontpack/win.htm`

> If you're wondering what fonts to use, a general guideline is to use sans-serif fonts (like Arial) for headlines and serifed fonts (like Times) for large portions of text.

## COLOR

`COLOR` specifies the color that the font will appear in. This can be displayed as a hexadecimal number or a color name.

Some interesting typographical effects can be achieved with these attributes, for example:

```
<!DOCTYPE HTML PUBLIC "-//W3C//DTD//HTML 3.2 Draft//EN">
<HTML>
```

```
<HEAD>
<TITLE>An example of the FONT element</TITLE>
</HEAD>
<BODY>
<P>
<BASEFONT SIZE=2 FACE=VERDANA, ARIAL COLOR=BLACK>

<!--If the Verdana font isn't installed, Arial will be used
instead. If neither are available, the default font will be
used-- >

<FONT SIZE=5 FACE="VERDANA,ARIAL" COLOR=BLUE>T</FONT>he
first letter of this sentence should be three sizes larger
than the rest of the sentence. The first letter should also
be displayed in blue rather than black.

</BODY>
</HTML>
```

The result of this code is as follows:

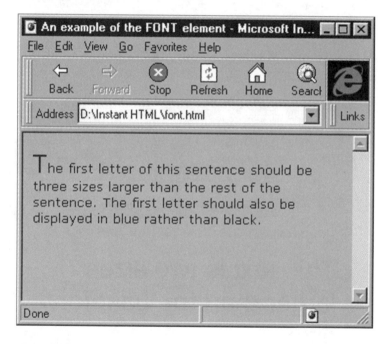

## <BASEFONT>

Notice that, in the code above, we used an element called
**<BASEFONT>**. This sets the default attributes for any text that has
not been formatted with the **<FONT>** element or a style sheet. The
syntax is:

**41**

```
<BASEFONT SIZE=n FACE="fontname1,fontname2,fontname3"
COLOR="#rrggbb">
```

The values for the attributes are the same as for **<FONT>**. The default value for the **SIZE** attribute is 3. You can specify the value for the **<FONT> SIZE** attribute, relative to the **<BASEFONT> SIZE,** like this.

```
<HTML>
<HEAD>
<TITLE>Relative font sizes</TITLE>
</HEAD>

<BODY BGCOLOR="#F9FFFF">

<BASEFONT SIZE=4 FACE="ARIAL">
<P>
<FONT SIZE=-1>This text is one size down from the basefont
size.</FONT>
<P>
<FONT SIZE=+2>This text is two sizes larger than the
basefont size.</FONT>

</BODY>
</HTML>
```

The result of this code is:

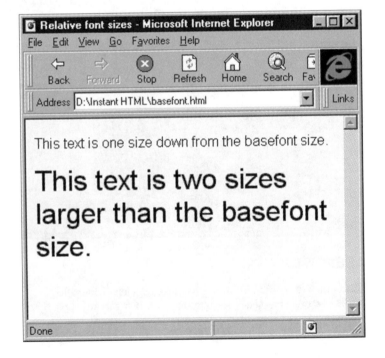

The simple addition of a minus or plus sign before the value means that the size becomes relative to the `<BASEFONT> SIZE` attribute. Unfortunately, you are still constrained to the 1 is smallest, 7 is largest limit. Choosing values outside this range won't work:

```
<!-- This is acceptable -->
<BASEFONT SIZE=1>
<FONT SIZE=+6>This will work as 1 + 6 = 7 </FONT>
```

```
<!-- This is wrong. The font size won't change -->
<BASEFONT SIZE=2>
<FONT SIZE=+6>This won't work as 2 + 6 = 8 </FONT>
```

When a + or - is used, the `<FONT> SIZE` attribute is always relative to the `<BASEFONT> SIZE` attribute, not the last `<FONT> SIZE`.

> The `<BASEFONT>` element should only be used once in a document, and should appear before any `<FONT>` elements.

# Using Physical and Logical Style Tags

HTML distinguishes between two groups of character-formatting tags: logical character-attribute tags and physical character-attribute tags. It may help to think of physical character-attribute tags as closely related to the direct formatting you could apply to text from a word processor, e.g. bold. The appearance of HTML text formatted with physical character-attribute tags is more likely to remain constant from one browser to another. Logical character-attribute tags in HTML can be thought of as like 'styles' in a word processor—the appearance of text formatted with a style in a word processor depends on how the style is defined in that word processor. Similarly, the appearance of HTML text formatted with logical character-attribute tags, depends upon the browser's interpretation of that logical character-attribute tag.

> The idea behind logical styles is that they can be rendered in the best way for that particular platform. For example, if you want to emphasize a word, `<EM>` might produce italics in a browser, but on a text-to-speech system, it could be rendered by increasing the volume slightly.

## Physical Tags

Physical tag styles do not vary from browser to browser. They include:

| | |
|---|---|
| **&lt;B&gt;** | Bold |
| **&lt;I&gt;** | Italic |
| **&lt;U&gt;** | Underscore |
| **&lt;TT&gt;** | Typewriter |
| **&lt;S&gt;** | Strikeout |
| **&lt;DFN&gt;** | Definition |
| **&lt;BLINK&gt;** | Blinking text (Netscape specific) |

and are rendered as follows:

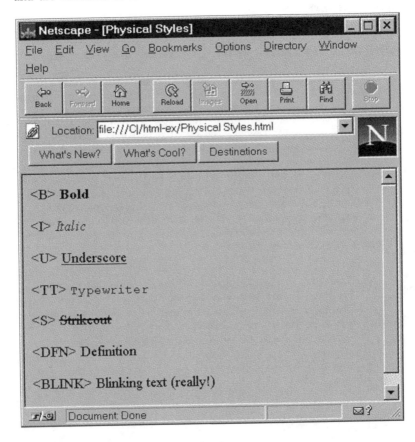

# Logical Tags

One of the things you should remember when building web pages is that HTML was designed to specify the relationships between the different parts of the document. Many tags are logical tags, and HTML does not specify how they should be represented. Logical style tags take on the preferences set for them within the browser, as well as being rendered differently depending on the browser vendor. For example, many browsers will let the user specify which size and shape of font will be used to display the **<H1>** tag. It will usually be larger than the **<H2>** tag, but you can't even be sure of that! Logical tags include:

| | |
|---|---|
| **<Hn>** | Headings |
| **<EM>** | Emphasis (usually italic) |
| **<STRONG>** | Strong (usually bold) |
| **<ADDRESS>** | Usually italic |
| **<CITE>** | Used for quoting text (usually italic) |
| **<CODE>** | Monospaced font (usually Courier) |
| **<SAMP>** | Monospaced font (usually Courier) |
| **<KBD>** | Monospaced font (usually Courier) |
| **<BIG>** | Makes text one size larger |
| **<SMALL>** | Makes text one size smaller |
| **<SUP>** | Renders text as superscript |
| **<SUB>** | Renders text as subscript |
| **<ABBREV>** | Logically denotes abbreviations |
| **<ACRONYM>** | Logically denotes acronyms |
| **<PERSON>** | Denotes a name for indexing purposes |
| **<Q>** | Denotes a short inline quotation |
| **<VAR>** | Denotes a variable name, usually rendered in italics |

**<CODE>**, **<SAMP>**, and **<KBD>** (keyboard) are particularly useful if your document contains actual code that you are trying to explain to your reader.

When viewed by the Netscape browser, relative tags appear as follows:

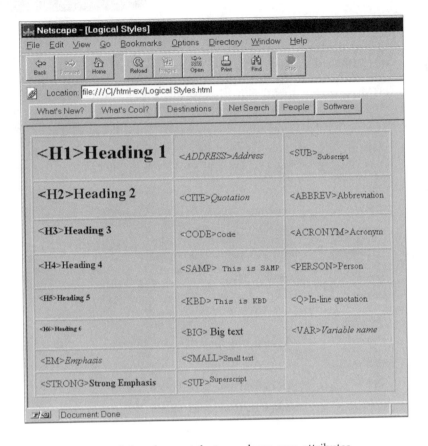

Note that none of the above style types have any attributes associated with them.

When deciding which type of tag to use, bear in mind that it's probably better to stick with the physical styles—at least, that way you can be sure that the page will be viewed the way you intended.

## <MARQUEE>

Internet Explorer supports the use of the **<MARQUEE>** element. This is used to produce scrolling text. Its attributes are:

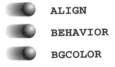 ALIGN

BEHAVIOR

BGCOLOR

DIRECTION

- HEIGHT
- HSPACE
- LOOP
- SCROLLAMOUNT
- SCROLLDELAY
- VSPACE
- WIDTH

## ALIGN

Aligns the marquee. The syntax is:

**ALIGN=alignment**

where **alignment** is one of **TOP**, **MIDDLE**, or **BOTTOM**. This attribute aligns the marquee with the top, middle, or bottom of the surrounding text.

## BEHAVIOR

Indicates how the marquee will move across the screen. The syntax is:

**BEHAVIOR=type**

where **type** is **SCROLL**, **SLIDE**, or **ALTERNATE**. **SCROLL** means the marquee will start completely off one side, scroll all the way across and off the other side, and then start again. This is the default. **SLIDE** will commence with the marquee completely off one side, it will then scroll in, stop when it reaches the far margin and then start again. **ALTERNATE** will bounce the marquee back and forth between the margins.

## BGCOLOR

Sets the background color of the scrolling text. The syntax is:

**BGCOLOR="#rrggbb"**

where **rrggbb** are hexadecimal values for red, green, and blue. You can also use predefined color names, such as **BLUE**, **RED**, **YELLOW**.

## DIRECTION

Sets the direction that the marquee scrolls in. The syntax is:

`DIRECTION=direction`

where **direction** is **LEFT** or **RIGHT**. The default is **LEFT**, which means the text scrolls to the left from the right.

## HEIGHT

Sets the height of the marquee. The syntax is:

`HEIGHT=n`

where **n** is the height of the marquee in pixels, or as a percentage of the screen height. To express the value as a percentage, you must append a **%** sign to the end of the value.

## HSPACE

Sets the width of the left and right margins of the marquee. The syntax is:

`HSPACE=n`

where **n** specifies the amount of space in pixels.

## LOOP

Determines how many times the marquee will scroll across the screen. The syntax is:

`LOOP=n`

where **n** specifies the number of times. If the value for **n** is set to **-1** or **INFINITE**, it will loop indefinitely.

## SCROLLAMOUNT

Specifies the number of pixels between each successive draw of the marquee text. The syntax is:

`SCROLLAMOUNT=n`

### SCROLLDELAY

Specifies the number of milliseconds between each successive draw of the marquee text. The syntax is:

```
SCROLLDELAY=n
```

### VSPACE

Specifies the top and bottom margins of the marquee. The syntax is:

```
VSPACE=n
```

where **n** is the amount of space in pixels.

### WIDTH

Sets the width of the marquee. The syntax is:

```
WIDTH=n
```

where **n** is the width of the marquee, expressed in pixels or as a percentage of the screen width. To specify a percentage, a **%** sign must be appended to the end of the value.

If you have Internet Explorer installed on your system, you can try the following example:

```
<MARQUEE DIRECTION=RIGHT BEHAVIOR=SCROLL SCROLLAMOUNT=10
SCROLLDELAY=200>This is a scrolling marquee!</MARQUEE>
```

# Summary

This chapter has shown you how to format and style text. You have seen how to break text up into manageable sections, and how to apply styles to make particular words or phrases stand out.

In the next chapter, we'll look at how you can use images in your documents to further enhance your pages.

# Graphics

The ability to display images of various types on the web is one of the biggest attractions for many people, and probably the main reason for its rapid growth rate. Images also present the biggest problems. As we could easily write three large books on this area alone, it makes sense to concentrate on the aspects that are important with respect to download times, the image formats available, and tricks and tips used by expert web authors.

# Images

Images are included within a document by using the **<IMG>** tag. Just looking around the web will reveal all sorts of amazing graphical effects that can be achieved with the use of this simple element. However, don't overdo it. Large images take a long time to download and will drive your audience crazy with frustration.

When you insert an image using the **<IMG>** element, it's loaded into the browser at the same time as all the other elements, and is effectively treated as text. Care must be exercised, though, if you expect your audience to print or save your pages. Images are not saved with the rest of the document, and many users turn off images to speed up download time on slower lines, therefore the document must be understandable without the images. Note that there is no end tag for the **<IMG>** element.

## <IMG>

Available attributes for the **<IMG>** tag are:

 SRC

 ALT

- ALIGN
- WIDTH
- HEIGHT
- BORDER
- HSPACE
- VSPACE
- USEMAP
- ISMAP

Of these, **SRC** is required, while the others are implied.

## SRC

This specifies the **So**u**RC**e of the picture or image to include. **SRC** always includes the file name, the path name is implied. The path name may be relative or absolute. The syntax is:

```
<IMG SRC="somepath/someimage.gif">
```

It's possible to specify a source file from anywhere—just put the full URL as the **SRC**:

```
<IMG SRC="http://www.someserver.org/directory/
someimage.gif">
```

## ALT

The importance of this attribute can't be over-emphasized. Its purpose is to present users with a text alternative if their system can't display graphics. Remember that many people turn off graphics or choose to have the graphics load after the text. A page full of graphics that have no **ALT** attribute defined will be meaningless unless graphics are turned on in the browser. The syntax is:

```
<IMG ALT="description">
```

where **description** is a sentence relating to the image specified by the **SRC** attribute. The description should be as clear and concise as possible. Many browsers will display the **ALT** text while waiting for the image to download, or instead of the image when images are turned off. Some will also use it when printing hard-copy versions of the page. The **ALT** attribute is also used by special browsers for the handicapped.

**52**

## ALIGN

Use this attribute to align the image. Images are aligned in a very similar manner to text. The syntax is:

```
<IMG ALIGN=alignment>
```

where **alignment** is **TOP**, **MIDDLE**, **BOTTOM**, **LEFT**, or **RIGHT**. These values are relative to the text around the image. So, **TOP** aligns the top of the image with the top of the line of text (or, sometimes, the highest element that appears prior to the current image); **BOTTOM** aligns the bottom of the image with the bottom of the line of text; **MIDDLE** aligns the middle of the image with the baseline of the text; **LEFT** places the image on the left margin; and **RIGHT** means the image will appear on the right margin.

> Netscape in particular has implemented other values for vertical alignment of images, such as **TEXTTOP**, **ABSMIDDLE**, and **BASELINE**. We suggest, however, that you stick to the normal **TOP**, **MIDDLE**, or **BOTTOM**, as using the more exotic values will give unpredictable results in other browsers.

## WIDTH and HEIGHT

Images are scaleable. That is, you can use the **WIDTH** and **HEIGHT** attributes to specify the size of box that you want the image to fit into, and the browser will scale the image to suit.

The syntax is:

```
<IMG WIDTH=n HEIGHT=n>
```

where **n** is the width and height in pixels.

Using **WIDTH** and **HEIGHT** with the **&lt;IMG&gt;** element helps the page to load faster. This is because the browser can get on with laying out the rest of the page, as it knows the dimensions of the image before loading it. Without **WIDTH** and **HEIGHT**, one big image at the top of a page can stop the whole page from displaying until the image is loaded.

Another advantage is that if the user has image loading turned off in their browser, a box the size of the image will be displayed instead. This way, the formatting of the rest of the pages is left unchanged. If the attributes were missing and images were turned off, a default icon would be shown; as this is unlikely to be the same size as the image, text flow and other formatting would be different from what you intended.

> Note that although using **WIDTH** and **HEIGHT** will scale the image size to the required dimensions, the image file size remains the same. The attributes are useful for making minor adjustments to the image size, but it should not be used for large changes. If you want to significantly reduce the size of an image, do so using an image editing program. Otherwise the reduced image will take the same amount of time to load as the larger version.

## BORDER

A border can be inserted around an image with the **BORDER** attribute. The border is invisible in Internet Explorer but visible in Netscape Navigator. If the image is a hyperlink, then the border will be drawn in the appropriate hyperlink color. The syntax is:

```
<IMG BORDER=n>
```

where **n** is a numerical value in pixels. Setting **n** to 0 will turn the border off. Setting **n** to any other value will alter the thickness of the border; 1 is narrowest.

Assigning 0 to the **BORDER** attribute can be useful if you have a non-rectangular image that acts as a hyperlink, though it can confuse people if it is not clear that the image is clickable. The default value for **BORDER** is 1.

## HSPACE and VSPACE

These attributes are used to control the white space around an image. The syntax is:

```
<IMG HSPACE=n VSPACE=n>
```

where **n** is a numerical value in pixels.

## ISMAP and USEMAP

**ISMAP** and **USEMAP** are used with image maps which are discussed in the next chapter. **ISMAP** indicates to the browser that the image is a server-side imagemap, while **USEMAP** is used with client-side imagemaps and indicates to the browser which map file to use.

**54**

# Formats

At the present time, there are only two formats that are widely supported:

- GIF image format
- JPEG image format

## GIF Image Format

GIF (Graphics Interchange Format) is the most widely supported graphics format. It is capable of displaying images in black and white, gray scale or color. The one drawback of the GIF image format is that it is limited to displaying a maximum of 256 colors or gray scales. When you save an image in GIF format, the software searches for the 256 colors that best represent the colors in the image, and creates a color table.

The GIF format stores images in a compressed state. Because of the type of compression used, it is particularly effective for large areas of a single color, such as icons, company logos, etc. The compression technique is not suitable for photographic images—in this case, it is invariably better to use the JPEG format.

There are two versions of the GIF format: GIF87 and GIF89a. GIF89a has the advantage of being able to make a single color in the image transparent. This can lead to some stunning effects if used creatively. For instance, you could have a background image with a transparent GIF format image on top so that the background shows through, like this:

The code for this is:

```
<HTML>
<HEAD>
<TITLE>Transparent GIF images</TITLE>
</HEAD>

<BODY BACKGROUND="backgnd.gif">

<IMG SRC="logo.gif">

</BODY>
</HTML>
```

The words Instant HTML are, in fact, a graphic called **logo.gif**.
Because the image was saved in GIF format and the background
color of the image (which was, in fact, white) was set to transparent,
the background image (**backgnd.gif**) shows through.

Images destined to be downloaded over the web should be as small
as possible. The physical size of the image is not significant. What is
significant is the size of image file. The larger the file, the longer the
download time. The easiest way to reduce the file size for a GIF
format image is to reduce the number of colors that it contains.
Another good reason for reducing the number of colors is that many
computers can only display 256 colors at one time. This means that a
browser will quite happily display one GIF image containing 256
colors. However, if it tries to display two GIF files at the same time,
and they both have 256 colors that are different, the browser will
'dither' the colors—in other words, it will find the best compromise
between the two images. This often results in a complete mess with
neither image looking the way you expected it to.

A useful feature of the GIF image format is its ability to produce an
**interlaced** image. Normally a browser will load an image from top to
bottom. On a slow connection, the user will not see the whole image
until it has completely downloaded. With interlaced GIF files, the
whole image is displayed at once in a very low (blocky) resolution
which then builds up to a high resolution as the rest of the file
downloads. Although the time taken for either file type to download
is the same; the interlaced file appears to load faster because the
whole image can be seen at once. Many programs and utilities that
can produce interlaced and transparent GIF format files are available
on the Internet.

You can also use GIF89a to produce crude animation. We
discuss this, and other features of the **<IMG>** tag, in
Chapter 8.

# JPEG Image Format

The JPEG (Joint Photographic Experts Group) image format, pronounced *jaypeg*, was designed specifically for storing photographic images. Image compression is via a **lossy** compression technique, which means that the higher the compression ratio, the greater chance there is of the image not looking like the uncompressed version, as parts of the image are lost and then 'made up' on the fly according to an algorithm. This is not noticeable to the eye for most images, except at very high compression levels, though you should note that JPEG is very bad for text or images with hard edges. The JPEG image format is capable of storing images in millions of colors as opposed to the GIF format's 256. Interlacing and transparency are not supported by JPEG itself, but Netscape have introduced the Progressive JPEG format which produces a similar effect to interlaced GIF.

> You should be aware that some older browsers do not support the use of in-line JPEG images.

# PNG Format

A relatively new format that is rapidly gaining in popularity is PNG. In comparison to GIFs, this format produces smaller, faster loading files that can be viewed on different platforms without loss of quality. It produces interlaced images displaying the first image preview when just 1/64 of the image data has been downloaded (GIFs produce the first preview after 1/8 of the image data has been downloaded). PNGs will therefore display detail much quicker than GIFs. Another advantage is that you can include meta-information with the file which will, for example, allow the image to be located in a search based on its description rather than its file name. Although the PNG format is not suitable for photographic images, it can handle images that are a lot more complicated than GIF images, including ray traced scenes.

## The Single Pixel GIF Trick

This is a useful trick used by many web authors to achieve precise control over layout and formatting. We're not sure who thought of the original idea, but credit usually goes to David Siegel, who's web site is well worth a visit if you are at all interested in layout and design issues relating to web documents. His home page can be found at:

```
http://www.dsiegel.com/
```

It basically works like this. You have an image, in this case **dot_clear.gif**, which is an image consisting of one invisible pixel. When you want to space over or down, use this code:

```
<IMG SRC="dot_clear.gif" HSPACE=x VSPACE=y>
```

where **x** is the number of pixels horizontally, and **y** is the number of pixels vertically. This makes a clear rectangle of any size that you can use as a spacer to move things about.

Here's an example:

```
<HTML>
<HEAD>
<TITLE>Single pixel GIF trick</TITLE>
</HEAD>

<BODY BGCOLOR=WHITE>

<!-- Set the basefont first -->
<BASEFONT="ARIAL">

<IMG SRC=dot_clear.gif HSPACE=8 VSPACE=10>
This paragraph starts indented because<BR>
we have utilised the single pixel GIF<BR>
trick.<BR>

<IMG SRC=dot_clear.gif HSPACE=12 VSPACE=8>
This paragraph also starts with an<BR>
indent, but the indent is larger because<BR>
the value of HSPACE has been increased.

</BODY>
</HTML>
```

This is what it looks like in the browser:

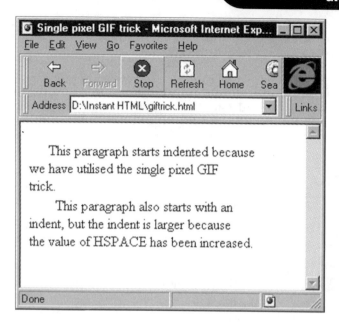

As you are coding your pages, it may be useful to use a colored pixel instead of a clear one. This makes it easier to understand exactly what's going on in your document. If we replace the **dot_clear.gif** with **dot_black.gif**, we get:

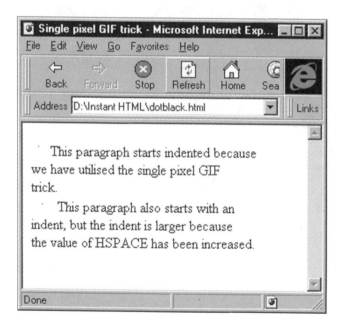

You can now see exactly what effect the image is having on the document. Don't forget to replace the visible dot with the invisible one when you've finished though!

Some HTML purists will no doubt tell you that this is a workaround that wastes bandwidth. Well, to a certain extent they're correct, but the image is extremely small and will be cached by the browser, so it will only ever be downloaded once, and then pulled from the user's system cache when required.

# Audio

There are several ways to add audio to your documents:

- RealAudio
- TrueSpeech
- Using the **<A>** tag to link to an audio file
- The **<BGSOUND>** tag

## Using Plug-ins

There are various plug-ins that you can get which will launch when you click on a link. The first is a technology known as **RealAudio**, or RA for short. This does, however, require RealAudio software at the server side. While many file formats require the whole file to be downloaded before anything is displayed, RealAudio is able to play the audio in streaming mode, which means that it plays during the download and usually does not even save the file. RealAudio is also able to synchronize sound and pictures so that the web page, or one or more of the frames in the page, are changed automatically at specified points in the audio stream. For an example, go to **www.backpage.co.uk**.

TrueSpeech is another plug-in based software option for browsers. It gives about the same quality result as RealAudio but requires no special server or file converters. Windows Sound Recorder can convert WAVs to TrueSpeech format and any web server can serve TrueSpeech sound with only one configuration change. TrueSpeech has been licensed by Microsoft, Intel, and other large corporations, and is growing in popularity.

# Using the Anchor Tag

Plug-ins are all well and good, but probably the simplest way of including sound in your documents is by using the anchor tag to enclose a sound file:

```
<A HREF="soundfile.au">This is a sound!</A>
```

The anchor tag is used to insert hyperlinks into an HTML document. We cover this in the next chapter.

You can insert a number of different sound format files into your documents. The WAV file format is probably the most widely supported.

# <BGSOUND>

Microsoft's Internet Explorer supports audio in the form of the **<BGSOUND>** element. The syntax is:

```
<BGSOUND SRC=url LOOP=n>
```

where **SRC** is the URL of the file to play.

**LOOP** specifies how many times the sound file will be played. If **n=1** or **INFINITE**, the sound will loop indefinitely. In the following example, the sound file **file.wav** will loop 6 times.

```
<BGSOUND SRC="http://www.myserver.com/sounds/
bell.wav" LOOP=6>
```

Note that the sound will start to play as soon as it has finished downloading. The user does not have to click on a link of any kind.

Be careful when using sound in your documents. A constantly repeating sound can be even more annoying than overusing blinking text. It is better to have one short sound that grabs your readers attention than a 20 minute long midi file that irritates.

Note also that people without soundcards won't hear any sounds, and many people turn sound off anyway. The only reason for using sound is for a special-effect—it should be short, or else easily ignored.

# Summary

In this chapter, we have explored how you can brighten up your web site using images. We have looked at the `<IMG>` tag and its attributes, and also discussed the different graphic file formats that are widely supported by browsers. We also took a brief look at how sound can be incorporated into your HTML documents.

We'll be coming back to the `<IMG>` tag both in Chapter 4, which discusses creating hyperlinks, and in Chapter 8, which looks at how you can animate your web site.

# Linking to Other Files

The heart of any HTML document is its hypertext links. Hypertext links give the user the ability to retrieve or display a different document in your own or someone else's collection simply by clicking the mouse on a word, phrase, or image.

## Hypertext Links

Your documents should be a collection of several separate pages connected together via hypertext links. No single document should be so long that the reader has to constantly scroll up and down to find the information they need. Where possible, break large documents down into smaller parts to limit the amount of scrolling. This also has the advantage of reducing download time if the reader is interested in just one part of the document.

## Creating Hypertext Links

To include hypertext links within your document, all you need to know is the document's unique address and how to include an **anchor** in your HTML code.

### URLs

Every single document on the Internet has its location defined by a unique address, known as a URL or Uniform Resource Locator. URLs are made up of the document's name preceded by the directory path, the domain name of the server where the document is located and the server's communication protocol, like this:

```
protocol://server domain name/path/filename
```

For example:

```
http://www.this_server.com/docs/mydocument.html
http://www.wrox.com/
ftp://ftp.shareware.com/pub/file.zip
```

> HTTP stands for HyperText Transfer Protocol. It is the mechanism used by web servers to transfer data back and forth between itself and the web pages.

The first of the above addresses is known as an **absolute** URL. This leaves nothing to chance and includes all the parts of the URL format—protocol, server, pathname, and document name.

The second example is similar, but doesn't refer to an exact file. In this instance, the server will return a previously configured default file, usually **index.html**.

The third example is another absolute URL, but rather than pointing to a web server by using HTTP, the server indicated is actually an FTP or File Transfer Protocol server. Other servers can also be specified such as **Telnet://**, **Gopher://**, etc.

Inside an HTML document we can use an additional type of reference, such as:

```
images/redball.gif
document.html#moreinfo.html
```

The first refers to a file relative to the current file, in this case in a lower subdirectory. The second refers to an anchor location inside a file.

## \<A> - The Anchor Tag

The anchor tag is used to define both the source and destination of a hypertext link. Anything that appears between the start anchor tag **\<A>**, and the end anchor tag **\</A>** becomes activated by the browser, allowing the user to click on that part of the document to take them somewhere else. Hypertext links are not just limited to text. You can also use images as hyperlinks by placing the image between the anchor tags in the same way that you would place text.

Allowable attributes for the anchor tag are:

  HREF

  NAME

REL

REV

TARGET

TITLE

## *HREF*

This defines a hypertext jump and points to the document that you want to link to. The syntax is:

`HREF=url`

where **url** is the address of the document that you want the link to take you to. If the document is on the same computer, then you can just specify the file name (and path if the file isn't in the same directory as the current document). In this case, you do not include the **http://machine/** part of the specifier. Where possible, it is usually best to specify addresses in a relative format because that will allow you to move all the files together to a new server without changing any of the hyperlinks.

## *NAME*

Defines a target for an internal hypertext link. The syntax is:

`NAME=name`

where **name** defines a point in the document that you want to be able to jump to. To specify this point as a link, use a **#** sign before the **name**. We'll look at how you use **NAME** in a moment.

## *REL*

Specifies a relative relationship. The syntax is

`REL=relationship`

This isn't widely used and should be avoided wherever possible.

## *REV*

Specifies the revision number.

**REV=revision**

Again, this isn't widely used and you should avoid using it if you can.

## TARGET

Indicates that the link should be loaded into the specified window. This attribute allows you to open the linked document in a separate window, so that the user can browse that page and follow any links, then close the window and return to the original document. The syntax is:

**TARGET=window**

where **window** is one of the following values:

| | |
|---|---|
| **window** | Loads the linked document into the specified window. If the window doesn't exist, the document will be loaded into a new window. The name of the window must start with an alphanumeric character. |
| **_blank** | Loads the link into a new blank window. This window isn't named. |
| **_parent** | Loads the document into the immediate parent of the current document. |
| **_self** | Loads the document into the current window. |
| **_top** | Loads the document into the main browser window. |

> Note that this is a nonstandard extension, and is not supported in all browsers. In addition, its action can be a little surprising to the user. We recommend that you don't use it.

## TITLE

Specifies the title that appears when the hyperlink is selected. The syntax is:

**TITLE=name**

This hasn't been implemented in Internet Explorer 3.0 or Netscape 3.0.

# Using Text as a Hyperlink

Have a look at the following example. This particular example uses text as the hyperlink:

```
<!DOCTYPE HTML PUBLIC "-//W3C//DTD HTML 3.2 Draft//EN">
<HTML>
<HEAD>
<TITLE>A hypertext link</TITLE>
</HEAD>

<BODY>
Clicking<A HREF="index.html"> right here</A> will open the
index.html page we saved earlier
</BODY>
</HTML>
```

> Note that there are spaces placed before the words 'right' and 'will'. This is because the tag itself has no effect on the document formatting. If you leave out the spaces, the sentence would be interpreted by the browser as **Clickingright herewill open the index.html page we saved earlier.** While this has no detrimental effect on the browser, it doesn't do anything for presentation!

If you execute this on the browser, you will see the following:

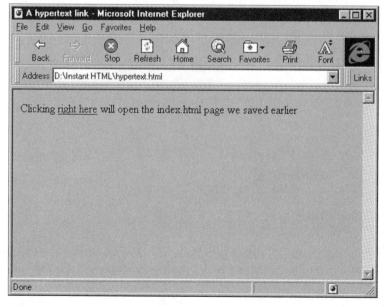

Clicking on the words right here will result in the browser requesting the file **index.html** and opening it. The line of code that achieves this:

```
Clicking<A HREF="index.html"> right here</A> will open the
index.html page we saved earlier
```

uses **<A>** to define the text right here as an anchor to **index.html**. We have added the attribute **HREF** or Hypertext **REF**erence to inform the browser of the file to fetch when the link is clicked. It is important to realize that the **HREF** we have defined is a **relative** link. In other words, the file to fetch is either in the same directory as the file being displayed, or in the search path. Had the file we wanted to open been on another server, the full URL would have to be included:

```
Clicking <A HREF="http://www.server.com/webstuff/
index.html"> right here</A> will open the index.html page
we saved earlier
```

# Using an Image as a Hyperlink

Now we will use an image or graphic as the hypertext link. One important thing to remember is that the image needs to look like it's clickable. You can achieve this by choosing an image which depicts the function or intended destination of the hyperlink.

```
<!DOCTYPE HTML PUBLIC "-//W3C//DTD HTML 3.2 Draft//EN">
<HTML>
<HEAD>
<TITLE>A hypertext link using an image</TITLE>
</HEAD>

<BODY>
<P>
To move to the previous or next page click on the buttons
below
<P>
<A HREF="first.html">
<IMG SRC="previous.gif" WIDTH=85 HEIGHT=22>
</A>
<A HREF="third.html">
<IMG SRC="next.gif" WIDTH=85 HEIGHT=22>
</A>
</BODY>
</HTML>
```

The main thing to note here is that we've replaced the text between the anchor tags with an image which we can click on to take us where we want to go. Let's take a closer look:

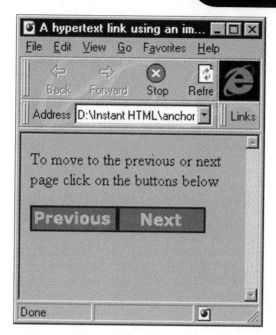

The important part of the code is this:

```
<P>
To move to the previous or next page click on the buttons
below
<P>
<A HREF="first.html">
<IMG SRC="previous.gif" WIDTH=85 HEIGHT=22>
</A>
<A HREF="third.html">
<IMG SRC="next.gif" WIDTH=85 HEIGHT=22>
</A>
```

The first thing we've done is to tell the reader what the images are
for, even though in this case the images show quite clearly what they
do. Next we have an anchor which points to the **first.html**
document. Then we have another anchor pointing to **third.html**.
Both anchors contain **<IMG>** tags for the relevant images that we
want displayed. As the images are contained within the anchor tags,
they become hyperlinks to the documents defined by the **HREF**
attribute of their corresponding anchor elements.

## Using the NAME Attribute

To help with the organization of your documents you can use the
**NAME** attribute with the **<A>** tag. The **NAME** attribute allows you to

define a name that refers to a location inside a document. It is then possible to use this name as the target of a hypertext link to jump to a location inside a document. Let's say your first page was a list of contents for the rest of your documents. If the list is long, your user will be forever scrolling up and down to find what they want. Using the **NAME** attribute, you can have a hypertext link at each logical break point in the list that returns the user to the top of the document. Have a look at this example:

```
<!DOCTYPE HTML PUBLIC "-//W3C//DTD HTML 3.2 Final//EN">
<HTML>
<HEAD>
<TITLE>The NAME attribute</TITLE>
</HEAD>
<BODY>
<H1>
<A NAME="top">List of contents</A>
</H1>
<P>
<H2>Introduction</H2>
Part 1<BR>
Part 2<BR>
Part 3<BR>
Part 4<BR>
<A HREF="#top">Back</A> to the top of this list

<P>
<H2>Chapter 1</H2>
Part 1<BR>
Part 2<BR>
Part 3<BR>
Part 4<BR>
Part 5<BR>
<A HREF="#top">Back</A> to the top of this list

<P>
<H2>Chapter 2</H2>
Part 1<BR>
Part 2<BR>
Part 3<BR>
Part 4<BR>
<A HREF="#top">Back</A> to the top of this list
</BODY>
</HTML>
```

Let's take a closer look at the code:

```
<H1>
<A NAME="top">List of contents</A>
</H1>
```

The first thing to notice is that we have made the **List of
contents** text into an anchor, although since there are no characters
inside the anchor tag, there is no clickable text associated with this
anchor. In this case we have given the **NAME** attribute the value **top**.
We could have used almost any value here, but as the purpose of
this target is to return the reader to the top of the document, **top**
makes sense.

Further down the code we have:

```
<A HREF="#top">Back</A> to the top of this list
```

Here we have chosen the word **Back** to be our hypertext link that
will return us to the top of the page. Take a close look at the anchor.
Note the **#top** specified as the hypertext link. When the reader clicks
on the link, the browser finds the **NAME** attribute with the value of
**top** in the current document, and displays that line as its first line.

The **NAME** attribute can also be used as a target to a particular word,
phrase or image in a different document. For example, in the
example above, it may be the case that the list of contents is on one
server, and the documents themselves are on a different server. So to
make the link between the list and the particular part of the
document we want to display, we could have:

```
<!DOCTYPE HTML PUBLIC "-//W3C//DTD HTML 3.2 Draft//EN">
<HTML>
<HEAD>
<TITLE>The NAME attribute</TITLE>
</HEAD>
<BODY>
<H1>
<A NAME="top">List of contents</A>
</H1>
<P>
<H2>Introduction</H2>
Part 1<BR>
Part 2<BR>
Part 3<BR>
Part 4<BR>
<A HREF="#top">Back</A> to the top of this list

<P>
<H2>Chapter 1</H2>
Part 1<BR>
Part 2<BR>
Part 3<BR>
Part 4<BR>
Part 5<BR>
```

```
    <A HREF="#top">Back</A> to the top of this list

    <P>
    <H2>Chapter 2</H2>
    Part 1<BR>
    Part 2<BR>
  <A HREF="http://www.myserver.com/docs/chapt2.html#part3">
  Part 3</A><BR>
    Part 4<BR>
    <A HREF="#top">Back</A> to the top of this list
    </BODY>
    </HTML>
```

What we've done here is turn the text **Part 3** into a hypertext link
that will request the document **chapt2.html** from
**www.myserver.com**. Note the appended **#part3** after the document
to be requested. The new page will open with part 3 at the top of
the browser window, even though parts 1 and 2 come before it.

> Note that in Netscape Navigator, if the HTML page
> referred to in **HREF** is held in the same directory as the
> HTML being executed, then the path should be omitted
> from the anchor. If not, Navigator will try to add the path
> to the current path name and this will cause an error, e.g.
> **http://www.wrox.com/http://www.wrox.com/**
> **eg.htm#part3**.

The code required in the target document **chapt2.html** would look
like:

```
<!DOCTYPE HTML PUBLIC "-//W3C//DTD HTML 3.2 Draft//EN">
<HTML>
<HEAD>
<TITLE>Chapter 2</TITLE>
</HEAD>
<BODY>
<H1>
Chapter 2
</H1>
Part 1<BR> Text in part 1
Part 2<BR> Text in part 2
<A NAME="part3">Part 3</A><BR> Text in part 3
Part 4<BR> Text in part 4

</BODY>
</HTML>
```

The important bit is:

```
<A NAME="part3">Part 3</A><BR> Text in part 3
```

Here we have explicitly named the text 'Part 3' as **part3**. Once this is done, we can then use the name as a target for any hypertext link from any other document. When the file opens, it will always display the line containing the **NAME** attribute whose value is set to **part3** at the top of the browser window.

# Imagemaps

Imagemaps allow users to access different documents by clicking different areas in an image. You can implement imagemaps in two ways: by storing imagemap information on a server or by including imagemap information in your document. Imagemaps implemented by information from the server are known as **server-side imagemaps**, those implemented from the document are known as **client-side imagemaps**.

## Server-side Imagemaps

Server-side imagemaps are supported by even the oldest browsers, however they do have disadvantages when compared to the newer client-side imagemaps. The first is that the user must have access to the server where the information is stored in order to be able to activate the map. If they're working offline, the map won't work. Second, each time the map is clicked, the browser requests information from the server. This increases the time taken to process the mouse click as well as using bandwidth.

Also, with client-side maps you get to see the URL you are hovering over, whereas with server-side maps you see just an x-y coordinate. You also have the server-side CGI map program permissions to worry about.

A server-side imagemap requires three files:

- The image itself
- A file containing the coordinates for the map
- A server script to process the request

Server-side imagemaps are processed in the following order:

- The user clicks on the image and the browser transmits the current coordinates and image name to the server.
- The server checks the relevant imagemap file, and sends back the URL information to the browser.

The browser then sends the server the request for the URL.

> Note that you should always supply text-based hyperlinks that correspond to the URLs defined by the imagemap for use by text-based browsers You should also use the `ALT` attribute with the `<IMG>` element to inform text-based browsers that the image is in fact an imagemap.

## Creating a Server-side Imagemap

The steps involved in creating a server-side imagemap are as follows:

 Create the image.

 Create the imagemap file to define the clickable regions.

 Write a CGI script to handle the processing of the information from the imagemap.

 Write the code into your document to specify the imagemap.

### Creating the Image

Creating an image is straightforward. You can use any drawing package you have available. Here's an example graphic for an imagemap:

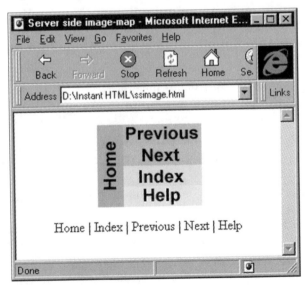

This is just a straightforward GIF format image. Note the text-based hyperlinks included for navigation by text-only browsers.

## Imagemap HTML Code

To specify an imagemap in your HTML document, you use the following syntax:

```
<A HREF="mapdirectory/example.map">
<IMG SRC="imagemap.gif" ISMAP>
</A>
```

Note the inclusion of the **ISMAP** attribute of the **<IMG>** tag. This is required to inform the browser that the image is an imagemap. Also, the **HREF** attribute of the **<A>** tag points to the map file, rather than to a URL as in the case of a normal hypertext link.

## Imagemap Files

The map file is a plain text file which defines the different regions on your image. There are two common formats for imagemaps: CERN and NCSA. CERN in Switzerland, and NCSA in America, both produced early versions of browsers which is where these formats originated. The CERN server can now be found on the W3C server at this address:

**http://www.w3.org/**

In addition, the popular Apache server uses a slightly different (but easier to use) format. Which one you use will depend upon your service provider. Both types allow you to define four kinds of region:

- Circles
- Rectangles
- Polygons
- Points

To move to a URL when any area of the image that isn't covered by one of the regions is clicked, you can use the keyword **default**. The syntax for the two types is different, as shown here:

NCSA Syntax:

```
default URL
circle URL center-x,center-y radius
rect URL left-x,top-y right-x,bottom-y
```

```
poly URL x1,y1 x2,y2 x3,y3 ... xn,yn
point URL x,y
```

CERN Syntax:

```
default URL
circle (center-x,center-y) radius URL
rectangle (left-x,top-y) (right-x,bottom-y) URL
polygon (x1,y1) (x2,y2) (x3,y3) ... (xn,yn)  URL
point (x,y) URL
```

As you can see, the main difference is that the CERN map has parentheses around each pair of coordinates and the URL is on the far right as opposed to the left.

An example NCSA map might look like this:

```
default http://www.myserver.org/test/index.html
rect http://www.myserver.org/test/help.html 50,25 100,50
rect http://www.myserver.org/test/news.html 101,151 51,76
```

This would define two rectangular areas on the image, one referencing **help.html** the other **news.html**. If the user clicks on an area of the image that isn't covered by the two rectangles, the default URL **index.html** will be referenced.

For more information, you should consult your service provider, or visit these addresses:

- **http://www.w3.org/pub/WWW/Server.html**—list of HTTP servers

- **http://www.w3.org/hypertext/WWW/Daemon/ Status.html**—the CERN server

- **http://hoohoo.ncsa.uiuc.edu/**—the NCSA server

- **http://www.apache.org/**—the Apache server.

In both formats, **x** values are measured in pixels starting at zero from the left and increasing towards the right. **y** values are measured in pixels starting at zero from the top and increasing as you move downwards. If two adjacent areas overlap each other, precedence is given to the one that appears first in the coordinates specified in the map file.

> You can find out the coordinates of different areas of your image by using your graphics package. As you move the cursor over each boundary point, the package will display the coordinates. Paint, for example, displays the coordinates in the status bar at the bottom.

There are several good utility programs available that can do most of the work for you when it comes to generating the map file. First, they display the image, then you draw the areas on the image, and lastly the program generates the map file for you in the format you request. All you have to do is upload it to the server. MapThis! is a good freeware program for this purpose; it can be found at this address:

`http://apb104.rh.psu.edu/pub/www/editors/mapthis/`

### CGI Scripts

The program that determines which area of the image was clicked and ensures the correct action is taken is a CGI script. The name for the default server script for handling map files is **htimage** for CERN and **imagemap** for NCSA. Quite often you can use the default script already on the server with no modifications.

# Client-side Imagemaps

Client-side imagemaps are defined in the HTML document rather than by the server. This kind of imagemap has the following advantages:

- They can be used offline
- They reduce network traffic and server loading
- They are quicker
- The destination for an area is shown in the browser window

At the present time, client-side imagemaps are still relatively new although most major browser vendors support their use.

## Creating a Client-side Imagemap

To include a client-side imagemap in your document, you use the <MAP> and <AREA> elements to actually create the map and define the links, and then point the browser at the map using the

<USEMAP> attribute of the <IMG> tag. The following code displays the image **map1.gif** and uses the map file **map1**:

```
<MAP NAME="map1">
<AREA SHAPE="RECT" COORDS="0, 0, 16, 16"
HREF="Sample1.htm">
<AREA SHAPE="RECT" COORDS="16, 0, 16, 16" NOHREF>
<AREA SHAPE="RECT" COORDS="0, 16, 16, 16"
HREF="Sample2.htm">
<AREA SHAPE="RECT" COORDS="16, 16, 16, 16"
HREF="Sample3.htm">
</MAP>
<IMG BORDER=0 SRC="map1.gif" USEMAP="#map1">
```

Let's have a look at the different elements.

# <MAP>

The **<MAP>** element specifies the name of the map and includes one or more **<AREA>** elements to specify areas of the image which can be clicked to move to a different document. The syntax is:

```
<MAP NAME="name">
```

The attribute **NAME** defines the name of the map, which is used with the **USEMAP** attribute of the **<IMG>** tag to direct the browser to the correct map.

# <AREA>

The **<AREA>** tag is used to define the different hot spots that the user can click on to link to another document. This tag has the following attributes:

- SHAPE
- COORDS
- NOHREF
- HREF
- TARGET

## *SHAPE*

**SHAPE** defines the shape of the active link. The syntax is:

```
SHAPE=shape
```

where **shape** is **RECT**, **CIRCLE**, or **POLYGON**. The default is **RECT**.

In addition, you can use **SHAPE=default** to provide a default target when a location outside your mapped shapes is selected.

### COORDS

Defines the coordinates of the shape. For a rectangle, you need to define four coordinates:

```
COORDS=x1,y1 x2,y2
```

For a circle, you define three coordinates:

```
COORDS=centerx, centery, radius
```

and for a polygon, you give a series of coordinate pairs that define the shape.

> If the shapes you define overlap, the browser searches sequentially through the list of **<AREA>** elements in the map and uses the first one listed.

### NOHREF

**NOHREF** indicates that the area defined will not be a hyperlink and therefore won't lead anywhere when clicked.

### HREF

Specifies the document that will be loaded when the area of the image is clicked. The syntax is:

```
HREF=url
```

## A Simple Client Map

Here's a very simple example of a client-side map, showing how the various elements are put together.

```
<!DOCTYPE HTML PUBLIC "-//W3C//DTD HTML 3.2 Draft//EN">
<HTML>
<HEAD>
<TITLE>An example map</TITLE>
</HEAD>
<BODY>
<IMG SRC="mapgif.gif" USEMAP="#simplemap">
<P>Here is any text you like.<BR>
<P>Somewhere in the document we specify a map section,
which is never seen in the browser.
<MAP NAME="simplemap">
```

**79**

```
<AREA SHAPE="rect" COORDS="0,0,50,100"
HREF="previous.html">
<AREA SHAPE="rect" COORDS="50,0,100,100" HREF="next.html">
</MAP>
</BODY>
</HTML>
```

The important parts are the `<IMG>` tag, which specifies both an image and a `USEMAP` attribute, and the `<MAP>` tag, which has the `NAME` attribute linking it to the earlier `<IMG>` tag, and contains the mapping and URL information the client needs to perform the jumps when the image is clicked.

You can also define the map to use as an external link by including the URL of the file containing the `<MAP>` tag. This is useful as it means that you don't have to type the code over and over again if you want to reuse the map in multiple documents, but isn't widely supported.

As with server-side imagemaps, you can use a utility program to define the coordinates for the map file, and then import it to your HTML document if you wish.

# Summary

This chapter has shown you how to add hypertext links to your documents. We introduced URLs (Uniform Resource Locators) which are the addresses used to uniquely identify the location of a document. We looked at how they are referenced within a browser and also inside HTML code. We also introduced the `<A>` tag which refers to both the source and destination of a link. In particular, we looked at how the `NAME` attribute can be used to jump to a specific location within a document. Lastly, we looked at how images, known as imagemaps, can be used as hypertext links, both on the server side and the client side.

Chapter

5

# Tables

Tables are fully supported by the latest versions of Netscape Navigator and Internet Explorer. They offer full backward compatibility with Netscape Navigator 1.1N, and are supported by the draft specification of HTML 3.2.

## Creating a Table

You can use tables for many different purposes. The obvious use is for structuring information, such as timetable data, technical data, etc. Tables can also be used to improve the layout of your document—for example, you can use tables to place text in columns like a newspaper, or to align images.

## A Basic Table

All tables are contained within the **<TABLE>** and **</TABLE>** tags. Within these tags, you use other tags to specify how many columns and rows there are, as well as the data that each column and row contains.

Have a look at the following code:

```
<!DOCTYPE HTML PUBLIC "-//W3C//DTD HTML 3.2 Draft//EN">
<HTML>
<HEAD>
<TITLE>A basic table</TITLE>
</HEAD>

<BODY>

<TABLE>
  <TR><TD>Wright <TD>S. <TD>steve@stevewri.demon.co.uk
  <TR><TD>Mouse  <TD>M. <TD>mouse@anywhere.com
```

```
  <TR><TD>Fudd <TD>E. <TD>elma@myplace.org
  </TABLE>

  </BODY>
  </HTML>
```

If you view this, you'll see:

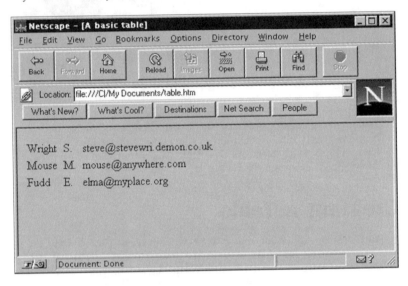

This is the simplest form of a table. Note that, by default, the table is left aligned.

The important lines of code are:

```
<TABLE>
  <TR><TD>Wright <TD>S.   <TD>steve@stevewri.demon.co.uk
  <TR><TD>Mouse  <TD>M.   <TD>mouse@anywhere.com
  <TR><TD>Fudd   <TD>E.   <TD>elma@myplace.org
</TABLE>
```

You start every table with the **<TABLE>** tag and end it with
**</TABLE>**. Tables consist of a number of rows and columns, and you
define these with the **<TR>** (table row) and **<TD>** (table data) tags.
**<TR>** indicates a new row. It doesn't require an end tag, because the
next **<TR>** tag automatically implies that the previous row has
ended. The **<TD>** tag starts a new cell within a row. In the above
example, there are three 3 rows, each with 3 cells in them.

<TABLE>

# More Complex Tables

To create more sophisticated tables, you need to be aware of the full set of attributes that you can use with the table tags. We'll look at these now.

## <TABLE>

You can specify the following attributes for the **<TABLE>** tag. These attributes affect the entire table:

- **ALIGN**
- **BORDER**
- **CELLPADDING**
- **CELLSPACING**
- **COLS**
- **FRAME**
- **RULES**
- **WIDTH**

### ALIGN

Defines the alignment of the entire table, relative to the margins of the browser. The syntax is:

```
<TABLE ALIGN=type>
```

where **type** is either **LEFT**, **RIGHT**, or **CENTER**. The default is **LEFT**.

---

If you use **ALIGN=LEFT** or **ALIGN=RIGHT**, text will flow round the table. To avoid this you can use <BR CLEAR=value> after the </TABLE> tag, where **value** is **LEFT** or **RIGHT**.

---

### BORDER

Draws a border around both the table itself and all the individual cells in it. The syntax is:

```
<TABLE BORDER=n>
```

where **n** is the width of the border in pixels. Setting **BORDER=0**, or omitting the attribute, will result in no visible border.

Using **BORDER** on its own, with no value, will result in a border width of 1 pixel.

## CELLPADDING

Specifies the amount of space between the sides of a cell and its contents. The syntax is:

`<TABLE CELLPADDING=n>`

where **n** is the amount of space in pixels.

## CELLSPACING

Specifies the amount of space between the frame of the table and the cells in the table. The syntax is:

`<TABLE CELLSPACING=n>`

where **n** is the amount of space in pixels.

## COLS

Specifies the number of columns in the table. The syntax is:

`<TABLE COLS=n>`

where **n** is the number of columns. This attribute is useful if you have a large table, as it will speed up the processing.

## FRAME

Specifies which outer borders of the table are displayed. **FRAME** allows more precise control than the **BORDER** attribute of the **TABLE** tag. The syntax is:

`<TABLE FRAME=type>`

where **type** can be one of the following:

| | |
|---|---|
| **VOID** | No outer borders are displayed. |
| **ABOVE** | Displays the top border. |
| **BELOW** | Displays the bottom border. |
| **HSIDES** | Displays the top and bottom borders. |
| **LHS** | Displays the left border. |
| **RHS** | Displays the right border. |

**VSIDES**   Displays the left and right borders.

**BOX**   Displays a border on all sides of the table frame.

**BORDER**   Displays a border on all sides of the table frame.

**FRAME** acts upon the outer border around the table. By default, all outer borders are displayed. Note that if both the **FRAME** and **BORDER** attributes of the **\<TABLE\>** tag are used, **FRAME** takes precedence. So if **BORDER** is set to 4 and **FRAME** to **VOID**, then only the vertical and horizontal lines between cells and rows will be shown. Specifying **\<TABLE BORDER=n\>** has the same effect as **FRAME=BORDER**, and **\<TABLE BORDER=0\>** has the same effect as **FRAME=VOID**.

## RULES

Specifies which inner borders of the table are displayed. The syntax is:

`<TABLE RULES=type>`

where **type** is one of the following:

**NONE**   No inner borders are displayed.

**GROUPS**   Displays horizontal borders between all table groups. Groups are specified by the **THEAD**, **TBODY**, **TFOOT**, and **COLGROUP** elements.

**ROWS**   Displays horizontal borders between all table rows.

**COLS**   Displays vertical borders between all table columns.

**ALL**   Displays a border on all rows and columns.

By default, all inner borders are displayed.

## WIDTH

Sets the width of the table. The syntax is:

`<TABLE WIDTH=n>`

where **n** is the width in pixels or as a percentage of the window. To set a percentage you must append a **%** sign to the end of the value.

# IE Extensions to <TABLE>

Microsoft have added a number of extensions which can be used with the **<TABLE>** tag to further enhance the look of tables:

- BACKGROUND

- BGCOLOR

- BORDERCOLOR

- BORDERCOLORDARK

- BORDERCOLORLIGHT

> BGCOLOR is supported by Netscape, but remember that if you use extensions, they will not, in general, work for anyone viewing your document with a different browser.

### BACKGROUND

Specifies a background picture. The syntax is:

`<TABLE BACKGROUND=url>`

The picture defined by **url** is tiled behind the text and graphics.

### BGCOLOR

Specifies the background color for the table. The syntax is:

`<TABLE BGCOLOR="#rrggbb">`

where **rrggbb** are hexadecimal values for red, green, and blue. Predefined color names can also be used, if they are supported by your browser.

### BORDERCOLOR

Specifies the color of the table border. The syntax is:

`<TABLE BORDERCOLOR="#rrggbb">`

Again, predefined color names can be substituted for the hexadecimal values, if they are supported by your browser.

### BORDERCOLORDARK

Used to create a 3D border. **BORDERCOLORDARK** specifies the dark side of a 3D border.

```
<TABLE BORDERCOLORDARK="#rrggbb">
```

This attribute can only be used with **BORDER**.

### BORDERCOLORLIGHT

Used to create a 3D border. **BORDERCOLORLIGHT** specifies the light side of a 3D border.

```
<TABLE BORDERCOLORLIGHT="#rrggbb">
```

This attribute can only be used with **BORDER**.

# &lt;TR&gt;

The **&lt;TR&gt;** element indicates the start of a table row. It has a corresponding end tag **&lt;/TR&gt;** but this can be omitted. Anything between the first **&lt;TR&gt;** element and the next will be on the same row. The **&lt;TR&gt;** element has its own attributes, which will affect the entire row of cells.

The attributes for **&lt;TR&gt;** are:

- **ALIGN**
- **VALIGN**
- **CHAR**
- **CHAROFF**

### ALIGN

**ALIGN** will align the text in the cells in the row. The syntax is:

```
<TR ALIGN=type>
```

where **type** is one of **LEFT**, **CENTER**, or **RIGHT**.

| | |
|---|---|
| **LEFT** | Text in that row is left aligned. |
| **RIGHT** | Text in that row is right aligned. |
| **CENTER** | Text in that row is centered. |

### VALIGN

**VALIGN** specifies the vertical alignment of text in the cells in the row.

The syntax is:

`<TR VALIGN=type>`

where type is one of **TOP, MIDDLE, BOTTOM,** or **BASELINE**

**TOP**        Text in that row is aligned with the top of each cell.

**MIDDLE**     Text in that row is aligned with the middle of each cell.

**BOTTOM**     Text in that row is aligned with the bottom of each cell.

**BASELINE**   Text in that row is aligned along a common baseline.

### CHAR

**CHAR** specifies the alignment character used with **ALIGN**. The default is a decimal point. The syntax is:

`<TR CHAR="character">`

### CHAROFF

**CHAROFF** specifies the offset to the first alignment character. The offset is normally from the left margin for Latin-based text. If a line doesn't include the alignment character, then it is shifted so that it ends at the alignment position. The syntax is:

`<TR CHAROFF="50%">`

# Microsoft Extensions to <TR>

Microsoft have added the following extensions to the standard attributes for **<TR>** for use with Internet Explorer:

- BACKGROUND
- BGCOLOR
- BORDERCOLOR
- BORDERCOLORLIGHT
- BORDERCOLORDARK

The values for these attributes are the same as for the corresponding **<TABLE>** attributes discussed earlier.

# <TD>

**<TD>** is the start of table data and creates a cell. The **<TD>** element has a corresponding end tag **</TD>** but, like **</TR>**, this can be omitted. Anything between the first **<TD>** tag and the next will be displayed in one cell, and each new cell in a row is defined by the next **<TD>** tag.

The **<TD>** element has its own set of attributes, which affect only that cell. These attributes will take precedence over the same attributes set by the **<TR>** tag. In turn, the **<TR>** tag attributes take precedence over the same attributes set by the **<TABLE>** tag. Allowable attributes for the **<TD>** element are:

- **ALIGN**
- **AXIS**
- **AXES**
- **CHAR**
- **CHAROFF**
- **COLSPAN**
- **ROWSPAN**
- **NOWRAP**
- **VALIGN**

## ALIGN, VALIGN, CHAR, and CHAROFF

The values for **ALIGN**, **VALIGN**, **CHAR** and **CHAROFF** are the same as for the **<TABLE>** and **<TR>** tags described previously.

## AXIS

**AXIS** provides an abbreviated name for a header cell, which can be used if the table is converted to another form. Notable if the table is converted to speech. The syntax is:

```
<TD AXIS="Fruit">
```

## AXES

This is a comma-separated list of names identifying the row and column headers for the current cell. Like **AXIS**, it may be used if the table is converted to speech.

The syntax is:

```
<TD AXES="Fruit,Type">
```

## COLSPAN

**COLSPAN** specifies the number of table columns that the cell spans. The syntax is:

```
<TD COLSPAN=n>
```

where **n** is the number of columns to span. **COLSPAN** allows you to join cells, just like you can in spreadsheet programs. If you want to include the same data in more than one adjacent column on a row, use **COLSPAN** to join the cells, and just enter that data once.

## ROWSPAN

**ROWSPAN** specifies the number of table rows the cell will span. The syntax is:

```
<TD ROWSPAN=n>
```

where **n** is the number of rows to span. Like **COLSPAN**, **ROWSPAN** allows you to join cells—you can include one set of data and make it span multiple rows.

## NOWRAP

**NOWRAP** stops the text from wrapping in the cell. The syntax is simply:

```
<TD NOWRAP>
```

This is useful to stop the text from wrapping within the cell when you are formatting your data, especially if only one cell would contain data that is likely to wrap to the next line. Use it with caution, though, since it can result in very wide cells.

# Microsoft Extensions to <TD>

Microsoft have added the following extensions to **<TD>** and these are supported by Internet Explorer:

 **BACKGROUND**

 **BGCOLOR**

 **BORDERCOLOR**

<TD>

 **BORDERCOLORLIGHT**

 **BORDERCOLORDARK**

They can take the same values as the extensions of the same names discussed earlier.

# Adding Row and Column Headings

Row and column headings can be included using the **<TH>** element. This is similar to the **<TD>** element, but emphasizes the text in the cell, and thus distinguishes it from text in **<TD>** cells. The attributes are the same as for the **<TD>** element.

# Adding a Caption

You can include a caption for your table by using the **<CAPTION>** element. This places a caption above your table.

You can align the caption using

```
<CAPTION ALIGN=type>
</CAPTION>
```

where **type** is **TOP**, **BOTTOM**, **LEFT**, or **RIGHT**.

> Note that Netscape supports just the **TOP** and **BOTTOM** values.

This element is valid only within the **TABLE** element, and should come immediately after the **<TABLE>** tag. It must have an end tag.

# Using Tables

Let's look at an example using some of the attributes we've just looked at:

```
<!DOCTYPE HTML PUBLIC  "-//W3C//DTD HTML 3.2 Draft//EN">
<HTML>
<HEAD>
<TITLE>Tables</TITLE>
</HEAD>
<BODY>
<TABLE BORDER=1>
<CAPTION>HP printers in use</CAPTION>
<TR align=center><TH><TH COLSPAN=3>Inkjet
```

```
<TH COLSPAN=2>Laser
<TR ALIGN=CENTER><TH><TH>Original<TH>500<TH>600<TH>2p<TH>4m
<TR ALIGN=CENTER><TH>Software<TD>0<TD>2<TD>1<TD>0<TD>2
<TR ALIGN=CENTER><TH>Hardware<TD>1<TD>1<TD>0<TD>1<TD>0
<TR ALIGN=CENTER><TH>Sales<TD>0<TD>0<TD>0<TD>1<TD>1
<TR ALIGN=CENTER><TH>Admin<BR>Office
<TD>0<TD>2<TD>0<TD>0<TD>0
</TABLE>
</BODY>
</HTML>
```

Viewed using Netscape, it looks like this:

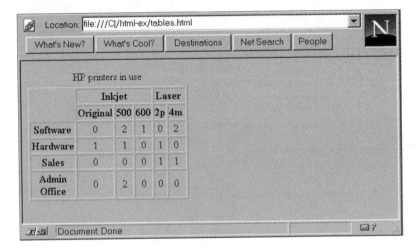

The code that commences the table is:

```
<TABLE BORDER=1>
<CAPTION>HP printers in use</CAPTION>
```

This simply sets the **BORDER** attribute to 1 to give a border 1 pixel wide and sets a caption.

We then have:

```
<TR ALIGN=CENTER><TH><TH COLSPAN=3>Inkjet
<TH COLSPAN=2>Laser
<TR ALIGN=CENTER><TH><TH>Original<TH>500<TH>600<TH>2p<TH>4m
```

These set the columnar headings for the table. The top left cell of the table should be empty, as it is the cross section of the heading column and first row, which includes the row headings. Therefore, we start off with a **<TR>** and an empty **<TH>**. The next cell includes the first main heading and is set to span 3 columns. The third cell includes another heading and spans 2 columns.

In the second row, we again have an empty first cell, and then include entries in each **<TH>** cell, as the subheadings for each column.

```
<TR ALIGN=CENTER><TH>Software<TD>0<TD>2<TD>1<TD>0<TD>2
<TR ALIGN=CENTER><TH>Hardware<TD>1<TD>1<TD>0<TD>1<TD>0
<TR ALIGN=CENTER><TH>Sales<TD>0<TD>0<TD>0<TD>1<TD>1
<TR ALIGN=CENTER><TH>Admin<BR>Office
<TD>0<TD>2<TD>0<TD>0<TD>0
</TABLE>
```

The next four lines of code specify the row headings and the data for the table. Each row begins with a header cell, and then includes four cells of data.

Each row in the table is set with **ALIGN=center** so the text in each cell is centered.

## Overriding Settings

We can jazz up the table above by adding colors. So for example, if you wanted to draw attention to the fact that printers are unevenly distributed in the Admin Office, you could replace the line of code shown for the Admin Office with:

```
<TR ALIGN=CENTER BGCOLOR=lime><TH>Drawing<BR>Office<TD>0<TD
BGCOLOR=fuchsia>2<TD>0<TD>0<TD>0
```

Here, the color is first set to lime for the whole row. If we had set a background color for the whole table, this line would override that color, but just for this line. We then add **BGCOLOR=fuchsia** in the third cell. This overrides the color previously set for the row, and turns the background of that cell, but that cell only, to fuchsia.

You could also override the center alignment that was set for each row by adding another **ALIGN** attribute in the cell you want to change.

## <COL>

This allows the specification of column-based attributes. It can be used to override the settings given in a **COLGROUP** (see below) for a particular column. It takes the same attributes as **COLGROUP**.

# <COLGROUP>

You can define a number of columns as belonging to a group using the **<COLGROUP>** element. This is useful if you want to apply the same properties to one particular group. For example, in our above example, we want the text in all cells to be centered. Instead of using **ALIGN=CENTER** with each **<TR>** element, we can use **COLGROUP**.

It takes the attributes **ALIGN**, **CHAR**, **CHAROFF**, and **VALIGN**, as previously described in the **<TR>** section. In addition, it takes the attributes **SPAN** and **WIDTH**.

## SPAN

Specifies the number of consecutive columns in a group. The syntax is:

```
<COLGROUP SPAN=n>
```

where **n** is the number of columns.

## WIDTH

Specifies the default width for each of the grouped columns. The general syntax is:

```
<COLGROUP WIDTH=n>
```

## Using Column Groups

Take a look at this new improved version of our printer table:

```
<!DOCTYPE HTML PUBLIC  "-//W3C//DTD HTML 3.2 Draft//EN">

<HTML>
<HEAD>
<TITLE>Tables</TITLE>
</HEAD>
<BODY>
<TABLE BORDER=1>
<COLGROUP SPAN =6 ALIGN=CENTER>
<CAPTION ALIGN=TOP>HP printers in use</CAPTION>
<TR><TH><TH COLSPAN=3>Inkjet<TH COLSPAN=2>Laser
<TR><TH><TH>Original<TH>500<TH>600<TH>2p<TH>4m
<TR><TH>Software<TD>0<TD>2<TD>1<TD>0<TD >2
<TR><TH>Hardware<TD>1<TD>1<TD>0<TD>1<TD>0
<TR><TH>Sales<TD>0<TD>0<TD>0<TD>1<TD>1
```

```
<TR><TH>Admin<BR>Office<TD>0<TD>2<TD>0<TD>0<TD>0

</TABLE>
</BODY>
</HTML>
```

> Although COLGROUP is in the 3.2 standard, you will find
> that it doesn't function in Netscape Navigator 3.0. Also
> worth mentioning is the fact that text in the <TH> tag is
> automatically center aligned, and this overrides any
> alignment you may assign in the COLGROUP tag.

This produces the same result as the earlier code, except that it is
quicker to write and easier to read.

There is just one <COLGROUP> entry, meaning we are defining just
one group. Therefore the alignment set for this group will be applied
to all the columns.

If we had wanted to set different alignments for the inkjet entries
and the laser printer entries, we could have used the following code:

```
<COLGROUP ALIGN=CENTER>
<COLGROUP SPAN=3 ALIGN=LEFT>
<COLGROUP SPAN=2 ALIGN=RIGHT>
```

In this case, the entries in the first column are centered, the entries in
the next three columns (the inkjet details) are left-aligned, and the
data in the next two columns (the laser printer details) are right-
aligned.

## Table Head, Foot, and Body Elements.

HTML 3.2 introduces the idea of tables being composed of three
sections, a header, a body, and a footer, using the tags <THEAD>,
<TBODY>, and <TFOOT>. By default, tables consist of just a body,
which ensures backward compatibility in the absence of explicit tags.

The principal use for these is when a table is so large it's split across
multiple pages. When the table is printed, header and footer rows
will be displayed on each of the pages the table appears in, while
the body rows flow normally. If it is displayed on a screen, then the
browser may display the body section as a separate scrolling region,
inside the header and footer rows. The <TFOOT> section must come
before the <TBODY> section.

Each tag may have the **ALIGN**, **CHAR**, **CHAROFF**, and **VALIGN**
attributes discussed earlier, and there must be at least one row

(`<TR>`) in each section if that section is defined.

To split your table into sections, surround the row information with the section tags, like this:

```
<THEAD>
some rows
</THEAD>
<TFOOT>
some rows
</TFOOT>
<TBODY>
some rows
</TBODY>
```

## Other Elements Inside Tables

You can include any other element you like inside a table cell. In other words, headers, paragraphs, lists, images, hypertext links, and even other tables (known as **nesting**). This practice is now becoming very popular among experienced authors as it affords a relatively simple way to lay out a complex document. Here's a more complex example showing how to incorporate some of these effects:

```
<!DOCTYPE HTML PUBLIC "-//W3C//DTD HTML 3.2 Draft//EN">
<HTML>
<HEAD>
<TITLE>An example of tables</TITLE></HEAD>
<BODY BGCOLOR=white>

<TABLE BGCOLOR=white CELLPADDING=2  BORDER=0 WIDTH=100%>

  <TR  ALIGN=RIGHT VALIGN=CENTER>

        <TD><IMG SRC="1.gif">
        <TD><IMG SRC="2.gif">
        <TD><IMG SRC="3.gif">
        <TD><IMG SRC="4.gif">

  <TR BGCOLOR=aqua VALIGN=TOP>

        <TD BGCOLOR=white><IMG SRC="coffee.gif"
                    ALT="Coffee cup">
        <TD VALIGN=CENTER>Guess what? you can now order
                    our range of coffee beans online!
        <TD ALIGN=RIGHT VALIGN=CENTER><B>For a limited
                    period, we are giving away a free coffee
                    cup with every purchase made</B>
        <TD BGCOLOR=aqua>

<!—begin nested table—>
```

```
<TABLE BGCOLOR=white CELLPADDING=0 BORDER=0 WIDTH=95%
ALIGN=RIGHT>

  <TR>

        <TD>Why not check out our online tips for
                    making better coffee?
        <TD BGCOLOR=pink>Better still, leave us your
                    own hints and tips!

</TABLE>

<!--end of nested table-->

  <TR>

        <TD COLSPAN=2 VALIGN=TOP WIDTH=50%>Welcome to our
            very special web site. From here you can
            find out everything you ever wanted to
            know about coffee, including how to make
            it, where the beans come from, what
            varieties are available and much, much more.
        <TD COLSPAN=2 VALIGN=TOP BGCOLOR=silver><FONT
            COLOR=white><B>Ever wondered what goes on in a
            coffee making factory, then check this out.
            Our indispensible guide to coffee making shows
            you everything from harvesting to
            packaging.</B></FONT>

</TABLE>
</BODY>
</HTML>
```

This code, viewed in Internet Explorer, is rendered as:

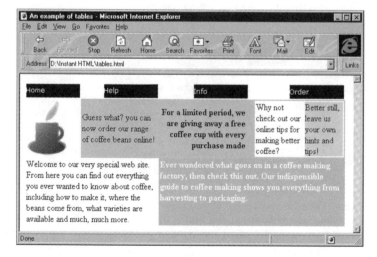

97

Breaking down the code, we have:

```
<BODY BGCOLOR=white>

<TABLE BGCOLOR=white CELLPADDING=2 BORDER=0 WIDTH=100%>
```

First of all, we've set the background color of the page to white with
the **BGCOLOR** attribute of the **<BODY>** tag. This is important as our
table will have no borders and we want to give the impression of
'page formatting' rather than a table. Next, we start the table with
the **<TABLE>** tag and set some attributes. We first set the overall
background color of the table to white with the **BGCOLOR** attribute.
Next is **CELLPADDING=2**; this means that there will be 2 pixels of
space between each cell's borders and its contents. We've set **BORDER**
to 0 so that no borders will be shown around the table and the
**WIDTH** is set to 100%, meaning the table will take up the entire
width of the browser window.

Next, we have:

```
<TR  ALIGN=RIGHT VALIGN=CENTER>

        <TD><IMG SRC="1.gif">
        <TD><IMG SRC="2.gif">
        <TD><IMG SRC="3.gif">
        <TD><IMG SRC="4.gif">
```

**<TR>** starts the first row of cells. **ALIGN=RIGHT** means that any data
in the cells will be right aligned. **VALIGN=CENTER** sets the vertical
alignment of the data within the cells to the center. The four **<TD>**
tags define four separate cells each containing an image. As there are
no attributes applied to the **<TD>** tags, the properties will be
inherited from the previous **<TR>** tag.

Next:

```
<TR BGCOLOR=aqua VALIGN=TOP>

        <TD BGCOLOR=white><IMG SRC="coffee.gif"
                ALT="Coffee cup">
        <TD VALIGN=CENTER>Guess what? you can now order
                our range of coffee beans online!
        <TD ALIGN=RIGHT VALIGN=CENTER><B>For a limited
                period, we are giving away a free coffee
                cup with every purchase made</B>
        <TD BGCOLOR=aqua>
```

**<TR>** starts the next row of cells. Notice that the **BGCOLOR** attribute
has been set to aqua for the entire row, as well as **VALIGN=TOP**,
which will vertically align the data in the cells to the top. The first

`<TD>` tag contains an image, **coffee.gif**. We have overridden the default table row color of aqua with white as defined by the **BGCOLOR=white** attribute. The second `<TD>` tag contains some text. This cell will be shown in aqua as it will inherit its color from the preceding `<TR>` tag. The third `<TD>` tag will align the text within the cell to the right as defined by the **ALIGN=RIGHT** attribute. The fourth `<TD>` tag contains no data, but the color is set to aqua. This is done so that we don't end up with a cell at the end of the row that appears in white. It will also contain a nested table, the code for which is:

```
<TABLE BGCOLOR=white CELLPADDING=0 BORDER=0 WIDTH=95%
ALIGN=RIGHT>

  <TR>

        <TD>Why not check out our online tips for making
                  better coffee?
        <TD BGCOLOR=pink>Better still, leave us your own
                  hints and tips!

  </TABLE>
```

As this is a nested table, it starts with a `<TABLE>` tag. We've set the default color for the nested table to white, and given it a width of 95%. This gives the illusion of the text being 'on top' of the table below. `<TR>` starts the only table row, and the two `<TD>` tags define two cells in the row, the second having a background color of pink. The `</TABLE>` tag ends the nested table.

Then we go back to the main table:

```
  <TR>

        <TD COLSPAN=2 VALIGN=TOP WIDTH=50%>Welcome to
                  our very special web site. From here you
                  can find out everything you ever wanted
                  to know about coffee, including how to
                  make it, where the beans come from, what
                  varieties are available and much, much
                  more.
        <TD COLSPAN=2 VALIGN=TOP BGCOLOR=silver><FONT
                  COLOR=white><B>Ever wondered what goes
                  on in a coffee making factory, then
                  check this out. Our indispensible guide
                  to coffee making shows you everything
                  from harvesting to packaging.</B></FONT>

  </TABLE>
```

`<TR>` starts our next row. The first `<TD>` tag has the **COLSPAN** attribute set to 2 so that the cell will span two columns. We have set the **WIDTH** to 50% so that it gives our table a less uniform look. The second `<TD>` tag is also set to span 2 columns and its background color is set to silver, to separate it from the previous cell. Finally, the `</TABLE>` tag ends our table.

# Summary

In this chapter, we've looked at all the aspects of tables. We started with an example of the most basic table before considering all of the attributes available. We looked at how the formatting of individual cells can be affected, and how you can format an entire table and then override that format for specific cells. We also looked at the `<COLGROUP>` tag, and how this can be used to simplify your code. Finally, we looked at how nested tables can be used to format whole pages of graphics and text.

Bear in mind that tables may not always be formatted on someone else's system in the same way as they are on yours. At the present time, there are a lot of extensions to the basic table model put forward by the W3C. Using these extensions is likely to limit the number of people that can view your information effectively. If you are going to use tables with extensions, it's a good idea to provide alternative pages, formatted without tables, for those browsers incapable of utilizing them.

# 6

# Frames

Frames give you a way of organizing the way information is displayed. They allow you to divide up the main browser window into different sections (like panes in a window), and then display different documents in each section. For example, you could display a list of contents in one frame and the actual content in another. Other uses for frames include displaying logos, copyright notices, navigation buttons, etc. Using frames in this way means that you can provide a consistent look and feel to your web site; you could have, for instance, a narrow frame at the bottom of the window that is displayed constantly, and a second frame in which important new information is shown.

Once you start using frames, it's very easy to get carried away and use them for everything: logo at the top, navigation aids down the side, adverts at the bottom.... Be sparing with your use of frames, and remember that not everyone will be viewing your site at the same resolution as you. Leave enough room for the main frame, where the bulk of your information will appear.

# Creating Frames

To use frames, you need to create a document that uses the **<FRAMESET>** and **<FRAME>** elements to divide the main window into rectangular frames. It's important not to confuse their functions:

 **<FRAMESET>** is the container element, and defines how all your frames will behave.

 **<FRAME>** is the element that defines each individual frame, and how that particular frame will behave.

For each frame, you specify an HTML document that contains the content (text and images) to fill the frame.

# An Example Frame

Let's start with a simple example:

```
<HTML>
<HEAD>
<TITLE>Simple frame example</TITLE>
</HEAD>

<FRAMESET ROWS="100%" COLS="45%,*">
 <FRAME SRC="index.html">
 <FRAME SRC="giftrick.html">
<NOFRAMES>
Sorry, our default version of this document contains
frames.<BR>You can view our frame-free version by going
<A HREF="indexnf.html">here.</A>
</NOFRAMES>
</FRAMESET>
</HTML>
```

> Note that there's no `<!DOCTYPE>` tag for this code, as the
> current draft of HTML 3.2 (as of writing) doesn't actually
> define frames at all.

What we're doing here is defining the number and placement of the
frames, as well as which documents to show in each frame. The
HTML document that contains only the frame control information is
often called a **navigation frame**, while documents that contain the
actual data are often called **contents frames**.

## Examining the Code

The first section of code:

```
<HTML>
<HEAD>
<TITLE>Simple frame example</TITLE>
</HEAD>
```

is what you would expect. Notice that there is no **<BODY>** element.
It's not needed. This page will never be viewed—it just sets up the
pages and frames that *will* be viewed. The following section of code
begins the setup of the frames:

```
<FRAMESET ROWS="100%" COLS="45%,*">
 <FRAME SRC="index.html">
 <FRAME SRC="giftrick.html">
```

**<FRAMESET>** is a container element. We have set the **ROWS** attribute to 100%, meaning that there will be just one row which will occupy the whole of the browser window. The **COLS** attribute specifies two columns. The first of these is set to a width of 45% of the browser window; the second column specification (marked with a *), means that this width will be relative to the width of the first column. As there are only two columns, the width of the second will be 55% of the browser window's width. In this particular instance, we could have just as easily specified the exact column widths; in other words, **COLS="45%,55%"**. However, relative widths come into their own when you have 3 or more columns with odd percentage values, as they mean you don't have to spend time on working out the other percentages.

Next come the two **<FRAME>** elements. These tell the browser which files to load in each frame. The browser will load the files in the order in which they are coded.

## <NOFRAMES>

This bit of code is specifically for browsers that don't support frames:

```
<NOFRAMES>
Sorry, our default version of this document contains
frames.<BR>You can view our frame-free version by going
<A HREF="indexnf.html">here.</A>
</NOFRAMES>
```

Frame-compliant browsers will ignore this tag, whereas those that don't support frames will ignore everything—including **<NOFRAMES>** and **</NOFRAMES>**—and will therefore display the alternative text 'hidden' between these two tags. You may wish to provide a link in your frame pages for the non-frame version. Many users, especially those with lower screen resolutions, may prefer versions that don't utilize frames.

> **Don't put anything in a frame document other than valid <HEAD> and <FRAMESET> elements. Doing so will result in the browser ignoring the <FRAMESET> elements.**

When you view the page, you will see something like this:

**103**

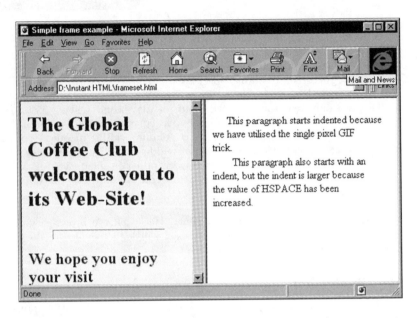

You should note that the `<FRAME>` and `<NOFRAMES>` elements must be contained within the `<FRAMESET>` container:

```
<FRAMESET ATTRIBUTES>
     <FRAME ATTRIBUTES>
     <NOFRAMES>
     . . .
     </NOFRAMES>
</FRAMESET>
```

Notice also, that it is only the `<NOFRAMES>` tag which requires a corresponding end tag `</NOFRAMES>`.

> While you are experimenting with frames, you may notice problems using the 'reload/refresh' option on your browser. Some browsers only reload the current frame when reload is selected. Whilst this is often appropriate when viewing a document across a slow modem link, it may not be what you want if you are experimenting with frame layouts! Look instead for an option to reopen the entire document.

# `<FRAMESET>` and `<FRAME>` Attributes

`<FRAMESET>` and `<FRAME>` have their own sets of attributes which we'll look at now.

# <FRAMESET>

The **<FRAMESET>** tag can take the following attributes:

- COLS
- FRAMEBORDER
- FRAMESPACING
- ROWS

## COLS

Defines the columns within a document containing frames.

`COLS=column_width`

where **column_width** is the width of individual columns, specified as a percentage of the browser window. You may also specify relative widths with the use of an asterisk. For example:

`COLS="20%,*,*"`

will define 3 columns: the first will be 20% of the width of the browser window and the second and third will be equal in width but relative to the first—in other words, each will be 40% of the browser window.

## FRAMEBORDER

Specifies that the frame will be shown with a 3D border.

`FRAMEBORDER=1 | 0`

The default value is 1. Setting **FRAMEBORDER=0** will display the frame with no border. In Netscape Navigator 3.0, you can use **yes** or **no** instead of the values 1 and 0.

## FRAMESPACING

**FRAMESPACING** can be used to add space between frames.

`FRAMESPACING=spacing`

where **spacing** is the amount of space in pixels. One use of this attribute is to produce newspaper style columns.

## *ROWS*

Defines the number and height of the rows in a frame document.

`ROWS=height_of_rows`

where **height_of_rows** is specified as a percentage of the browser window height, or as a relative measurement using asterisks (*). Including this attribute in your code will appear to speed up the loading of a frame document, since the number of rows is specified before the rest of the code is loaded.

> **FRAMEBORDER** and **FRAMESPACING** inherit their attributes from their containing `<FRAMESET>` element. If you want all frames to have the same **FRAMEBORDER** and **FRAMESPACING** attributes, you need only set the attributes once in the containing `<FRAMESET>` element.

# `<FRAME>`

`<FRAME>` can take the following attributes:

- ALIGN
- FRAMEBORDER
- MARGINHEIGHT
- MARGINWIDTH
- NAME
- NORESIZE
- SCROLLING
- SRC

## *ALIGN*

Sets the alignment of the frame and the surrounding text. The syntax is:

`ALIGN=alignment`

where **alignment** is one of these values:

TOP          Text outside the frame is aligned with the top of the frame.

| | |
|---|---|
| **MIDDLE** | Text outside the frame is aligned with the middle of the frame. |
| **BOTTOM** | Text outside the frame is aligned with the bottom of the frame. |
| **LEFT** | The frame is placed against the left border of the browser window, and text outside the frame flows around it to the right. |
| **RIGHT** | The frame is placed against the right border of the browser window, and text outside the frame flows around it to the left. |

## FRAMEBORDER

Renders a 3D edge border around the frame. The syntax is:

```
FRAMEBORDER=value
```

where **value** is 0 or 1. 1 (default) inserts a border. 0 displays no border. This will override the **FRAMEBORDER** attribute set using the **<FRAMESET>** element.

## MARGINHEIGHT

Defines the amount of space between the top and bottom edges of a frame and its contents.

```
MARGINHEIGHT=height
```

where **height** is the amount of space in pixels. This value can't be less than one (i.e. contents touch the frame border) or so big that nothing will fit in the frame.

## MARGINWIDTH

Defines the amount of space between the left and right edges of a frame and its contents.

```
MARGINWIDTH=width
```

where **width** is the amount of space in pixels. As with **MARGINHEIGHT**, the value must be 1 or greater.

You should generally use **MARGINHEIGHT** and **MARGINWIDTH** as a pair; specifying one without the other can lead to some unexpected effects.

**107**

## NAME

Allows you to specify a name for the frame.

**NAME=name**

This allows you to label a particular frame. A labeled frame is capable of displaying redirected hypertext links from another frame. In other words, you could click on a link in one frame, and the new document will be loaded into the labeled frame. To accomplish this, you use the **TARGET** attribute for the **<A>** anchor tag. We'll look at an example in a moment.

## NORESIZE

Prevents the user from resizing the frame. By default, the user can resize the frames by dragging the borders. Including **NORESIZE** will prohibit the user from doing this. This attribute should be used carefully, as the user may be viewing your documents at a lower resolution than you and may prefer to resize the frame rather than scroll up and down or left and right.

## SCROLLING

Creates a frame with or without scrollbars. The syntax is:

**SCROLLING=value**

where **value** is one of the following:

**YES**  Scrollbars are always displayed, even if the page content fits within the frame.

**NO**  No scrollbar capacity, even if the page content is too large for the frame.

**AUTO**  Only enable scrollbars if the page content is too large for the frame displaying it.

Again, you need to be careful with this. Setting **SCROLLING=NO** and **NORESIZE** will render your document unreadable to someone viewing the page at a lower resolution than yours.

## SRC

Specifies the source file for the frame.

**SRC=url**

# Targets for Hyperlinks

In Chapter 4, we looked at how windows could be given individual names which could then be used within the **<A>** tag, together with the **TARGET** attribute, to locate a specific location within an HTML document. The **TARGET** attribute is more useful when used with frames. In fact, it was specifically introduced to get around the problem of what happens when a hyperlink is selected inside a frame. Depending on how the data is structured, it may be appropriate to load the new document into the current frame, a different frame, or even replace the whole browser window with the new document.

You specify how you would like hyperlinks in your frame to behave by using the **TARGET** attribute in the same way as with windows:

**<A HREF="moreinfo.html" TARGET="_self">More Info</A>**

In this case, we have specified the target as **_self**, which means load the new document into the current frame. This is generally the default if no target has been specified. The target can be either the name of a frame, as described earlier in the chapter, or an implicit name. Four implicit names are defined:

- **_blank**—Loads a page into a new window, effectively opening a second instance of the browser.
- **_self**—The current frame.
- **_parent**—Used with nested frames. If the current frame is a child, then update the parent frame.
- **_top**—Update the whole browser window.

If you use frames on your page, remember that all external links should have the **TARGET** set to **top**—otherwise the external document may be unintentionally loaded into a frame of the current document. This can produce some strange, and undesirable layouts!

## Named Frames

We'll now look at an example that uses the name of a frame as a target. First, the frameset document:

```
<HTML>
<HEAD>
<TITLE>Example of targets</TITLE>
</HEAD>
```

```
<!-- Define the frames for display -->
<FRAMESET COLS=25%,*>

   <FRAME SRC="target.html">
   <FRAME SRC="intro.html" NAME="main_view">

<NOFRAMES>
Unfortunately, your browser is not capable of displaying
frames. You should consider updating your browser. For your
convenience we have provided a <A HREF="http://
www.aserver.com/documents/noframes/intro.html">"noframes"</
A> site for your use.
</NOFRAMES>

</FRAMESET>
</HTML>
```

Notice the second **<FRAME>** element:

```
<FRAME SRC="intro.html" NAME="main_view">
```

The **NAME** attribute has been given a value of **main_view**. We can now refer to this label from any other document. Loading the above code gives:

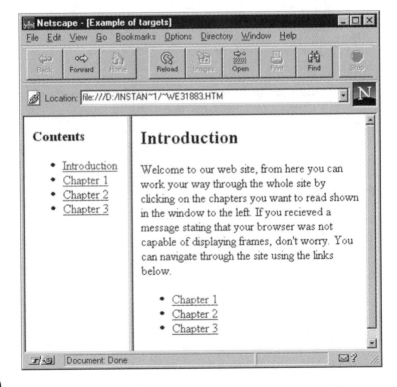

The code for the **target.html** document looks like this:

```
<!DOCTYPE HTML PUBLIC "-//W3C//DTD HTML 3.2 Draft//EN">
<HTML>
<HEAD>
<TITLE>Example of targets</TITLE>
</HEAD>

<BODY BGCOLOR="White">

<!-- list of contents -->
<H3>Contents</H3>
<UL>
<LI><A HREF="intro.html" TARGET="main_view">
Introduction</A>
<LI><A HREF="ch1.html" TARGET="main_view">Chapter 1</A>
<LI><A HREF="ch2.html" TARGET="main_view">Chapter 2</A>
<LI><A HREF="ch3.html" TARGET="main_view">Chapter 3</A>
</UL>
</BODY>
</HTML>
```

Notice how each list item is a hypertext link and that each link
specifies the **TARGET** attribute as **main_view**. Clicking on these links
will cause the relevant document to be loaded in the target window
rather than the window where the link itself resides; so clicking on
the link Chapter 1 produces this:

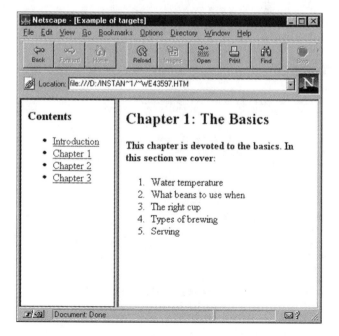

# Frame Layout

General frame layout is similar to table layout. If you place six frames, they will flow from left to right, and top to bottom:

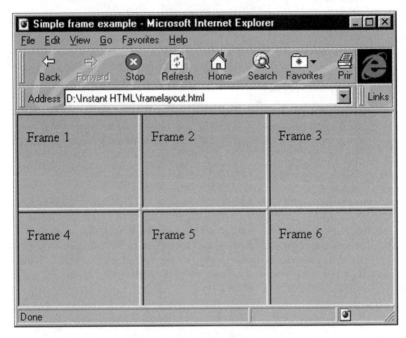

The code for this is:

```
<HTML>
<HEAD>
<TITLE>Simple frame example</TITLE>
</HEAD>

<FRAMESET ROWS="50%,*" COLS="33%,*,*">
 <FRAME SRC="frame1.html">
 <FRAME SRC="frame2.html">
 <FRAME SRC="frame3.html">
 <FRAME SRC="frame4.html">
 <FRAME SRC="frame5.html">
 <FRAME SRC="frame6.html">
<NOFRAMES>
Sorry, this document contains frames, you need to upgrade
your<BR>
browser to the latest version. You can view the first
frame<BR>
in the set <A HREF="index.html">here.</A>
</NOFRAMES>
```

```
</FRAMESET>
</HTML>
```

The important bit is:

```
<FRAMESET ROWS="50%,*" COLS="33%,*,*">
```

Here we have created two rows: the first has a height 50% of the browser window. The second will also be 50%, as it is relative to the first. There are 3 columns, each 33% of the window's width.

# Nested Frames

There is only so much you can do with the frames we've looked at so far. However, frames can be nested by incorporating multiple **<FRAMESET>** tags within a top-level **<FRAMESET>**, thus allowing you to create more sophisticated pages.

```
<HTML>
<HEAD>
<TITLE>Nested frames</TITLE>
</HEAD>

<FRAMESET COLS="50%,*">
   <FRAMESET ROWS="50%,*">
      <FRAME SRC="frame1.html">
       <FRAME SRC="frame2.html">
   </FRAMESET>
   <FRAMESET ROWS="33%,33%,*">
      <FRAME SRC="frame3.html">
      <FRAME SRC="frame4.html">
      <FRAME SRC="frame5.html">
   </FRAMESET>
</FRAMESET>

<NOFRAMES>
Sorry, this document contains frames, you need to upgrade your<BR>
browser to the latest version. You can view the first frame<BR>
in the set <A HREF="index.html">here.</A>
</NOFRAMES>
</FRAMESET>
</HTML>
```

This piece of code produces the screenshot shown on the following page.

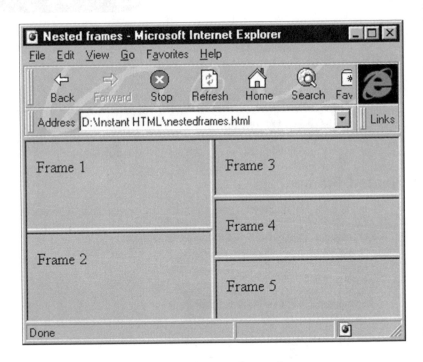

So let's take a look at the code, section by section:

```
<FRAMESET COLS="50%,*">
   <FRAMESET ROWS="50%,*">
      <FRAME SRC="frame1.html">
      <FRAME SRC="frame2.html">
   </FRAMESET>
```

The first line defines our frameset as 2 columns, each 50% of the width of the browser window. The second line starts another frameset within the first, and defines 2 columns each 50% of the width of the browser window. Lines 3 and 4 define 2 rows within the nested frameset. The fifth line ends the nested frameset. Then we have:

```
<FRAMESET ROWS="33%,33%,*">
      <FRAME SRC="frame3.html">
      <FRAME SRC="frame4.html">
      <FRAME SRC="frame5.html">
   </FRAMESET>
```

Here, the first line starts the second nested frame, and defines 3 rows all 33% of the width of the browser window. The second, third, and fourth lines define the documents to load within the three frames, and the last line ends the nested frameset.

**114**

Lastly:

```
</FRAMESET>
```

ends the opening frameset element.

# Floating Frames using <IFRAME>

Floating frames, defined by the **<IFRAME>** tag, are specific to Internet Explorer. They can be thought of as a cross between the normal HTML **<FRAME>** tag and the **<IMG>** tag used to place graphics in a page.

They are not part of the normal **<FRAMESET>** container, but are simply included in an HTML document in the same way as any other element. Have a look at the following example:

```
<HTML>
<HEAD>
<TITLE>Floating frames</TITLE>
</HEAD>

<BODY>
<P>
This text is part of a<BR>
normal HTML document,<BR>
the code for the<BR>
floating frame is in<BR>
this document.

<IFRAME ALIGN=RIGHT SRC=float.html>

</BODY>
</HTML>
```

This results in the screenshot shown on the following page.

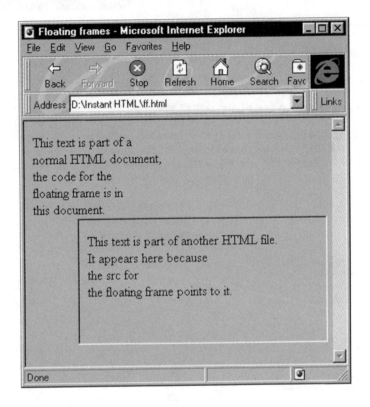

The **\<IFRAME>** element has the following attributes:

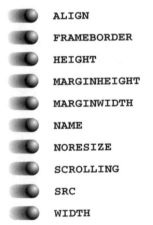

- **ALIGN**
- **FRAMEBORDER**
- **HEIGHT**
- **MARGINHEIGHT**
- **MARGINWIDTH**
- **NAME**
- **NORESIZE**
- **SCROLLING**
- **SRC**
- **WIDTH**

## ALIGN

Defines the alignment of the frame with respect to the surrounding text. The syntax is:

```
ALIGN=alignment
```

where **alignment** is one of the following values:

| | |
|---|---|
| **TOP** | Text outside the frame is aligned with the top of the frame. |
| **MIDDLE** | Text outside the frame is aligned with the middle of the frame. |
| **BOTTOM** | Text outside the frame is aligned with the bottom of the frame. |
| **LEFT** | The frame is aligned along the left border of the browser window, and text flows around it to the right. |
| **RIGHT** | The frame is aligned along the right border of the browser window, and text flows around it to the left. |

## FRAMEBORDER

Places a 3D border around the frame. The syntax is:

```
FRAMEBORDER=value
```

where **value** is 0 or 1. 1 is the default. Setting **FRAMEBORDER=0** will mean no border is displayed.

## HEIGHT and WIDTH

Controls the height and width of a floating frame:

```
HEIGHT=n
WIDTH=n
```

where **n** is the height or width in pixels.

## MARGINHEIGHT and MARGINWIDTH

Defines the amount of space between the top and bottom edges and the left and right edges of the frame and its contents.

```
MARGINHEIGHT=height
MARGINWIDTH=width
```

where **height** and **width** are the amounts of space in pixels.

### NAME

Provides a target name for the frame.

`NAME=name`

### NORESIZE

Prevents the user from resizing the frame.

### SCROLLING

Creates a scrolling frame.

`SCROLLING=value`

where **value** is **YES**, **NO**, or **AUTO**.

### SRC

Specifies the source file for the frame.

`SRC=url`

# Summary

In this chapter, we have looked at frames which were originally introduced by Netscape, but are now more widely supported.

We have seen how to arrange the screen into different areas, which can be useful for providing additional navigation features, and how to lay out the frames on the browser window. We have also seen how to control the updating of frames when hyperlinks inside a frame are selected.

We have looked at how to allow for browsers that don't support frames, and lastly, we looked at a feature specific to Internet Explorer: the floating frame.

# Forms

One of the advantages that web sites have over traditional media, such as magazines and television, is that the web allows for the immediate processing of feedback and interaction from the 'audience'.

Forms provide a way to prompt the user for information, and then carry out actions based on that input. For example, forms are commonly used to validate users before allowing them to download the latest beta copy of software. From a programming perspective, all HTML forms are broken into two parts: the client-side and the server-side. The client-side is the form itself—that part of the document that accepts user input and submits it to the server. Once the data is submitted, it is up to the server to process it correctly— the browser simply assumes that the server-side will know what to do. If no script or other service exists to process the data, the browser should return an error. For the moment, we will concern ourselves with the client-side: that is, the creation of the form itself.

# Creating a Form

To create a form, you use the **<FORM>** element to enclose one or more **<INPUT>** elements. The **<FORM>** element specifies the action to take when the user has provided the information. The **<INPUT>** elements define the type and function of the input controls in the form.

Forms can be placed anywhere inside the body of an HTML document. You may also have multiple forms in one document, so long as one form ends before another begins (i.e. they can't overlap or nest). Normal body text and images can be included inside the **<FORM>** tags. This is useful for labeling user input fields, providing instructions and formatting. There are no special layout options, so you use the same tags as you would for normal text and images.

# <FORM>

There are three required attributes for the **<FORM>** element:

- **ACTION**
- **ENCTYPE**
- **METHOD**

## ACTION

This attribute is used to specify the URL that will receive the data passed by the form. The syntax is simply:

**ACTION=url**

The URL doesn't have to be the same machine as the one that hosts the HTML document, although it often is. If you make a mistake in this section, browsers will generally return an error, since they won't be able to submit the form data.

You may also specify that the form data be e-mailed to a particular address, rather than passing it to a server script. This is easily accomplished, by using **mailto:sombody@somewhere.com** as your **ACTION**. This might, for example, be useful in automatically subscribing someone to a listserver or the like. Since listservers already take subscriptions by e-mail request, you may be able to properly format your form data so that the listserver will automatically process the request without you having to write any interfacing scripts, and so on.

## ENCTYPE

At the moment, this isn't commonly used, but it's present in HTML 3.2. Unless otherwise specified, it defaults to **"application/x-www-form-ulrencoded"**. This attribute is supposed to be used to indicate the desired method of encoding the form data.

## METHOD

This attribute defines the method used to send the data to the server. The syntax is:

**METHOD=method**

where **method** is **POST** or **GET**.

**POST** is the preferred method, and should be used in all cases—unless you have a compelling reason for not doing so. This method sends the data to the server as an actual data stream, and therefore avoids placing certain limits on the maximum submission length. Although **POST** is generically preferred, one reason why you may not wish to use it is that some firewalls are configured to intercept and destroy the data stream, causing the form to be interpreted as empty.

**GET** is an older method, and should normally be avoided. With this method, the data is passed in the URL itself:

```
http://hoohoo.ncsa.uiuc.edu/cgi-binquery?Name=123&
Submit=Submit
```

Note that the question mark separates the original URL from the data being passed. This has the advantage of allowing the form results to be bookmarked (useful in the case of searches), but has the disadvantage of being limited in length since the data is assigned to an environment variable on the server. In addition, the form data (as it is a URL) is often stored in the server logs for anyone to find.

# Name/Value Pairs

All form elements use **NAME** and **VALUE** attributes. The names are specified in the **NAME** attributes of form input elements, and the values are given initial values by various forms of markup, and edited by the user. Data is sent as name/value pairs, separated by ampersands (&), where the name is that given in the **NAME** attribute, and the value is that given in the **VALUE** attribute, or replaced by the user. Each name/value pair is URL encoded, i.e. spaces are changed into plusses and some characters (accented letters, etc.) are encoded into hexadecimal. The basic processing procedure is to split the data by the ampersands. Then, for each name/value pair, you should URL decode the name, then the value, and then the process as needed. See the example used in our discussion of **GET**, or type a query into a search engine like AltaVista, and look at the URL it gives you to see how name/value pairs work in real life.

# An Example Form

We'll look at each element in detail in a moment. For now, let's look at a simple example:

```
<!DOCTYPE HTML PUBLIC "-//W3C//DTD HTML 3.2 Draft//EN">
<HTML>
<HEAD>
<TITLE>Test Form</TITLE>
</HEAD>
```

```
<BODY>
<FORM METHOD=GET ACTION="http://hoohoo.ncsa.uiuc.edu/cgi-
bin/query">

Name: <INPUT TYPE=TEXT NAME=Name SIZE=40>

<P>

Color: <INPUT TYPE=RADIO NAME=color VALUE="W"> White
 <INPUT TYPE=RADIO NAME=color VALUE="R"> Red
 <INPUT TYPE=RADIO NAME=color VALUE="O"> Other

<P>

Value: <SELECT NAME=value SIZE=1>

        <OPTION>Below $10,000
        <OPTION>Between $10,000 & $30,000
        <OPTION>Above $30,000

  </SELECT>

<P>

<INPUT TYPE=SUBMIT>

</FORM>
</BODY>
</HTML>
```

This displays as:

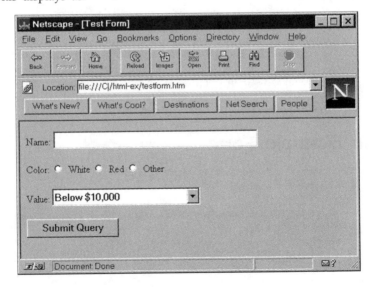

```
<FORM METHOD=GET ACTION="http://hoohoo.ncsa.uiuc.edu/cgi-
bin/query">
```

This line of the example starts the form, and sets the URL of the
server and method to use when sending the form's data.

Next come four elements separated by paragraphs. Each is defined
by an **<INPUT>** element containing the **TYPE** attribute.

```
Name: <INPUT TYPE=TEXT NAME=Name SIZE=40>

<P>
```

First is a straightforward text entry field. This one is forty characters
long; it will accept longer entries, but they will scroll off the end of
the box and therefore be invisible.

```
Color: <INPUT TYPE=RADIO NAME=color VALUE="W"> White
  <INPUT TYPE=RADIO NAME=color VALUE="R"> Red
  <INPUT TYPE=RADIO NAME=color VALUE="O"> Other
```

The next element contains three radio buttons. The user is only
allowed to choose one button at a time, and therefore must select
from only one of the alternatives. The data will be passed to the
script by the **VALUE** listed (in this case, **W**, **R**, or **O**).

```
Value: <SELECT NAME=value SIZE=1>

        <OPTION>Below $10,000
        <OPTION>Between $10,000 & $30,000
        <OPTION>Above $30,000

  </SELECT>

<P>

<INPUT TYPE=SUBMIT>

</FORM>
```

Next is a pull-down menu comprising 3 options, of which only one
is visible at the start. Upon clicking on the pop-up box, the menu
will appear and offer the three options shown.

The last element is a Submit button. This starts the form processing by the browser/server. We might also have placed a Reset button here, but more on that later.

# Entering Data

The `<FORM>` tag, used to declare the opening and closing of a form, says nothing about what data it will collect. This is left to the various data entry tags: `<INPUT>`, `<TEXTAREA>`, and `<SELECT>`, each of which is only meaningful within a form.

## <INPUT>

The full list of attributes for the `<INPUT>` tag is as follows:

- **TYPE**
- **NAME**
- **ALIGN**
- **CHECKED**
- **MAXLENGTH**
- **SIZE**
- **SRC**
- **VALUE**

Of these, **TYPE** and **NAME** are required.

### TYPE

Specifies what type of control to use. The syntax is:

`TYPE=type`

where **type** is one of the following:

**CHECKBOX**    Shown as a number of checkbox fields. Each checkbox has the same name. A selected checkbox will generate its own unique name/value pair. The default value is 'on'.

<INPUT>

| HIDDEN | The user will see no field, but the value of the field (set by **VALUE**) will be submitted with the form. This allows you to send information to the server that you don't want the user to see, and can be used in a variety of inventive ways, depending on the application. |
|---|---|
| IMAGE | An image which you can click to submit the form. The coordinates of the selected point on the image are sent to the server along with the data from the form. This is basically a complicated way of making a fancy Submit button, although it can be used for other purposes. |
| PASSWORD | This works in the same way as the **TEXT** attribute, except that text is not displayed as you enter it. The text is displayed as 'bullets' so that people looking over your shoulder cannot read it. It doesn't actually encrypt the transmission (which would be nice, if you were using this to transmit passwords). |
| RADIO | Provides a selection of alternatives from which only one can be chosen. Each button should be given the same name. The selected radio button is the only one to generate a name/value pair when the form is submitted. |
| RESET | This button resets all the fields to their initial default values. Setting the **VALUE** attribute will alter the label on the button itself. |
| SUBMIT | This button submits the form to the server. Setting the **VALUE** attribute will alter the label on the button. If the **NAME** attribute is set, the button will generate a name/value pair. If not, it will simply submit the form. |
| TEXT | Produces a single line text field for user input. Used in conjunction with **MAXLENGTH** and **SIZE**. |

The default control type is **TEXT**.

## *NAME*

Specifies the name of the control. The syntax is:

**NAME=name**

The name is sent back to the server, so you must pick a name that your processing script will expect. For example, if your database is expecting a 'FirstName' entry, and you call it '1stname' in the form, you will get errors, since the database won't know what it is supposed to do with the value you've sent it.

**125**

## ALIGN

If **TYPE=IMAGE**, use this attribute to define how the next line of text will be aligned with the image. The syntax is:

`ALIGN=alignment`

where **alignment** is **TOP**, **MIDDLE**, or **BOTTOM**. These values have the same effect as with inline images.

## CHECKED

Ensures a checkbox or radio button is selected when the form loads. The syntax is simply:

`CHECKED`

This is useful for 'presetting' certain values, in order to make them the default choice.

## MAXLENGTH

Sets how many characters you can enter into a text box. The syntax is:

`MAXLENGTH=n`

It's generally not a good idea to set this value, as you never know how much space a person will need for their name, address, etc. A form which won't let you enter all the data you need can be very annoying. Only use **MAXLENGTH** if you have a good reason to do so—for example, if your processing script has strict limits on the size of an input field.

## SIZE

Specifies the size of the control. The syntax is:

`SIZE=size`

where **size** is the size in characters. In our previous example, we set the size to 40. This means that the text-entry box will appear to be 40 characters long. Note that this is not the same as setting a maximum length. If the **SIZE** attribute is set to a smaller value than **MAXLENGTH**, the characters will scroll. The **TEXTAREA** control uses a special format that can set both height and width, instead of **SIZE**:

```
<textarea rows="number" cols="number">.
```

## SRC

Used when **TYPE=IMAGE** to specify the image to be used.

```
SRC=url
```

This attribute behaves in exactly the same way as for inline images.

## VALUE

Specifies the default value of text or numeric controls. The syntax is:

```
VALUE=value
```

This value will be passed to the server unless it's replaced by user input. For Boolean controls (i.e. checkboxes), this specifies the value to be returned when the control is selected.

# <TEXTAREA>

This tag produces a multiline text box area for user input. When the form is submitted, each line of text is sent to the server separated by a carriage return and line feed (**%0D%0A**). For the sake of simplicity, and if you value your sanity, you should probably avoid trying to automatically parse the contents of a text area—there usually isn't any compelling reason to do so that can't be more elegantly achieved with checkboxes and selects.

The attributes of **<TEXTAREA>** are:

 **NAME**

 **COLS**

 **ROWS**

## NAME

Gives the text area a unique name. The syntax is:

```
NAME=name
```

### COLS

Sets the width of the text area. The syntax is:

`COLS=n`

where **n** is the width in characters.

### ROWS

Sets the height of the text area. The syntax is:

`ROWS=n`

where **n** is the height in characters.

> The end tag `</TEXTAREA>` is required. Text that is placed between the start and end-tags sets the control's initial value.

## <SELECT>

The `<SELECT>` tag is used to produce a list of options or a drop-down menu list from which one or more selections can be made. This tag can be extremely useful, if employed carefully.

Allowable attributes are:

 MULTIPLE

 NAME

 SIZE

### MULTIPLE

Indicates that multiple items can be selected. If **MULTIPLE** is not specified, only one option can be chosen. Depending on your operating system, you would hold down the *Ctrl*, *Alt*, or command keys to click multiple selections.

### NAME

Defines a unique name for the list. The syntax is:

**NAME=name**

### SIZE

Specifies the height of the list control, and therefore how many options are visible at one time. The syntax is:

**SIZE=n**

where **n** is the number of options that will be shown at once. If **SIZE=1**, only one option will be visible, and the rest will appear in a pop-up box when the control is clicked. If you set **SIZE** to be more than one, it will create a scrollable box with more than one entry visible at one time.

> Use **SELECTED** to mark the default entry in a drop-down list.

# Examples

The following example shows a single choice select box:

```
<!DOCTYPE HTML PUBLIC "-//W3C//DTD HTML 3.2 Draft//EN">
<HTML>
<HEAD>
<TITLE>An example of a form</TITLE>
</HEAD>

<BODY BGCOLOR="White">

<FORM METHOD="POST" ACTION="http://aserver.com/cgi_bin/
script.cgi">

<P>
Please complete this form to let us know how we are
doing.
<P>
How easy did you find our site to navigate:
```

```
<P>
<SELECT NAME="navigate" SIZE=5>
 <OPTION>Very easy to navigate
 <OPTION>Easy to navigate
 <OPTION>Reasonably easy to navigate
 <OPTION>Hard to navigate
 <OPTION>Very hard to navigate
</SELECT>
</FORM>

</BODY>
</HTML>
```

The result is:

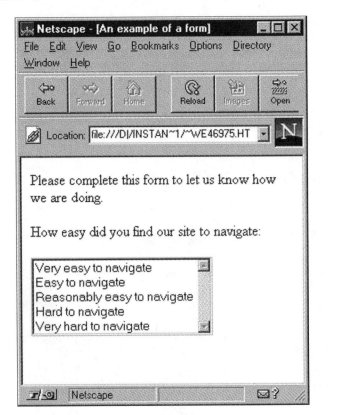

The first part of the code:

```
<FORM METHOD="POST" ACTION="http://aserver.com/cgi_bin/
script.cgi">
```

starts our form, and sets the method and action to take when the form is submitted to the server.

```
<P>
Please complete this form to let us know how we are
doing.
<P>
How easy did you find our site to navigate:
<P>
```

Next, we have some general text explaining the form. We could have used any normal HTML formatting commands we liked here, e.g. headings, etc. The last **<P>** element means that the select box itself will be contained in its own paragraph. If we had a lot of select boxes, this would make the whole thing look neater.

```
<SELECT NAME="navigate" SIZE=5>
  <OPTION>Very easy to navigate
  <OPTION>Easy to navigate
  <OPTION>Reasonably easy to navigate
  <OPTION>Hard to navigate
  <OPTION>Very hard to navigate
</SELECT>
</FORM>
```

**SELECT** defines the select box and the 5 **OPTION** tags define our 5 options. As we set the **SIZE** attribute of **SELECT** to 5, all options will be visible. Had we been short of space, we could have set the **SIZE** attribute to 2 and let the user scroll through the options. Note we have not set the **MULTIPLE** attribute, as we want the user to choose only one option. The **SELECT** box is ended with the **</SELECT>** tag and the form is ended with the **</FORM>** tag.

Here's a more complex example showing how tables can be used to format a form:

```
<!DOCTYPE HTML PUBLIC "-//W3C//DTD HTML 3.2 Draft//EN">
<HTML>
<HEAD>
<TITLE>An example of a form</TITLE>
</HEAD>

<BODY BGCOLOR="White">
<P>
Please complete the following form in full.
<P>
```

```
<B>Your details:<B/>

<TABLE>
<FORM METHOD=POST ACTION="http://www.aserver.com/cgi_bin/
script.cgi">
 <TR>
        <TD>Name:
        <TD><INPUT TYPE=text NAME=name SIZE=30>

 <TR>
        <TD>Street/road No:
        <TD><INPUT TYPE=text NAME=number SIZE=30>

 <TR>
        <TD>Town:
        <TD><INPUT TYPE=text NAME=town SIZE=30>

 <TR>
        <TD>State:
        <TD><INPUT TYPE=text NAME=state SIZE=30>

 <TR>
        <TD>ZIP:
        <TD><INPUT TYPE=text NAME=zip SIZE=30>

 <TR>
        <TD>Telephone No:
        <TD><INPUT TYPE=text NAME=tel SIZE=30>

 <TR>
        <TD>Fax No:
        <TD><INPUT TYPE=text NAME=fax SIZE=30>

 <TR>
        <TD>E-mail:
        <TD><INPUT TYPE=text NAME=email SIZE=30>
 </TR>

</FORM>
</TABLE>
</BODY>
</HTML>
```

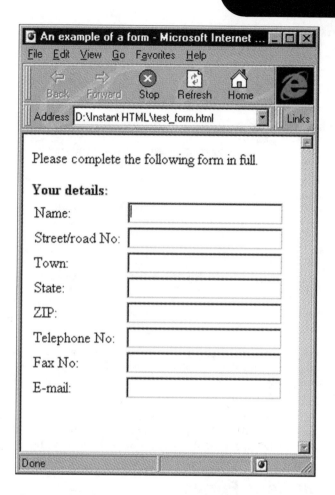

Notice how all the text input boxes line up with each other. This is because we have defined each text input box as a separate cell in a table. Had we not used a table, it would be very difficult to align the boxes correctly. The actual layout of forms can use any of the formatting elements that you would normally use for plain HTML text. In this example, we have used a single table to contain the form text and input areas.

Breaking the code down, we have:

```
<P>
Please complete the following form in full.
<P>
<B>Your details:<B/>
```

This defines a couple of paragraphs to set the scene.

```
<TABLE>
<FORM METHOD=POST ACTION="http://www.aserver.com/cgi_bin/
script.cgi">
```

Next, the **<TABLE>** tag starts the table. The **<FORM>** tag starts the form within the table, and sets the method to post and the action.

```
<TR>
        <TD>Name:
        <TD><INPUT TYPE=text NAME=name SIZE=30>
```

The next part starts the first table row containing two cells. The first cell contains the description of what should go in the text input box defined by the second cell. This continues down until we have defined all the input boxes we want.

```
<TR>
        <TD>E-mail:
        <TD><INPUT TYPE=text NAME=email SIZE=30>
   </TR>

</FORM>
</TABLE>
```

The last part, shown above, is the last table row and two cells. The form is ended with the **</FORM>** tag and the table is ended with the **</TABLE>** tag.

> Note how the last table row has its associated end tag included. This is because Netscape exhibits a bug which adds extra space to the table unless it is included.

# Testing Your Forms

When you are creating your own forms, it may be useful to test them before you actually try to use them. There is a special test server running at the National Center for Supercomputing Applications (NCSA) which makes it easy to do this. NCSA has created a server that will take the data from any form, and return it to you as an HTML page that explains what data your form is sending. To use this handy service, simply write your test forms with the following opening tags (pick one, depending on what sort of form submission mechanism you are using):

```
<FORM ACTION="http://hoohoo.ncsa.uiuc.edu/cgi-bin/
post-query" METHOD=POST>
```

```
<FORM ACTION="http://hoohoo.ncsa.uiuc.edu/cgi-bin/
query" METHOD=GET>
```

Please note that the NCSA maintains **hoohoo.ncsa.uiuc.edu** out of charity, and doesn't maintain any record of test form submissions. If you use their machine as the **ACTION** target for the purpose of testing out your forms, you must remember to change the URL to your real target before 'going live' with the form! If you forget, any data entered into your form will disappear into the depths of "**hoohoo**" and you will not be able to retrieve it.

# Processing Forms

As previously discussed, forms are a two-part equation. Once you've designed your form and got the client-side working, you are going to need a program on the server to process the form's data. When you come to programming a form, remember that there's a good chance that someone else has already designed a program that does most of the things you want; you'll just need to modify it to meet your particular requirements. Have a look around the web and you'll find several sites with programs that you can use specifically for this purpose. They are often freeware programs that just require an acknowledgment to the original author.

## The Common Gateway Interface

The Common Gateway Interface, or CGI, is the recognized method of communication between the HTTP server and gateway programs. Any data sent to the server from the client has to be processed by a gateway program, the CGI handles the data between the server and the program.

Gateway programs can be of several types. They can be compiled programs, such as C or C++, or executable scripts written in languages like Perl, which is the most common at the moment. Writing CGI programs can be fairly involved, depending on what you want to do, so we recommend checking out the following sources of information:

```
http://hoohoo.ncsa.uiuc.edu/cgi/
http://www.lpage.com/cgi/
http://snowwhite.it.brighton.ac.uk/~mas/mas/courses/
html/html3.html
```

135

# Summary

This chapter has shown you how you can create your own forms to interact with users. We have discussed **<FORM>** and its associated tags: **<INPUT>**, **<TEXTAREA>**, and **<SELECT>**. We have also looked at name/value pairs and their importance, relative to forms. Remember that the layout of a form is important—your user must be able to navigate their way through the form easily. This can be achieved by incorporating forms into tables, as we've seen in this chapter. Obviously, you have to check that your form works, so we have also provided pointers as to how this can be achieved. Finally, the server processing handled by CGI mustn't be forgotten. This is a large area, and not covered by this book, but the pointers at the end of the chapter will get you started on the right foot.

# Animation and Other Media <OBJECTS>

This chapter covers the HTML tags that you need to make your web pages come to life with animated graphics, in-line video, sound, and other media objects. The chapter begins with an explanation of one of the easiest and most effective ways of grabbing a web surfer's attention: animation! We then delve into the specific HTML tags that can be used to give your web pages that cutting-edge look and feel.

## Getting Animated!

One of the fastest ways to get your web pages activated is by incorporating GIF animation into them. But before we get into that, we'll take a look at the animated GIF format.

## Animated GIF Images

We looked at the GIF format in Chapter 3, but neglected to mention one important feature, which is that GIF is not just a single-image file format. It also allows multiple images to be stored in a single file, which can be rendered into an animation sequence. Even though the GIF89a standard has been around for more than six years, most browsers do not support animated GIFs. These older browsers will display only the first image in a GIF animation sequence.

Before browsers supported animated GIFS, most animation was done with server push or client pull, which will be discussed later in the chapter.

> For more information on GIF animation please visit:
> `http://home.netscape.com/comprod/products/`
> `navigator/version_3.0/index.html`

# Creating a Simple GIF Animation

Before you can begin, you'll need two things: an animation editor, and a graphics tool that can save or convert files to GIF89a. If you haven't got either of these tools, you can get a great animation editor from **`http://www.ulead.com`**, called PhotoImpact GIF Animator 1.0, on a free 30-day trial. There's also a good graphics tool, Paint Shop Pro 4.1, from **`http://www.jasc.com`**, also on a free 30-day trial.

> All information in the following steps references PhotoImpact GIF Animator and Paint Shop Pro as the tools being used.

Open up your graphics tool and create a new image. The size doesn't really matter, but for this process let's keep it small e.g. 100x100. On your new image draw a red circle. Now save this file as **`image1.gif`**. Create another image with the same attributes, but make the circle blue this time. Now save this file as **`image2.gif`**. Finally, create just one more image, with the same attributes, but this one is going to be green. Now save this file as **`image3.gif`**.

Next, open up your animation editor and start a new file. Find the button to add images to this file; then find **`image1.gif`**, **`image2.gif`**, and **`image3.gif`,** and select them to be inserted into your animation editor.

Find the line where it says Global Information, and select it. You'll notice that the upper portion of the tool changes to reflect the currently selected item. Find the Looping information, and enter 500 in this box. This is the number of times your animation will loop.

Now select **`image1.gif`**, and again you will see the upper portion of the window change to reflect the currently selected item. Find the Delay information and, in this box, enter 20. This is the amount of time, based on 1/100th of a second, before your next image will be displayed.

After setting that information for **`image1.gif`**, repeat this for **`image2.gif`** and **`image3.gif`**. Now save the file as **`myanim.gif`**, and open up your browser. Either use the open function of the

## 138

browser to open your **myanim.gif** file, or simply drag and drop it into the browser. No HTML is required for viewing.

## Incorporating an Animated GIF into HTML

To incorporate this animated image into your web page, you simply use the **<IMG>** tag:

```
<IMG SRC="MYANIM.GIF" WIDTH=100 HEIGHT=100 ALT="MY
FIRST ANIMATION">
```

An animated GIF is treated the same way as any other image file on your web page. So, congratulations on creating your first animated GIF file! We realize it's quite rudimentary, but it's a place to start. For more information and references on animated GIFs, visit: **http://members.aol.com/royalef/gifnext.htm**.

# Vendor-specific Tags for Other Media

The HTML 2.0 Proposed Standard only provided one method for incorporating media into HTML documents: the **<IMG>** tag. This element has certainly proved worthwhile, but it is, of course, restricted to image media—which means that it's usefulness is limited as richer media finds its way onto the Web.

One upshot of this is that browser developers have implemented their own tags for referencing other media from the web. For example, Microsoft has added the dynamic source (**DYNSRC**) attribute to the **<IMG>** tag for in-line video and audio support. Netscape implemented the use of the **<EMBED>** tag, for embedding different documents into an HTML document. And Sun Microsystems implemented the use of the **<APP>** or **<APPLET>** tag for executable code.

Let's start by taking a closer look at these tags—to gain a better idea of what they are and how you can use them in your own web pages.

# Netscape's <EMBED> Tag

Netscape originated the **<EMBED>** tag to allow different media, of varying data types, to be embedded into an HTML document. The types of media that are supported under the current version of Netscape Navigator (without having to download any plug-ins) are:

QuickTime **MOV**ies (via a shipping plug-in)

LiveAudio (**MIDI**, **AIFF**, **AU**, **WAV**)

LiveVideo (**A**udio **V**ideo **I**nterleave)

Now that you can see the different multimedia types that are supported, let's discuss how you can take advantage of them using the **EMBED** tag.

# Attributes of the Netscape <EMBED> Tag

The **<EMBED>** tag has three default attributes:

SRC

WIDTH

HEIGHT

It may also contain optional parameters that can be sent to the plug-in handling the embedded data type. These parameters are dependent upon which plug-in is being used.

## SRC

The URL of the source document.

## WIDTH and HEIGHT

Specifies the width and height of the embedded document.

```
WIDTH=n
HEIGHT=n
```

where **n** is the number of pixels.

## PARAMETER_NAME

Optional parameters sent to plug-ins.

```
PARAMETER_NAME=value
```

There can be an infinite number of parameters passed to a plug-in. Parameters are specific to the particular plug-in that is being used.

## Using Netscape's <EMBED>

What follows is an example of the **<EMBED>** tag, used here to embed a QuickTime movie to play as an in-line video in Netscape Navigator:

```
<EMBED SRC="EXAMPLE.MOV" WIDTH=160 HEIGHT=120
PLAY_LOOP=2>
```

This example also illustrates a parameter (**PLAY_LOOP=2**) being passed into the QuickTime plug-in, within Netscape, to play the movie twice.

> For more information on Netscape authoring tags, please visit: **http://home.netscape.com/assist/net_sites**

# Microsoft's <EMBED> Tag

Now that we have seen how the **<EMBED>** tag works with Netscape, it is important to discuss the support which the new release of Microsoft Internet Explorer 3.0 has implemented. Microsoft has provided support for the **<EMBED>** tag to provide backward compatibility with earlier HTML documents. There is a catch, however, and that catch is syntax.

> Any version of Microsoft Internet Explorer prior to and including 2.0 does not support the **<EMBED>** tag.

## Attributes of the Microsoft <EMBED> Tag

For Microsoft Internet Explorer, the preferred tag for inserting objects into web pages is the **<OBJECT>** tag, which we'll discuss in more detail later. The **<EMBED>** tag is, for the most part, implemented in the same fashion as Netscape: Microsoft has just implemented a few extra attributes. The full set of attributes is as follows:

- `WIDTH`
- `HEIGHT`
- `SRC`
- `NAME`
- `OPTIONAL PARAM`
- `PALETTE`

WIDTH, HEIGHT, and SRC are the same as for Netscape's <EMBED> tag.

### NAME

The name used by other objects or elements to refer to this object.

```
NAME=ID
```

### OPTIONAL PARAM

Specifies any parameters that are specific to the object. Multiple parameters can be passed.

```
OPTIONAL PARAM="value"
```

The OPTIONAL PARAMETER is equivalent to the PARAMETER_NAME attribute in Netscape.

### PALETTE

Sets the color palette to the foreground or background color.

```
PALETTE=foreground|background;
```

# Using Microsoft's <EMBED>

We saw an earlier example where the <EMBED> tag was used with Netscape Navigator; we have taken that same example and modified it to implement an in-line video in Internet Explorer:

```
<EMBED SRC="EXAMPLE.AVI" WIDTH=120 HEIGHT=160
AUTOSTART="TRUE" PLAYCOUNT="2">
```

You will notice that we are, once again, passing parameters into the Microsoft ActiveMovie control. ActiveMovie is Microsoft's Audio and Video technology, and comes with the full version of Internet Explorer. The above code plays the video when your web page is loaded (AUTOSTART="TRUE") and sets it to play twice (PLAYCOUNT="2").

> For more information on ActiveMovie, please visit:
> http://microsoft.com/imedia/activemovie/
> activem.htm

As you can see, both <EMBED> tags are used for the same purpose, but implemented slightly different. This is important to remember when developing your web pages, if you want to ensure that your sounds and videos can be viewed by all.

# Netscape's LOWSRC Attribute

The **LOWSRC** attribute is a Netscape-only extension to the **<IMG>** tag (version 2.0 and above) that lets you specify a low-resolution graphic to be displayed before the main graphic (defined by **SRC**) is loaded. Normally, the **LOWSRC** image is a low-resolution version of the **SRC** image, which speeds up display times; but it doesn't have to be. With some careful planning, it's possible to utilize this attribute for simple animation. For instance, the **LOWSRC** image could be a picture of the sun, while the **SRC** image is a picture of the moon. The **LOWSRC** attribute is included like this:

```
<IMG LOWSRC=sun.gif SRC=moon.gif>
```

> Remember that this is a Netscape-only extension, and so any other browser will only display the image defined by SRC.

**LOWSRC** must be used together with **SRC**, otherwise no image will be displayed. It is important to remember that using the **LOWSRC** attribute of the **<IMG>** tag provides the most basic level of animation. The animation effect is simply a two-frame animation: one file loads first, and then on the second pass of the page loading, the second file loads.

> For more information on Netscape's **LOWSRC** attribute of the **<IMG>** tag, please visit: http://home.netscape.com/ eng/mozilla/3.0/handbook/javascript/ atlas.html#reference_topics. This page discusses JavaScript-specific information, but has information related to **LOWSRC**.

# Microsoft's DYNSRC Attribute

Microsoft Internet Explorer 2.0 and above supports the use of the attribute **DYNSRC**, which stands for **DYN**amic **S**ou**RC**e. This attribute must be used as part of the **<IMG>** tag. Its purpose is to allow the embedding of in-line video clips (**.AVI**). It also supports the embedding of VRML Worlds (Virtual Reality Worlds).

A simple example of how to use **DYNSRC** is as follows:

```
<IMG DYNSRC="video.avi" src="image.gif">
```

Where **video.avi** is the URL of the file to open, and **image.gif** is the URL of the image to be displayed for browsers that do not support the **DYNSRC** attribute.

## Controlling the DYNSRC Attribute

There are several additional attributes which can be used in conjunction with the **DYNSRC** attribute and the **<IMG>** tag, that give both the developer and the user more control. The full set of **DYNSRC** attributes for the **<IMG>** tag are as follows:

### DYNSRC

Specifies the location of a video clip or VRML world to be displayed in the window.

```
DYNSRC=url
```

### SRC

Specifies the location of the image to insert.

```
SRC=url
```

### WIDTH and HEIGHT

Specifies the size at which the image and video are drawn.

```
WIDTH=n
HEIGHT=n
```

where **n** is the width or height in pixels. If the image or the video's actual dimensions differ from those specified, it is stretched to match what is specified. Internet Explorer also uses these attributes to draw a placeholder of appropriate size for the image before it's loaded.

### START

Specifies when the file specified by the **DYNSRC** attribute should start playing.

```
START=start-event
```

where **start-event** is one of these values:

**FILEOPEN**  Start playing as soon as the file has finished opening. This is the default.

**MOUSEOVER**   Start playing when the user moves the mouse pointer over the animation.

Both values can be set, but they must be separated with a comma. You would use both values together, if you wanted the video to play as soon as the web page opens, and then again, whenever the user moved the mouse over it.

## LOOP

Specifies how many times a video clip will loop when activated.

**LOOP=n**

where **n** is the number of times. If **LOOP=-1** or **LOOP=INFINITE** is specified, it will loop indefinitely.

## CONTROLS

If you include the **CONTROLS** attribute once the video is present, it will display a set of controls under the video. These controls consist of Play and Stop.

# The DYNSRC Attribute in Action

The following is an example of **DYNSRC**, using the full set of attributes associated with it:

```
<IMG DYNSRC="EXAMPLE.AVI" SRC="EXAMPLE.GIF" WIDTH=160
HEIGHT=120 START="FILEOPEN,MOUSEOVER" CONTROLS>
```

When implementing **MOUSEOVER**, it doesn't make sense to implement the **LOOP=INFINITE** attribute. This is because **MOUSEOVER** will be ignored, because you have set the video to loop infinitely; therefore the mouse event is ignored infinitely.

As mentioned at the beginning of this section, the **DYNSRC** attribute is only supported by Microsoft Internet Explorer 2.0 and above.

For more information on Microsoft's **DYNSRC**, please visit:
http://microsoft.com/workshop/author/newfeat/
ie30html-f.htm

# Other Ways of Incorporating Animation

We have looked at some of the tags that can be used to create animation and animation effects. But there are also other ways to achieve animation. In this section, we'll discuss two ways to provide a pseudo-animation effect using client pull and server push.

## Client Pull

Client pull provides the ability to automatically load a new document in the specified time, or reload a document on a regular basis. This can be put to several uses—including, of course, crude (very crude) animation or presentation.

As an example, let's say that your web site is a series of 10 pages, linked together by Previous and Next hypertext links, and that each page is a continuation of the previous. Using client pull, you could get each page to load in turn, after a preset time period, eventually returning to the beginning. All this can be achieved with no interaction from the user. Implemented this way, you are presenting the user with a rolling demo of your web site.

The code needed to achieve this lies within the **<META>** tag(s) of your web page. We looked at the **<META>** tag back in Chapter 1. It is used to embed meta-information not defined by other HTML tags. This meta-information can be extracted by web servers to identify, index, or perform other specialized functions.

Let's take a look at the HTML code that would create a rolling demo of your web site. We'll assume it includes ten pages.

```
<HTML>
<HEAD>
<TITLE>My Rolling Web Page DEMO</TITLE>
<META HTTP-EQUIV="REFRESH" CONTENT="30"; URL="http://
www.yourserver.dom/pg2.html">
</HEAD>
<BODY>
This is page 1 of my rolling web page demo
</BODY>
</HTML>
```

Once the user has received the first page, everything is done automatically! Notice the **<META>** tag, which says: after 30 seconds go to **http://www.yourserver.dom/pg2.html**.

When you have this, you can simply take the same code, save it to another file, and call this one **pg2.html** for page 2. With page 2 (**pg2.html**), we have to modify some of the code as shown:

```
<HTML>
<HEAD>
<TITLE>My Rolling Web Page DEMO</TITLE>
<META HTTP-EQUIV="REFRESH" CONTENT="30"; URL="http://
www.yourserver.dom/pg3.html">
</HEAD>
<BODY>
This is page 2 of my rolling web page demo
</BODY>
</HTML>
```

Once you're done with page 2, move on to page 3 and follow the same steps, saving the **pg2.html** file as **pg3.html** for page 3. And then modify the code as shown:

```
<META HTTP-EQUIV="REFRESH" CONTENT="30"; URL="http://
www.yourserver.dom/pg4.html">
```

Notice that each time we create a new page, we update the **<META>** tag's **URL** attribute to the next page in the sequence. You should also change the page number in the body of the web page, so that you know where you are. And maybe we should only make it 5 pages <G>!

Once you have created and modified all the pages, you're going to need a web server to make them work—because this is client-to-server interaction.

# Server Push

Server push is the complement of client pull. Client pull and server push differ in the sense that server push takes advantage of a connection that's held open, whereas client pull's HTTP connections are never held open: the client is told when to open a new connection. One of the advantages of server push is that the server has control over what data gets sent and when that data is received. One disadvantage, however, is that most server pushes will not work through a proxy server, or behind a firewall.

With that in mind, it must be said that server push is an older technology which is not regularly used or integrated into today's ever-changing technological environment. There will be other alternatives to this method in the future—you'll see!

> For more information on either client pull or server push, visit: `http://home.netscape.com/assist/net_sites/pushpull.html`

# <OBJECT >

The **<OBJECT>** tag is a new HTML extension introduced by Microsoft Corporation for the inclusion of Microsoft Component Object Model (COM) objects (e.g. ActiveX Controls and ActiveX documents or DocObjects) and a wide variety of different media types and plug-ins.

The **<OBJECT>** tag supersedes the role of the **<IMG>** tag: it supplies a general solution for coping with new media types, and provides backwards compatibility with existing browsers. The **<OBJECT>** tag allows web developers to specify the data, properties, and parameters for initializing objects that are to be inserted into HTML documents, as well as the code that is to be used to display and manipulate that data.

The **<OBJECT>** tag is not currently a part of the HTML standards set by the World Wide Web Consortium (W3C).

> Previously, the W3C's draft specification for the **<OBJECT>** tag was known as the **INSERT** draft. So, any references on the web that discuss the **<INSERT>** tag are actually referring to the **<OBJECT>** tag.

The next version of HTML is forecast to add support for the **<OBJECT>** tag, client-side scripting, style sheets, and extensions to fill-out forms. But, of course, this is subject to change.

> For more information on the W3C, visit: `http://www.w3c.org` or for current information regarding the W3C Technical Reports & Publications, visit: `http://www.w3.org/pub/WWW/TR/`

Currently, Microsoft Internet Explorer 3.0 is the only browser that natively supports the **<OBJECT>** tag. Netscape Navigator does support usage of the **<OBJECT>** tag through a plug-in from Ncompass Labs. Have no fear, though: when Netscape with a plug-in crosses the **<OBJECT>** tag, it simply ignores it and keeps moving on.

For more information on Ncompass Labs plug-in for ActiveX objects and scripting, please visit: http:// www.ncompasslabs.com

Now with that said, let's take a look at the **<OBJECT>** tag's attributes, and see how you can use an object in your web page.

# The <OBJECT> Tag's Attributes

**<OBJECT>** has the following attributes:

- **ALIGN**
- **BORDER**
- **CLASSID**
- **CODEBASE**
- **CODETYPE**
- **DATA**
- **DECLARE**
- **HSPACE**
- **VSPACE**
- **ID**
- **NAME**
- **SHAPES**
- **STANDBY**
- **TYPE**
- **USEMAP**
- **WIDTH**
- **HEIGHT**

## *ALIGN*

Determines where to place the object on the web page.

```
ALIGN=value
```

where **value** is **TEXTTOP**, **MIDDLE**, **TEXTMIDDLE**, **BASELINE**, **TEXTBOTTOM**, **LEFT**, **CENTER**, or **RIGHT**.

> Note that the proposed Netscape extensions for the ALIGN attribute of the <IMG> element are context-sensitive, as are some of the implementations of ALIGN=TOP.

## BORDER

Specifies the width of the border to be drawn around the object.

`BORDER=n`

where **n** is an integer. For **BORDER=0**, no border is drawn.

## CLASSID

Specifies a URL that identifies an implementation for the object.

`CLASSID=class_identifier`

In some object systems, this is a class identifier; it's the information used to create an object on your web page. The class identifier tells your browser to draw an object of a specified type.

## CODEBASE

Allows you to specify the URL location of the object to be used.

`CODEBASE="url"`

Many ActiveX controls need to be installed on your system for you to be able to use them in your web pages. The **CODEBASE** attribute points to a location where the object can be downloaded and installed on your system for use.

## CODETYPE

Specifies the Internet Media Type of the referenced **CLASSID** attribute, before the object is actually downloaded.

`CODETYPE="media_type"`

Browsers may use the value of the **CODETYPE** attribute to skip over unsupported media types, without the need to download unnecessary objects. See **TYPE** for more details on media types.

## DATA

Specifies a URL pointing to the object's data.

## 150

```
DATA="url"
```

An example would a **JPEG** file for an image.

## DECLARE

Declares the object without instantiating it.

```
DECLARE CLASSID=class_identifier
```

Use this when you are creating cross-references to objects that occur later in the document, or when you are using the object as a parameter within another object.

## HSPACE and VSPACE

Specify the amount of space on each side of the object, and above and below the object.

```
HSPACE=n
VSPACE=n
```

## ID

Used to define the object for the entire web page.

```
ID="name"
```

This can be used for naming positions within documents for use as destinations of hypertext links. Additionally, it may also be used by the browser, or objects within the document, to find and use other objects embedded in the document.

## NAME

Provides a way for browsers that support **FORM**s to determine whether an object within a **&lt;FORM&gt;** block should participate in a submit.

```
NAME="url"
```

If the **NAME** attribute is specified, and the **DECLARE** attribute is absent, the browser should include the value of the **NAME** attribute and data obtained from the object, along with information from the other **&lt;FORM&gt;** elements.

## SHAPES

Indicates that the contents of the **&lt;OBJECT&gt;** tag contain anchors, with hypertext links associated with shaped regions on the object.

This **SHAPE** attribute is used in a similar fashion to client-side imagemaps, but the syntax is different. Below is an example of how to use the **SHAPE** attribute:

```
<OBJECT DATA="EXAMPLE.GIF" SHAPES>
    <A HREF=PAGE1.HTML SHAPE=RECT COORDS="0,0,118,28">
PAGE 1</A>
    <A HREF=PAGE2.HTML SHAPE=RECT COORDS="118,0,184,28">
PAGE 2</A>
    <A HREF=PAGE3.HTML SHAPE=RECT COORDS="184,0,276,28">
PAGE 3</A>
    <A HREF=PAGE4.HTML SHAPE=RECT COORDS="276,0,373,28">
PAGE 4</A>
</OBJECT>
```

## STANDBY

Specifies a short text string which the browser can show while downloading an object.

```
STANDBY="string"
```

## TYPE

When a browser requests a file, that file is accompanied by information which tells the browser about the type of data that is being transferred.

```
TYPE="media_type"
```

One of these headers is known as the Internet Media Type or MIME content type. From this header, the browser will know whether or not it can handle that particular type of media.

A few examples are:

```
text/html          image/jpeg
text/plain         image/gif
video/avi          audio/wav
video/mpeg         audio/aiff
image/pjpeg        x-world/x-vrml
```

The advantage of using **TYPE** is that it allows non-compliant browsers to quickly bypass media that they don't understand, and go straight to an alternative. For example, if a browser can't handle the specified media and **TYPE** isn't specified, the browser will first download the object and then display a message explaining that it doesn't know how to handle it. However, if **TYPE** is specified, the browser won't download the video to begin with—therefore saving time and bandwidth.

### USEMAP

Specifies a URL for a client-side imagemap. This is, generally, only used for static images.

### WIDTH and HEIGHT

Specify the width and height of the object in pixels.

```
WIDTH=n
HEIGHT=n
```

That concludes the list of the **<OBJECT>** tag attributes. Not all of these attributes are required for the **<OBJECT>** tag to work—it depends on the object you are inserting.

## An Introduction to ActiveX Controls

ActiveX controls are objects that can be inserted into web pages or other applications. If you are a Visual Basic developer, you will be very familiar with ActiveX controls, as they were formerly known as OLE controls or OCXs.

There are several ActiveX controls that are included with Internet Explorer 3.0, which give you the ability to make your own web pages come alive by providing special formatting features, animation, video, and much more.

Currently, there are more than 1,000 ActiveX controls available, with functionality ranging from a simple label control to a control that gives you the ability to see another desktop across the Internet. If you can think of a particular control that you need for some specialized purpose, chances are that someone has probably created it.

You can add ActiveX controls to your Web pages by using the **<OBJECT>** tag. The **<OBJECT>** tag includes a set of parameters that you use to specify which data a particular control should use. These parameters then allow you to control the appearance and behavior of that control.

> For more information on ActiveX Controls and Technology, please visit: **http://microsoft.com/ workshop**

# Showing an ActiveX Movie

If you remember, earlier in the chapter we mentioned Microsoft ActiveMovie. ActiveMovie, or AM, is Microsoft's Audio and Video technology and comes with the full version of Internet Explorer. Well, to cut a long story short, ActiveMovie enables you to play back popular media formats on the web, including progressive playback of **MPEG** Audio and Video, **AVI** files, QuickTime **MOV**ies, **AU**, **WAV** Files, **MIDI**, and **AIFF**.

We are going to show you one more way of putting in-line video into your web page, by giving you an example of how to implement the ActiveMovie ActiveX Control, also known as an object, into your web page. Take a look at the following code:

```
<HTML>
<HEAD>
<TITLE>ActiveMovie Example</TITLE>
</HEAD>
<BODY>

<OBJECT ID="ActiveMovie1" WIDTH=163 HEIGHT=250
 CLASSID="CLSID:05589FA1-C356-11CE-BF01-
00AA0055595A">
    <PARAM NAME="_ExtentX" VALUE="3471">
    <PARAM NAME="_ExtentY" VALUE="2942">
    <PARAM NAME="ShowDisplay" VALUE="1">
    <PARAM NAME="ShowControls" VALUE="1">
    <PARAM NAME="MovieWindowWidth" VALUE="160">
    <PARAM NAME="MovieWindowHeight" VALUE="142">
    <PARAM NAME="AutoStart" VALUE="-1">
    <PARAM NAME="Appearance" VALUE="1">
    <PARAM NAME="FileName" VALUE="http://microsoft.com/
                      ie/media/movie/hunt15.mpg">
</OBJECT>

</BODY>
</HTML>
```

As you can quickly see, there are a number of **<PARAM>** tags included within the **<OBJECT>** tag itself: these are all specific parameters for the ActiveMovie object. If you wanted to embed a different object in your page, the properties for that object would be different, and you would need to enter those different parameters. We are not actually going to spend any time explaining each of the properties, but rather, give you a pointer to where you can get more information on ActiveMovie: **http://microsoft.com/mediadev/ video/usingam.htm**

One quick note, to mention is that you will see how the **FileName** property of the ActiveMovie control is set to an MPEG Video (**.mpg**) at Microsoft. This video is used on their site for an ActiveMovie demonstration, so we are just linking to it for our demonstration as well. You will also notice that there is no **CODEBASE** for the ActiveMovie object, because it is shipped as part of the full version of Internet Explorer 3.0. Try the code, and check out the video!

# Java Animation and Graphics Applets

Java is one of the newest programming languages to have hit the streets. It's well known that you can use Java in HTML documents— we'll now look at how you can do this.

## <APPLET>

First things first: Java is currently supported by Microsoft Internet Explorer 3.0, Netscape Navigator 3.0, and Sun Microsystems's HotJava browser. More importantly, Java, or specifically the **<APPLET>** tag, is being incorporated into the HTML 3.2 specification from the World Wide Web Consortium.

Since the focus of this chapter is animation and multimedia, we are going to discuss how you can use Java to aid animation. You must remember, though, that Java is a powerful programming language, and shouldn't be mistaken simply for an animation tool. Also, we are not going to address how to build Java applets here: you will learn how to use an **<APPLET>** in your web pages that have already been developed. Creating a Java applet is another book in itself.

### The <APPLET> Tag's Attributes

Java is implemented in a browser by using the **<APPLET>** tag. The **<APPLET>** tag has several attributes associated with it, which are as follows:

 ALIGN

 ALT

 CODE

 CODEBASE

- HEIGHT
- WIDTH
- NAME
- HSPACE
- VSPACE

## ALIGN

Determines where to place the applet on the web page.

`ALIGN=value`

where value is **TEXTTOP**, **MIDDLE**, **TEXTMIDDLE**, **BASELINE**, **TEXTBOTTOM**, **LEFT**, **CENTER**, or **RIGHT**.

## ALT

Defines the alternative text to be displayed if the **<APPLET>** tag is not supported.

## CODE

Specifies the name of the Java class to be executed.

`CODE="java.class"`

An example is **CODE="Animator.class"**

> One important note to remember is that Java class files are case-sensitive. So be sure that whatever you place in your HTML is case correct.

## CODEBASE

Specifies the location of the Java class file. This parameter is optional, but is always needed if the Java class is not in the same directory as the referencing HTML document. The syntax is:

`CODEBASE="path|url"`

where **path** is equivalent to a relative path and **url** is the uniform resource locator for a class. This allows for the inclusion of applets in your web pages from remote systems. An example is:

`CODEBASE="http://java.sun.com/applets/Animator/"`

### HEIGHT and WIDTH

Specifies the height and width of the applet.

```
HEIGHT=n
WIDTH=n
```

where **n** is the height or width in pixels.

### NAME

Specifies the name of the applet.

```
NAME=name
```

### VSPACE and HSPACE

Defines how many pixels of space are reserved above and below the applet, and to either side of it.

```
VSPACE=n
HSPACE=n
```

## Incorporating the <APPLET> Tag into HTML

Here is an example of how to incorporate the **<APPLET>** tag in your web pages:

```
<APPLET CODEBASE="JAVA" CODE="YOURJAVA.CLASS"
WIDTH=200 HEIGHT=200>
```

Java applets have the ability to accept parameters from your HTML web pages. These parameters are passed to the applet by using the **<PARAM>** tag. These parameters allow for information to be passed into a Java applet; a simple example would be passing a color into an applet to change the color of text. Here is the syntax for the **PARAM** tag:

```
<PARAM NAME="PARAMETER_NAME" VALUE="PARAMETER_VALUE">
```

## Using the Animator Applet

The Animator applet is a general purpose animation tool that was produced by a developer at Sun Microsystems. This applet is available on the web at:

```
http://java.sun.com/applets/applets/Animator/
index.html
```

We encourage you to try this applet so that you can get an understanding of how Java handles animation. You can also get information about Animator by pressing the *Shift* key while clicking the mouse in an animation.

Here is the necessary HTML code to use the Animator applet in your web pages. As long as your browser supports Java, this example will work with a connection to the Internet. Note that all the attributes in the previous section are used within this example.

```
<HTML>
<BODY>
<APPLET CODEBASE="HTTP://java.sun.com/applets/applets/
Animator/" CODE="Animator.class" WIDTH=460 HEIGHT=160>
<PARAM NAME=IMAGESOURCE VALUE="HTTP://java.sun.com/
        applets/applets/Animator/images/Beans">
<PARAM NAME=ENDIMAGE VALUE=10>
<PARAM NAME=BACKGROUNDCOLOR VALUE="0X00FF00">
<PARAM NAME=SOUNDSOURCE VALUE="HTTP://java.sun.com/
        applets/applets/Animator/audio">
<PARAM NAME=SOUNDTRACK VALUE="spacemusic.au">
<PARAM NAME=SOUNDS
VALUE="1.au|2.au|3.au|4.au|5.au|6.au|7.au|8.au|9.au|0.au">
<PARAM NAME=PAUSE VALUE=200>
<PARAM NAME=STARTUP VALUE="HTTP://java.sun.com/
applets/applets/Animator/images/loading-msg.gif">
</APPLET>
</BODY>
</HTML>
```

This is how it looks running inside Internet Explorer 3.0:

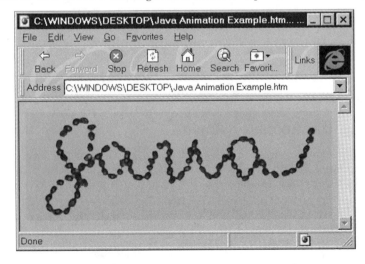

Using this Animator applet, you can create your own images and sounds by replacing the actual ones referenced within it. You're on your way to creating your very own Java animation.

# Summary

In this chapter, we've introduced and explained how to liven up your web pages with different techniques: animation, embedded documents, ActiveX Objects, and a Java applet or two.

We've looked at what GIF animation is, and how you can create a simple animation sequence with the right tools. We also showed you a few of the HTML tags that are specific to Netscape and Microsoft, how they work, and, more importantly, how you can use them in your web pages. We spent a bit of time discussing the 'older' approach to animation on the web: client pull and server push. Finally, we looked at some of the most exciting ways to bring your web pages alive—with ActiveX objects and Java applets.

# Chapter

# 9

# Scripting

While HTML offers a wide array of facilities for the display of text and graphics, it can't actually do much more than display a static web page. You're unable to alter the information in the page, or perform even simple calculations. Therefore, HTML's functionality is very limited; you actually need another programming language if you're going to achieve anything more interactive. One method at your disposal is the process of scripting.

Scripting can be used to make your pages interactive, together with the aid of a **scripting language**. Generally, a scripting language is a programming language that provides control in a host environment. They frequently lack some of the more advanced programming capabilities, however, such as file handling and graphics. Programs built by scripting languages can't be run as stand-alone applications, they can only be run within a browser that supports them. The programs created are known as **scripts,** and are included within the code of the HTML document. They are recognized by the browser as separate from the HTML code, and are interpreted and executed, rather than just displayed (as in HTML's case).

There are two main scripting languages available, JavaScript and VBScript. JavaScript was introduced on Netscape Navigator, while VBScript is native to Internet Explorer. We'll look at how you can run both JavaScript and VBScript, and the reasons you might use one instead of the other. First though, we'll look at how you include a script within your HTML code.

# <SCRIPT>

Scripts are enclosed by the **<SCRIPT>** tag, which tells the browser to begin parsing program information (i.e. it shouldn't display the text, it should execute it). The syntax is:

```
<SCRIPT LANGUAGE="scriptlanguage">
  script goes here...
</SCRIPT>
```

where **scriptlanguage** is usually either **JavaScript** or **VBScript**. You do not have to get the capitalization right when specifying your script language.

When the **<SCRIPT>** element is encountered, the interpreter is called. The code is executed in the order in which it appears in the document. Therefore, any reference to an object must appear in the text *after* the script element in which the object is defined.

As the introduction of the two main scripting languages has been a relatively recent innovation, many older browsers won't be able to run scripts. Since most browsers will simply ignore elements that they don't understand, you may find that your script is displayed right alongside the regular text. This is usually pretty unsightly, and is why you can 'hide' your **<SCRIPT>** element inside the HTML comment tags.

```
<SCRIPT LANGUAGE="VBScript">
  <!-- hide from older browsers
  ...
  Script goes here
  ...
  -->
</SCRIPT>
```

Browsers that understand **<SCRIPT>** will see the tag and run the script, while older browsers will simply ignore everything.

## SCRIPT Tag Attributes

The **<SCRIPT>** tag has the following attributes:

 LANGUAGE

 SRC

### LANGUAGE

Specifies the scripting language that is to be used. The syntax is:

**LANGUAGE="scriptlanguage"**

If the scripting language is not recognized by the browser, the code inside the **<SCRIPT>** tags will be ignored.

**162**

## SRC

Specifies a URL for a script, stored in a separate file, to be included as part of the current Web page. The syntax is:

```
SRC="url"
```

This is particularly useful when several Web pages all use the same script as it saves copying and pasting the script into each page's code. In this form, the script can be any relative or absolute URL. **.js** is the file extension for a JavaScript file.

# IE Extensions for &lt;SCRIPT&gt;

Internet Explorer 3.0 has introduced a couple of handy extensions to **&lt;SCRIPT&gt;**:

 FOR

 EVENT

## FOR

Associates the script within the **&lt;SCRIPT&gt;** tags with a particular object or control within the HTML document. The syntax is:

```
FOR="Object_name"
```

Using this method, each object in the document can have its own independent script, which is executed when the object associated with it is activated by an event—see the **EVENT** attribute for more details.

## EVENT

Specifies the event that causes a certain script to be executed. It can be used in conjunction with **FOR** to indicate the event of a specific control. The syntax is:

```
EVENT="Event_name"
```

Events are a subject in their own right. An **event** is a script called up by the result of either user or a system action. For instance, if you click on a mouse button, this generates an event. If you have a script associated with that event, that script is executed by the browser. Here are some of the most common events that a browser can react to:

 **onClick** occurs when a user clicks on a button.

**onChange** occurs when a user types text into a text box.

**onSelect** occurs when a user selects an item such as an option in a combo box, or list item in a list box.

If you wanted to associate a script with an event, which was triggered whenever a certain button, **Button1**, was clicked, you could use the following line:

```
<SCRIPT LANGUAGE="VBScript" FOR="Button1" EVENT="onClick">
```

# JavaScript

JavaScript was introduced by Netscape in order to extend and supplement HTML, and is often confused with Java, which is an entire programming language in its own right. JavaScript owes some of its syntax and structures to Java, but is quite different, and is used to manipulate Java applets. The basic aim of JavaScript was to provide programmers with a way to enhance the interactivity and capabilities of web pages without requiring server-side programming (this was an innovation when it was introduced).

## Alert Example

The first JavaScript example we'll look at simply responds to the user clicking a Click me button on a form with an appropriate message box. The entire HTML document is shown, in order to make it clear where the **<SCRIPT>** element is located:

```
<HTML>
<HEAD>
<TITLE>A Simple JavaScript Example</TITLE>
</HEAD>
<BODY>
<H3> Alert Example <H3><HR>
<FORM>
<INPUT TYPE="Button" NAME="MyButton" VALUE="Click me"
ONCLICK="DoIt();">
<SCRIPT LANGUAGE="JavaScript">
<!--
  function DoIt(){
alert('Click away');
  }
<!-- End of script-->
</SCRIPT>
</FORM>
</BODY>

</HTML>
```

When executed, the script looks like this:

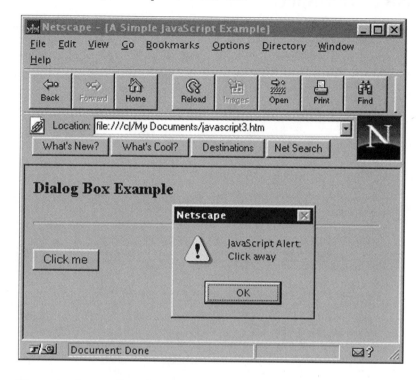

The script is actually called when the Click me button is pressed:

```
<INPUT TYPE="Button" NAME="MyButton" VALUE="Click me"
ONCLICK="DoIt();">
```

The name of the function is passed in the **ONCLICK** attribute, the browser locates it within the **<!--** tags:

```
<!--
  function DoIt(){
      alert('Click away');
  }
<!-- End of script-->
```

and that function is executed. If there was more than one function in this example, only function **DoIt** would be executed. All that function **DoIt** does is display a message in an alert box.

# SRC Example

Our next example utilizes another attribute of the **`<SCRIPT>`** element, namely the **`<SRC>`** attribute. In this example, we call up a script stored in a separate file, named **`script.js`**. The HTML is as follows:

```
<HTML>
<HEAD>
<TITLE>A Simple JavaScript Example</TITLE>
</HEAD>
<BODY>
<H3> SRC Example <H3><HR>
<FORM>
<SCRIPT LANGUAGE="JavaScript" SRC="script.js">
</SCRIPT>
</FORM>
</BODY>

</HTML>
```

The actual script is:

```
var book=prompt("Is this your first Wrox book?","no");
if (book=="yes")
  document.write("Lets hope it's not your last");
else if (book=="no")
  document.write("Keep coming back for more!");
```

If you run the program, you will see the following:

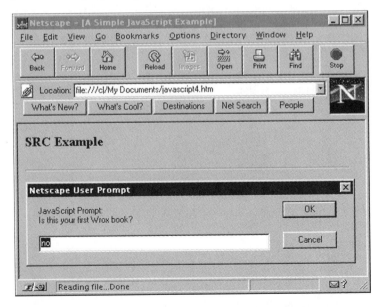

The first line of the script creates a variable called **book,** and
displays a user prompt, requesting an answer from the user.

```
var book=prompt("Is this your first Wrox book?","no");
```

The answer to the question is stored in the variable **book**, and then
tested against two values:

```
if (book=="yes")
 document.write("Lets hope it's not your last");
else if (book=="no")
 document.write("Keep coming back for more!");
```

> **The double equals sign is used to test for equality, i.e.
> does book = "yes"? One equals sign denotes that the value
> is assigned to a variable, i.e. book = yes**

A message is displayed on the HTML document depending on the
answer.

# Form Validation Example

The final example demonstrates the validation of form data. To spare
yourself server load time, you may, for example, wish to check form
data *before* it is passed to the server and thereby intercept any
common errors.

```
<!DOCTYPE HTML PUBLIC "-//W3C/DTD HTML 3.2 Draft//EN">
<HTML>
<HEAD>
<TITLE>A Simple JavaScript Example</TITLE>
<SCRIPT LANGUAGE="javascript">
<!--
function compute(form) {
 if (confirm("Are you sure?"))
       form.result.value= eval(form.expr.value)
 else
       alert("Please try again!");
       form.expr.value="";
}
<!-- End of Script-->
</SCRIPT>
</HEAD>

<BODY BGCOLOR="#FFFFFF">
<FORM>
Enter a Calculation:<BR>
<INPUT TYPE="text" NAME="expr" SIZE=15>
<P>
```

```
<INPUT TYPE="button" VALUE="Calculate"
ONCLICK="compute(this.form)">
<P>
Result:<BR>
<INPUT TYPE="text" NAME="result" SIZE=15>
<BR>
</FORM>
</BODY>
</HTML>
```

Enter a calculation into the text box and then click the Calculate button. Before the function proceeds, it asks you whether you wish to proceed:

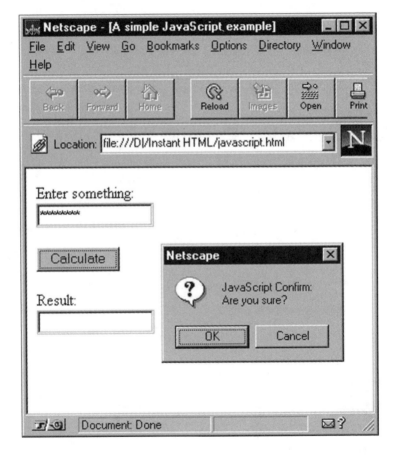

The main 'decision making' part of the program:

```
if (confirm("Are you sure?"))
```

displays a confirm dialog box and, if the OK button is pressed, executes the next line of code which evaluates the expression entered by the user.

```
form.result.value= eval(form.expr.value)
```

Otherwise, if the Cancel button has been pressed, an appropriate alert can be issued, and the top box is cleared for another go.

```
else
        alert("Please try again!");
        form.expr.value="";
```

> Please note that if you enter a non-numeric expression into the text box, it will cause an error.

Of course, this is only a small example of what you can do with JavaScript. Appendix F supplies a reference of the different commands and functions that are available in the language. If you wish to experiment further, you'll find some references at the end of this chapter as to where to look for more information.

# VBScript

VBScript was introduced by Microsoft as a competitor to JavaScript. It is broadly derived from VBA (Visual Basic for Applications) and like VBA is a cut-down version of Visual Basic. It includes most of the statements of Visual Basic, as well as many of the string, date, and number manipulation functions and the common control structures, but little else. There's no graphics or file handling functions available, so you are limited in what you can achieve. However, you must consider that, once you've opened a HTML page in your browser, the code is loaded into memory and can be executed at the push of a button. Many of the omitted functions could have been used to damage your system.

Currently, VBScript is not natively supported by Netscape Navigator, but it is picking many new followers, as Internet Explorer gains in popularity. The main attraction of VBScript is that it's a lot simpler to pick up than JavaScript, but offers a similar level of speed and power.

# Dialog Box Example

We'll now take a look at the simplest example possible in VBScript, one which waits for the user to click a button on a document, then displays a message when the user does.

```
<!DOCTYPE  HTML PUBLIC "-//W3C/DTD HTML 3.2 Draft//EN">
<HTML>
<HEAD>
<TITLE>A Simple VBScript Example</TITLE>
</HEAD>
<BODY>
<H3>Dialog Box Example</H3><HR>
<SCRIPT LANGUAGE="vbscript" FOR="MyButton" EVENT="OnClick"
>
<!--
MsgBox ("Greetings HTML programmer!")
-->
</SCRIPT>
<INPUT NAME="MyButton" TYPE="Button" VALUE ="Don't Click
me">
</BODY>
</HTML>
```

If you execute this script, you will get the following:

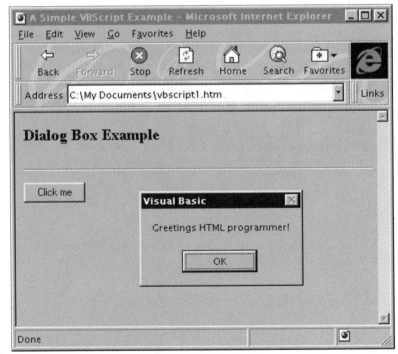

The main work is done within the **<SCRIPT>** tag:

```
<SCRIPT LANGUAGE="vbscript" FOR="MyButton" EVENT="OnClick">
```

The script is associated with the only button on the form, **MyButton**. It's primed to run when the **onClick** event occurs. There is just one line of code in the script:

```
MsgBox ("Greetings HTML programmer!")
```

This is a call to the **MsgBox** function, and supplied within the brackets and quotes in the message that you wish to display. The dialog box appears when **MyButton** is clicked, and disappears when the OK button is clicked. Let's take a look at something slightly more ambitious.

# Control of Flow Example

In this example, a dialog box appears when the user presses a button, but then it prompts the user for a response, and displays an different answer depending on the reply.

```
<!DOCTYPE  HTML PUBLIC "-//W3C/DTD HTML 3.2 Draft//EN">
<HTML>
<HEAD>
<TITLE>A Simple VBScript Example</TITLE>
</HEAD>
<BODY>
<H3>Control of Flow Example</H3><HR>
<SCRIPT LANGUAGE="vbscript" FOR="MyButton" EVENT="OnClick"
>
<!--
If MsgBox ("Didn't I tell you not to click
that?",36,"Control Structure Example")=6 Then
 MsgBox "Well why did you do it then?",,"The machine
answers back"
Else
 MsgBox "You obviously weren't paying attention",,"The
machine answers back"
End If
-->
</SCRIPT>
<INPUT NAME="MyButton" TYPE="Button" VALUE ="Don't Click
me">
</BODY>
</HTML>
```

If you run the script, you'll see it demonstrated:

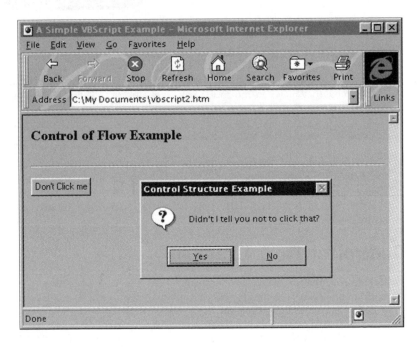

The actual VBScript code is very simple to follow. It relies on an **if...then...else** statement to do the work. The **MsgBox** function takes three parameters in this example:

```
If MsgBox ("Didn't I tell you not to click
that?",36,"Control Structure Example")=6 Then
```

The first parameter is the text of the message, the second is a code indicating that we want a dialog with a Yes and a No button, and the third provides the heading for the dialog box. When the user presses either the Yes or No button, a value is generated by **MsgBox**. The value 6 equates to the Yes button being pressed. If the value 6 is returned by **MsgBox**, we display one message:

```
MsgBox "Well why did you do it then?",,"The machine answers
back"
```

otherwise, we display another:

```
Else
  MsgBox "You obviously weren't paying attention",,"The
machine answers back"
```

We use **END IF** to indicate these are all the possible alternatives. Let's take a look at one last example.

# Form Validation Example

The following is a simple example of how VBScript can perform basic form validation:

```html
<!DOCTYPE HTML PUBLIC "-//W3C/DTD HTML 3.2 Draft//EN">
<HTML>
<HEAD>
<TITLE>A Simple VBScript Example</TITLE>
</HEAD>

<BODY>
<H3>Simple Validation Example</H3><HR>
<FORM NAME="ValidForm">
Enter a value between 1 and 10:
<INPUT NAME="Text1" TYPE="TEXT" SIZE=2>
<INPUT NAME="Submit" TYPE="BUTTON" VALUE="Submit">
</FORM>
<SCRIPT LANGUAGE="vbscript" FOR="Submit" Event="OnClick" >
<!--
  Dim TheForm
  Set TheForm = Document.ValidForm
  If ISNumeric(TheForm.Text1.Value) Then
  If TheForm.Text1.Value < 1 Or TheForm.Text1.Value > 10
Then
      MsgBox "Please enter a Number between 1 and 10."
  Else
      MsgBox "Thank you."
  End If
Else
  MsgBox "Please enter a Numeric value."
End If
-->
</SCRIPT>
</BODY>
</HTML>
```

Try entering some letters instead of a numeric value into the text box and the result is:

**173**

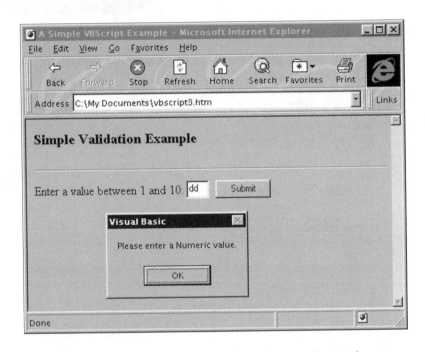

This example not only gets a number from the user, but it also refuses to accept any input other than a number between 1 and 10. It does this by checking the value given by the user on the form with the **IsNumeric** function to see if the user has actually entered a number at all. Without this check, you could end up causing an error if you tried to use the value at a later point in a calculation. The line that does this is:

```
If ISNumeric(TheForm.Text1.Value) Then
```

The script then checks to see if the number falls between 1 and 10.

```
If TheForm.Text1.Value < 1 Or TheForm.Text1.Value > 10 Then
    ...
```

If it does then the value can be accepted, but if not, it requests that the user tries again. That is basically all the script does.

Obviously, there is a whole lot more that you can do with VBScript. Appendix E gives a reference of the different commands and functions that are available in the language. If you wish to experiment further, you'll find some references at the end of this chapter as to where to look for more information.

# Other  Concerns

As  scripting  languages  are  still  in  their  relative  infancy,  there's  a
couple  of  points  you  should  take  heed  of.

## Compatibility

At  the  moment,  scripting  languages  aren't  fully  cross-platform.
JavaScript  is  supported  primarily  by  Netscape,  whereas  VBScript  is
supported  entirely  by  Microsoft.  What  works  in  one  browser  may  not
work  at  all  in  another—although  Microsoft  has  pledged  to  support
JavaScript  in  Internet  Explorer,  its  use  is  still  a  bit  problematic.
Navigator,  for  its  part,  cannot  run  VBScript  at  all  without  a
specialized  Script  plug-in,  available  from  Ncompass  labs  at  this  URL:

`http://www.ncompasslabs.com`

In  general,  be  careful  when  using  scripting  languages,  as  you  can
never  be  sure  that  your  intended  audience  will  be  able  to  execute  it.
The  best  thing  is  to  include  an  alternative  script-free  page,  which
everyone  will  be  able  to  view,  or  offer  a  link  to  the  site  from  which
they  can  download  a  browser  that  supports  the  scripting  language  of
your  choice.

## Security

As  with  any  Internet  technology,  scripting  has  introduced  a  number
of  security  concerns.  To  address  these  worries,  Netscape  has
constructed  JavaScript  so  that  it  cannot  access  the  local  file  system,  or
other  crucial  system  resources.  This  should  prevent  JavaScript  from
executing  hostile  instructions,  but  also  limits  its  power  somewhat  and
does  not  entirely  prevent  'unfriendly'  programming  (for  example,
spawning  endless  windows  until  the  browser  crashes,  or  writing  a
script  that  loops  eternally  to  slow  everything  down).  VBScript  is
somewhat  less  secure,  but  Microsoft  is  trying  to  address  any
concerns.

# Additional  Sources  of  Information

As  we've  mentioned  earlier,  there's  far  more  to  script  programming
than  we  could  possibly  cover  here.  Consequently,  we  recommend  that
you  have  a  look  at  the  following  resources:

JavaScript:

- `www.netscape.com`
- `www.gamelan.com`
- `www.inquiry.com/techtips/js_pro/`

VBScript

- *Instant VBScript* by Wrox Press. (ISBN 1-861000-44-8)
- `www.microsoft.com`
- `www.inquiry.com/thevbpro/vbscentral/gallery.html`

# Summary

In this chapter, we have considered what exactly a scripting language is, and why you'd want to use one. We looked at how the browser differentiates the script from the HTML, with the use of the `<SCRIPT>` tag. We then looked at how JavaScript works, and gave a couple of very basic programs. Next, we looked at some very basic VBScript programs. Finally, we looked at couple of concerns which affect both scripting languages, namely those of security and compatibility.

# Chapter 10

# Style Sheets

As we've seen, one of the original aims of the web was to separate information from presentation. HTML is a semantic markup language, and is concerned with the meaning of formatting in a document—not its visual representation. Contrary to popular belief, this is not a 'limitation' in HTML—it has some very important advantages, not least of which is the ability to define document appearance locally.

However, as the web has grown in popularity, the concept of a semantic markup language has been perceived as somewhat limiting. Authors have been seeking increasingly high levels of control over the appearance of their web documents, and haven't been content with restricting themselves to the basic HTML constructs. This demand is, in many ways, responsible for the state of HTML today; it is precisely the reason why the early Netscape extensions to HTML were adopted so rapidly. The newest way to give authors control over document appearance, without simultaneously sacrificing the content/presentation separation, is through style sheets.

## Using Style Sheets

There are currently two main ways to implement style sheets, both of which have ugly acronyms. The first is **Document Style Semantics and Specification Language**, or **DSSSL** for short. This is a remarkably large and complex standard, supported by the ISO, which also has a 'lite' version for use on the web called DSSSL-Online. The second way to implement style sheets is through **Cascading Style Sheets Level One**, or **CSS1** (in case you were wondering: no, there isn't a Level Two yet). CSS1 is designed to be easy to use and implement, so it has something of a lead over the more comprehensive (and difficult) DSSSL-Online. In addition, CSS1 will probably become the de facto standard for web style sheets, since the major browsers and the W3C have announced support for it. For this reason, we'll concentrate on CSS1 rather than DSSSL-Online.

# The Advantages of Using Style Sheets

There are three primary advantages of using style sheets. The first is their universality of application. This means that you can develop a style sheet and then apply it to any document or group of documents, by simply setting them so that they refer to the style sheet you've made (more on this in a moment). This universality has an added benefit: you can change the appearance of all pages by simply changing their style sheet.

The next advantage is that style sheets can convey greater typographic control than is normally possible. CSS1 provides a number of properties that can be used to create effects like drop-caps, overlapping text, shadowed text, and so on.

The third benefit is that style sheets, unlike other methods of display control, retain the content/presentation split. This means that style sheet information is separate from the actual text information. Aside from architectural concerns, this can result in smaller file sizes—five 10K documents can reference one 15K style sheet, instead of having five 25K documents that each contain their own style information.

# An Example

The following picture is actually all text, with no bitmaps (the giant 'we' appears in red type in the original).

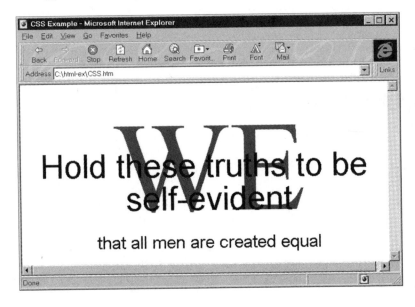

The actual HTML file that generated this page follows.

```
<HTML>
<HEAD>
<TITLE>CSS Example</TITLE>
<STYLE  TYPE="text/css">
<!--
BODY { background: white;
 color: black;
 font-size: 12px;
 font-family: Times }
P {    color: color: black;
 font-size: 18px;
 font-family: Times }
A:link { text-decoration: none;
 font-size: 20px;
 color: black;
 font-family: Arial }
.base {color: red;
 weight: medium;
 margin-top: 10px;
 font-size: 250px;
 line-height: 250px;
 font-family: Times }
.layer1 { color: black;
 margin-top: -130px;
 weight: medium;
 font-size: 65px;
 line-height: 65px;
 font-family: Arial }
.layer2 { color: black;
 margin-top: 30px;
 weight: medium;
 font-size: 35px;
 line-height: 45px;
 font-family: Arial }
-->
</STYLE>
</HEAD>
<BODY>
<CENTER>
<TABLE WIDTH=730 CELLPADDING=0 CELLSPACING=0 BORDER=0>
<TR>
<TD ALIGN=CENTER VALIGN=TOP>
<DIV CLASS=base>WE</DIV>
<DIV CLASS=layer1>Hold these truths to be self-evident<DIV>
<DIV CLASS=layer2>that all men are created equal</DIV>
</TD></TR>
</TABLE>
</CENTER>
</BODY>
</HTML>
```

Notice that this HTML file doesn't contain any images, not even the infamous **'pixel_clear.gif'** trick! This is an example of the sort of things that you can do with style sheets, without resorting to special workarounds or tricks. Anyone viewing this page would only have to download a little over 1K, which is significantly smaller than the equivalent page constructed from images. Now that you've seen what you can do with CSS1, we'll look at how you can do it.

# Implementing Style Sheets

There are four ways to incorporate style sheet functionality into your HTML documents, and they each have slightly different effects. It is important to decide which method suits your purpose, since they're not functionally identical.

## Using <LINK>

The first method is a special use of the **<LINK>** tag. This can be used to reference alternative style sheets, which can then be applied to the document at will. Unfortunately, this method doesn't actually *apply* the style sheet formatting unless the viewer makes a decision to do so. As a result, it's generally a bad idea to use this method for any formatting that is crucial to the document, since any viewers will need to specifically choose to view the formatting (and most won't). For extraneous formatting, such as minor font and color changes, this method may nevertheless be preferable to the others.

To use the **<LINK>** method, place the following bit of code in the **<HEAD>** element of your document:

```
<LINK REL=STYLESHEET TYPE="text/css" HREF="http://
foo.bar.com/style" TITLE="Style">
```

Obviously, you would need to change the **HREF** to point to your real style sheet. Note that this means you can apply style sheets that reside on completely different servers. This can be particularly useful in an intranet situation, where one department can set up several 'approved' styles for all documents to use. As a point of Internet etiquette, it would be a good idea to ask the original style sheet author for permission before 'borrowing' their style sheet in this manner.

## Using <STYLE>

The next way to use style sheets is to use the **<STYLE>** element, which was specifically invented for this purpose. The idea here is to enclose the style sheet data in the **<STYLE>** tag, so that it can be parsed and applied as the document is loaded. To this end, you would use the following code, placed in the **<HEAD>** of your document:

```
<STYLE TYPE="text/css"> ...style info goes here... </STYLE>
```

This seems quick and easy (and it is) but there are a few things you should be aware of before you use it. The first problem is that older browsers will ignore the **<STYLE>** tag, and will try to handle the style data as if it were normal text. This can be avoided by enclosing the whole thing in HTML comment tags, since style-aware browsers will still find the style information and handle it appropriately.

The second problem is that by using the **<STYLE>** tag in the manner described above, you will need to include a complete style sheet in every document! This not only increases the time needed to create a document, but increases the file sizes as well! In effect, this method erases two of the three advantages conferred by style sheets, and should be avoided if possible.

# Using @import

Fortunately, there is a way to automatically apply style sheets and still keep your file sizes down: you can use a special notation in CSS1 that was designed for this very purpose:

```
@import url (http://foo.bar.com/style);
```

This notation tells the browser to get the style sheet 'style' from the server at **foo.bar.com**. If you place this line in the **<HEAD>** of your document, the style will be automatically retrieved and applied before your document is displayed. Even better, you can override the imported style by simply declaring any changes in the document itself, using the CSS1 description format we'll be covering shortly (this lets you set up a 'baseline' style sheet, from which individual documents can diverge).

The only drawback to the **@import** notation is that it is not, at the moment, widely supported (this will change, but it is important to note). Until it is more widely supported, pages that use it will appear unformatted. In addition, all of the above methods apply their style sheets to the entire document; so you cannot style just one paragraph, unless you employ yet one more method of using style sheets.

# Using STYLE with Individual Tags

In order to apply CSS1 formatting to selected elements of your document, you can simply specify the CSS1 information as part of the tag you would like to affect.

```
<P STYLE="color: green">This paragraph will be green<P>
```

This is extremely flexible, and easy to use, but it does have the major drawback that you need to specify each tag individually (again, this removes the major advantages of style sheets). Consequently, we do not recommend using this method for extended periods, as it will rapidly become burdensome. The best method, at the moment, is probably to use **<STYLE>** wrapped in comment tags; but **@import** will be the most useful, once it is more widely supported.

# Creating Style Sheets

A style sheet is essentially a declaration of display rules, specifying the display attributes of particular HTML constructs. These rules are easy to write, consisting of combinations of tags, property names, and values.

## Syntax

All CSS1 declarations (they're officially termed 'selectors') follow the same format:

```
TAG { property: value }
```

For example, to set all level 1 headings to white, you could use either of the following statements:

```
H1 { color: white }
H1 { color: #FFFFFF }
```

As you can see, both of these lines declare that everything enclosed by an **<H1>** tag will have the color white (or hex #FFFFFF) applied to it.

> **We include a list of properties and their possible values at the end of this chapter.**

You can apply a single property to multiple tags by simply grouping those tags in the selector statement:

```
H1, H2, H3 { color: #000000 }
```

In this example, we've just set all three headings to display in black.

As well as grouping tags, you can also group properties. Simply enclose your multiple property declarations inside the curly braces:

```
H2 {
  color: #000000;
  font-size: 14pt;
  font-family: monaco;
    }
```

This example would display all level 2 headings in 14 point Monaco, in black. Note the use of a semicolon after each declaration—this divides one property from another, and must always be used (except after the last property, which obviously doesn't need to be separated).

> You can spread a selector across multiple lines to make your code easier to read. It has the same effect as placing it all on one line. In both cases, though, don't forget the closing brace.

# Inheritance

One of the best features of CSS1 is the ability to have one tag inherit the properties of an enclosing tag. This means that you don't need to specify every possible tag; if you neglect to set a property for **<EM>** it will simply acquire the characteristics of whatever tag encloses it. Consider the following:

```
<H3>Section Four: <EM>Colossal</EM> Widgets</H3>
```

If your style sheet specified that all **<H3>** items were to be in green, but didn't say anything about **<EM>**, then 'Colossal' would be green, just like the rest of the line. If, on the other hand, you carefully specified that **<EM>** was blue, it would appear as such. This system of inheritance follows through all of the possible properties, allowing you to set default values and then worry only about the exceptions to your rules (the best way to do this is to set all default properties to **<BODY>**, and then change things for all of the usual tags where necessary).

Even better, you can declare that one property will have a value that is relative to its parent property:

```
P { font-size: 14pt }
P { line-height: 120% }
```

In this instance, line height is defined as a percentage of font size, which will ensure that the paragraph is easy to read. This capability is most useful for revisions, since it automatically ensures that your line heights will instantly change whenever you change the font size! If you explicitly declared the line height, you would need to change it manually, which can be annoying, and easily forgotten in the heat of designing.

## Contextual Selectors

Another useful feature of inheritance is that it can be used to apply styles contextually. For example, we can not only set **<H3>** to green and **<EM>** to blue (as we've done above), but we can also set all instances of **<EM>** that occur in **<H3>** as yellow, without affecting either of other declarations! This is remarkably easy to achieve:

```
H3 EM { color: yellow }
```

Here the style sheet is specifying that any instance of **<EM>** that occurs inside **<H3>** will be shown as yellow. This does not affect any other instance of **<EM>**! You must be careful not to use a comma when you wish to use this sort of inheritance, or the declaration will be interpreted as meaning that both **<H3>** and **<EM>** should be yellow.

This technique can be applied in great detail: it's possible to specify that all emphasized words are in red, in small print, but only when they appear in a listing that is itself enclosed by **<I>**! These types of declarations are termed **contextual selectors,** since they select values based on their context. It is also possible to specify values for several contextual selectors in a single statement, by dividing them with commas. For example:

```
H3 EM, H2 I { color: yellow }
```

is the same thing as:

```
H3 EM { color: yellow }
H2 I { color: yellow }
```

# Classes

To provide even more control over how things are formatted, CSS1 introduces the concept of a 'class'. This is basically a subset of a previous declaration. If, for example, you stated that **<H3>** is blue, you can create a subset of **<H3>** that is white. This subset will retain any other properties you've given the parent, and must be referenced by name (in order to separate it from the parent.) For example:

```
H3 { font-size: 14pt, font-family: monaco }
H3.second { color: #FFFFFF }
```

To implement your newly-created class, you must call it explicitly, as shown:

```
<H3 CLASS=second>This is in white fourteen-point monaco<H3>
<H3>This is in the default color, fourteen-point monaco<H3>
```

To round things out, you can specify properties on a class-wide basis, with any properties of that class applying to all instances of that class—even when used with different tags! Declaring the properties of a class is easy:

```
.second { color: #FFFFFF }
```

Notice the period that appears before **second**—this is needed to indicate that you are defining the properties of a class. You can now apply the properties of **second** wherever you call it, without having to set up every conceivable combination of tag and class:

```
<H1 CLASS=second>Level One</H1>
<EM CLASS=second>Emphasis</EM>
```

In this example, both bits of text will be in white, and each will have whatever characteristics have been previously defined, without having to explicitly define the properties of **H1.second** and **EM.second**. You should know, however, that you can only use one class at a time per tag. So **EM.second.big** isn't valid—but this doesn't really matter, since most of the effects that it would have given you are already available through careful use of contextual selectors.

# Pseudo-classes and Pseudo-elements

By now you may have noticed that CSS1 hasn't really addressed some of the more commonly customized elements of HTML: for example, what color the links are on a page. Fortunately, CSS1 not only lets you control that, it actually adds on all of the additional control that it provides for other elements.

The mechanism for doing this is by 'pseudo-classes', which can be used to apply formatting based on link status (visited, not visited, active) and can be applied to normal classes as well. For example:

```
A:link { color: green }
```

This line breaks down like this: **A** indicates that the selector applies to an anchor element, **Link** indicates that the properties will apply

for an unvisited URL (other possible values are **visited** and
**active**), and the rest will set properties as usual.

Pseudo-elements are arguably more useful, since they allow a
relatively fine level of control over commonly-used typographical
elements. For example, they can be used to set special characteristics
for the first letter in a paragraph, for the first line, and so on. They
are relatively simple to use. In the following example, we set the first
letter of any paragraph to appear in red:

```
P:first-letter { color: red }
```

You may, of course, combine pseudo-elements with other classes and
selectors, in order to achieve the level of control you require.

> One of the first things budding CSS1 designers do is to
> go crazy with the control they've just acquired. Sure, you
> can make your links all appear in pink 24pt Times, but
> do you really want to? Changing properties, simply
> because you can, is a recipe for reader dissatisfaction. If
> nobody can figure out 'what is a link' versus 'what is just
> an emphasis', or 'why all of the lines are in 6pt type',
> nobody will be reading your page twice.

# Cascading Style Sheets

One of the niftiest, and most confusing, capabilities of CSS1 is the
ability to have style sheets **cascade**—hence the name *Cascading Style
Sheets*! This means that compliant browsers are supposed to allow
multiple style sheets control over the same document at the same
time. It is possible, for example, to have three separate style sheets
trying to format a document at once. This is actually more useful
than it sounds.

The idea is this: when an author sets up a document and refers to a
style sheet, they are expressing their preferred mode of display. Each
browser may also have a 'default style' of its own that it will prefer
to display pages with. As the browser interprets documents on the
web, it will display them in its default style. If, however, it runs
across a document that uses CSS1, it will give way to the preferences
stated in that style sheet. The basic idea appears to be that 'normal'
HTML documents have nothing to lose by being formatted according
to browser preferences, but that documents using CSS1 ought to be
displayed according to the way the author intended (or else they
wouldn't have been formatted that way in the first place).

Which style sheet 'wins' is determined on a selector-by-selector basis, so that the browser can win sometimes, and the author others. This can be influenced through the use of the **important** mark—if the browser has been set to display all type in 48 point (in the case of user disability, for example), the user will probably not appreciate your documents overriding that preference and forcing a display in 10 point type. The user can, accordingly, enforce their preference by writing a default style sheet, so that the critical selectors are marked as such:

```
H1, H2, H3 { color: black }
EM { font-size: 24pt! important }
```

In this case, the settings for **<H1>** and the others are of normal weight (they will be overridden by normal author settings), but **<EM>** is flagged important, and will override normal author settings. And yes, author settings marked **important** will override any user setting. (By the way, please don't use the **important** flag unless it is really very important. Using it just because you want to make sure you're forcing the user to see things the way you want them is asinine, to say the least.)

The method that browsers use to determine which instructions will be used are basically as follows:

- Determine if the settings for any element actually conflict. If not, any inherited values (from 'parent' tags) are used instead. If there aren't any, the default values are used.

- If there is a conflict, the values are sorted by weight (i.e. 'important' ones rank higher).

- Sort again by origin (author values are higher than reader values).

- Sort by specificity: if two values conflict, and one applies only to the situation at hand, but the other applies in all cases, then the restricted value will win.

- Apply selectors according to their ranking.

Notice that this system allows for the possibility of having effects from multiple style sheets all appearing at once on the page. This is actually a benefit, since it allows you to create multiple focused style sheets, and then apply them in different combinations.

# CSS1 Properties

There are more than two dozen properties in CSS1, and they are broken up into several major 'groups'. To help you use CSS1, we've listed all of the properties below (by group), with some of the crucial information for each.

## Font Properties

### font-family

| | |
|---|---|
| **Values:** | Name of a font family (e.g. New York) or a generic family (e.g. Serif) |
| **Default:** | Set by browser |
| **Applies to:** | All elements |
| **Inherited:** | Yes |
| **Percentage?:** | No |

You can specify multiple values, in order of preference (in case the browser doesn't have the font you want). To do so, simply specify them and separate multiple values by commas. You should end with a generic font-family (allowable values would then be **serif, sans-serif, cursive, fantasy,** or **monospace**). If the font name has spaces in it, you should enclose the name in quotation marks.

### font-style

| | |
|---|---|
| **Values:** | **normal, italic,** or **oblique** |
| **Default:** | **normal** |
| **Applies to:** | All elements |
| **Inherited:** | Yes |
| **Percentage?:** | No |

This is used to apply styling to your font—if a pre-rendered font is available (e.g. New York Oblique) then that will be used if possible. If not, the styling will be applied electronically.

### font-variant

| | |
|---|---|
| **Values:** | **normal, small-caps** |
| **Default:** | **normal** |
| **Applies to:** | All elements |
| **Inherited:** | Yes |
| **Percentage?:** | No |

**Normal** is the standard appearance, and so is the default. **Small-caps** uses capital letters that are the same size as normal lowercase letters.

## font-weight

| | |
|---|---|
| **Values:** | **normal**, **bold**, **bolder**, **lighter**—or numeric values from 100 to 900 |
| **Default:** | **normal** |
| **Applies to:** | All elements |
| **Inherited:** | Yes |
| **Percentage?:** | No |

Specifies the 'boldness' of text, which is usually expressed by stroke thickness. If numeric values are used, they must proceed in 100-unit increments (e.g. 250 isn't legal). **400** is the same as **normal**, and **700** is the same as **bold**.

## font-size

| | |
|---|---|
| **Values:** | <absolute>, <relative>, <length>, <percentage> |
| **Default:** | Medium |
| **Applies to:** | All elements |
| **Inherited:** | Yes |
| **Percentage?:** | Yes, relative to parent font size |

The values for this property can be expressed in several ways:

- Absolute size: legal values are **xx-small**, **x-small**, **small**, **medium**, **large**, **x-large**, **xx-large**

- Relative size: values are **larger**, **smaller**

- Length: values are in any unit of measurement—see the end of this chapter)

- Percentage: values are a percentage of the parent font size

## font

| | |
|---|---|
| **Values:** | <font-size>, [/<line-height>], <font-family> |
| **Default:** | Not defined |
| **Applies to:** | All elements |
| **Inherited:** | Yes |
| **Percentage?:** | Only on <font-size> and <line-height> |

This allows you to set several font properties all at once, with the initial values being determined by the properties being used (e.g. the default for **font-size** is different to the default for **font-family**). This property should be used with multiple values separated by spaces, or a comma if specifying multiple font-families.

# Color and Background Properties

## *color*

| | |
|---|---|
| **Values:** | Color name or RGB value |
| **Default:** | Depends on browser |
| **Applies to:** | All elements |
| **Inherited:** | Yes |
| **Percentage?:** | No |

Sets the color of any element. The color can be specified by name (e.g. green) or by RGB-value (which can be stated in hex '#FFFFFF', by percentage '80%, 20%, 0%', or by value '255,0,0').

## *background*

| | |
|---|---|
| **Values:** | **transparent**, color, URL (plus \<repeat\>, \<scroll\>, \<position\>) |
| **Default:** | **transparent** |
| **Applies to:** | All elements |
| **Inherited:** | No |
| **Percentage?:** | Yes, will refer to the dimension of the element itself |

Specifies the background of the document. **Transparent** is the same as no defined background. You can use a solid color, or you can specify the URL for an image to be used. The URL can be absolute or relative, but must be enclosed in parentheses and immediately preceded by **url**:

```
BODY { background: url(http://foo.bar.com/image/small.gif) }
```

It is possible to use a color and an image, in which case the image will be overlaid on top of the color. Images can have several properties set:

- \<repeat\> can be **repeat**, **repeat-x** (where **x** is a number), **repeat-y** (where **y** is a number) and **no-repeat**. If no repeat value is given, then **repeat** is assumed.

- \<scroll\> determines if the background will remain fixed, or if it will scroll when the page does. Possible values are **fixed** or **scroll**.

- \<position\> specifies the location of the image on the page. Values are by percentage (horizontal, vertical), by absolute distance (in a unit of measurement, horizontal then vertical), or by keyword (values are **top**, **center**, **bottom**, **left**, or **right**)

# Text Properties

### word-spacing

| | |
|---|---|
| Values: | **normal**, <length> |
| Default: | **normal** |
| Applies to: | All elements |
| Inherited: | Yes |
| Percentage?: | No |

Sets the distance between words. **Normal** distance is assumed, but any value can be given in a unit of measurement.

### letter-spacing

| | |
|---|---|
| Values: | **normal**, <length> |
| Default: | **normal** |
| Applies to: | All elements |
| Inherited: | Yes |
| Percentage?: | No |

Sets the distance between letters. Values, if given, should be in units of measurement.

### text-decoration

| | |
|---|---|
| Values: | **none, underline, overline, line-through, blink** |
| Default: | **none** |
| Applies to: | All elements |
| Inherited: | No |
| Percentage?: | No |

Specifies any special appearance of the text. Open to extension by vendors, with unidentified extensions rendered as an underline. This property is not inherited, but will usually span across any 'child' elements.

### vertical-align

| | |
|---|---|
| Values: | **baseline, sub, super, top, text-top, middle, bottom, text-bottom**, <%> |
| Default: | **baseline** |
| Applies to: | Inline elements |
| Inherited: | No |
| Percentage?: | Yes, will refer to the line-height itself |

Controls the vertical positioning of any affected element.

**191**

- **baseline** sets the alignment with the base of the parent.

- **middle** aligns the vertical midpoint of the element with the baseline of the parent plus half of the vertical height of the parent.

- **sub** makes the element a subscript.

- **super** makes the element a superscript.

- **text-top** aligns the element with the top of text in the parent element's font.

- **text-bottom** aligns with the bottom of text in the parent element's font.

- **top** aligns the top of the element with the top of the tallest element on the current line.

- **bottom** aligns by the bottom of the lowest element on the line.

### text-transform

| Values: | **capitalize, uppercase, lowercase, none** |
|---|---|
| Default: | **none** |
| Applies to: | All elements |
| Inherited: | Yes |
| Percentage?: | No |

- **capitalize** will set the first character of each word in the element as uppercase.

- **uppercase** will set every character in the element in uppercase.

- **lowercase** will place every character in lowercase.

- **none** will neutralize any inherited settings.

### text-align

| Values: | **left, right, center, justify** |
|---|---|
| Default: | Depends on browser |
| Applies to: | Block-level elements |
| Inherited: | Yes |
| Percentage?: | No |

Describes how text is aligned. Essentially replicates the **<DIV ALIGN=>** tag.

### text-indent

| | |
|---|---|
| **Values:** | \<length\>, \<percentage\> |
| **Default:** | Zero |
| **Applies to:** | Block-level elements |
| **Inherited:** | Yes |
| **Percentage?:** | Yes, refers to width of parent element |

Sets the indentation values, in units of measurement, or as a percentage of the parent element's width.

### line-height

| | |
|---|---|
| **Values:** | \<number\>, \<length\>, \<percentage\> |
| **Default:** | Depends on browser |
| **Applies to:** | All elements |
| **Inherited:** | Yes |
| **Percentage?:** | Yes, relative to the font-size of the current element |

Sets the height of the current line. Numerical values are expressed as the font size of the current element multiplied by the value given (for example, 1.2 would be valid). If given by length, a unit of measurement must be used. Percentages are based on the font-size of the current font size, and should normally be more than 100%.

## Box Properties

These values are used to set the characteristics of the layout 'box' that exists around elements. They can apply to characters, images, and so on.

### margin-top, margin-right, margin-bottom, margin-left, margin

| | |
|---|---|
| **Values:** | **auto**, \<length\>, \<percentage\> |
| **Default:** | Zero |
| **Applies to:** | All elements |
| **Inherited:** | No |
| **Percentage?:** | Yes, refers to parent element's width |

Sets the size of margins around any given element. You can use **margin** as shorthand for setting all of the other values (as it applies to all four sides). If you use multiple values in **margin** but use less than four, opposing sides will try to be equal. These values all set the effective minimum distance between the current element and others.

## padding-top, padding-right, padding-bottom, padding-left, padding

| | |
|---|---|
| **Values:** | **auto**, <length>, <percentage> |
| **Default:** | Zero |
| **Applies to:** | All elements |
| **Inherited:** | No |
| **Percentage?:** | Yes, refers to parent element's width |

Specifies how much space to insert between the border and the content (e.g. between the border of the image and the image itself). Functions similarly to the margin settings above.

## border-top, border-right, border-bottom, border-left, border

| | |
|---|---|
| **Values:** | <border-width>, <border-style>, <color> |
| **Default:** | Medium none |
| **Applies to:** | All elements |
| **Inherited:** | No |
| **Percentage?:** | No |

Sets the properties of the border element (box drawn around the affected element). Again, works roughly the same as the margin settings, except that it can be made visible.

> <border-width> can be given as **thin**, **medium**, **thick**, or in a unit of measurement.

> <border-style> can be given as **none**, **dotted**, **dashed**, **solid**, **double**, **groove**, **ridge**, **inset**, **outset**.

## width

| | |
|---|---|
| **Values:** | **auto**, <length>, <percentage> |
| **Default:** | **auto**, except for any element with an intrinsic dimension |
| **Applies to:** | Block-level elements |
| **Inherited:** | No |
| **Percentage?:** | Yes, refers to parent's width |

Sets the horizontal size of an element, and will scale the element if necessary.

## height

| | |
|---|---|
| **Values:** | **auto**, <length> |
| **Default:** | **auto** |
| **Applies to:** | Block-level elements |
| **Inherited:** | No |
| **Percentage?:** | No |

Sets the vertical size of an element, and will scale the element if necessary.

### *float*

| | |
|---|---|
| **Values:** | **left**, **right**, **none** |
| **Default:** | **none** |
| **Applies to:** | All elements |
| **Inherited:** | No |
| **Percentage?:** | No |

This controls the position of an element. The default value will place the element where it would appear in the text (i.e. normal positioning).

- **left** causes the left margin settings to control the positioning, with text flowing around to the right.

- **right** sets the positioning according to the right margins, with text flowing around to the left.

### *clear*

| | |
|---|---|
| **Values:** | **none**, **left**, **right**, **both** |
| **Default:** | **none** |
| **Applies to:** | All elements |
| **Inherited:** | No |
| **Percentage?:** | No |

This controls whether or not an element will allow text to flow around it to the sides by stating whether the element must have clear space around it or not.

- **none** means that the element doesn't require that it have clear space to either side of it, so text will flow around on both sides.

- **both** will prevent any text from flowing around the element, so it will exist by itself on a line.

## Classification Properties

These are used to put elements into display categories.

### *display*

| | |
|---|---|
| **Values:** | Block, in-line, list-item, none |
| **Default:** | According to HTML |
| **Applies to:** | All elements |

**195**

Inherited:      No
Percentage?:    No

This specifies whether an element is in-line (e.g. **<EM>**), block-level (e.g. **<H1>**), or a list item (e.g. **<LI>**). A value of **none** will turn the display of the element and all children off.

## list-style

Values:         <keyword>, <position>, <url>
Default:        Disc outside
Applies to:     Elements that are in lists
Inherited:      Yes
Percentage?:    No

Can be set several ways:

- <keyword> can have the values **disc**, **circle**, **square**, **decimal**, **lower-roman**, **upper-roman**, **lower-alpha**, **upper-alpha**, **none**; these values control the method used to list. The default is **disc**, which means that list items will be preceded by a bullet-point.

- <position> sets the indentation (or lack of) for list items and can have the values **inside**, **outside** with **outside** being the default.

- If a URL is given, the image found at the location will be used as a bullet point (the format for URLs is as with other elements—**url(http://foo.bar.com)**)

## white-space

Values:         **normal**, **pre**, **nowrap**
Default:        According to HTML
Applies to:     Block-level elements
Inherited:      Yes
Percentage?:    No

This specifies how white space should be handled in the element:

- As for normal HTML: extra white space beyond one space is ignored, breaks must be made with **<BR>**.

- As for **<PRE>**: all white space is left as typed, breaks left as typed.

- **nowrap**: where wrapping is done *only* on **<BR>**.

# Units of Measurement

There are two basic categories of unit: relative and absolute (plus percentages). As a general rule, relative measures are preferred, as using absolute measures requires familiarity with the actual mechanism of display (e.g. what kind of printer, what sort of monitor, etc.).

## *Relative Units*

Values:        **em, ex, px**

**em** is a typographic term, and refers to the height of a single character (in this case, the height of characters in the current element). **ex** refers to the height of the letter 'x' in the current element. The only exception to this is for <font-size>, where the units are relative to the parent element rather than the current element itself. **px** refers to a measurement in pixels, which is generally only meaningful for display on computer monitors, and is relative to the display being used.

## *Absolute Units*

Values:        **in, cm, mm, pt, pc**

**in** gives the measurement in inches, **cm** gives it in centimeters, **mm** in millimeters, **pt** is in typeface points (72 to an inch), and **pc** is in picas (1 pica equals 12 points). These units are generally only useful when you know what the output medium is going to be, since browsers are allowed to approximate if they must.

## *Percentage*

Values:        Numeric

This is given as a number (with or without a decimal point), and is relative to a length unit (which is usually the font size of the current element). You should note that child elements will inherit the computed value, not the percentage value (so a child will not be 20% of the parent, it will be the same size as the parent).

# Summary

Style sheets are exceedingly useful, if used in moderation. They aren't very widely supported yet, but they are guaranteed to enter wide use. As with most things, the best way to become intimately familiar with their use is to practice using them.

As a parting note, we would like to re-emphasize the need to use style sheets only as necessary—pointless manipulation will rapidly become irritating, rather than useful.

# Appendix A - Alphabetical List of Tags

Here we give a full listing of all the tags and their attributes. We have also marked which tags and attributes are part of the HTML 2.0 and HTML 3.2 standards, and which are supported by the two leading browsers: Internet Explorer 3.0 and Netscape Navigator 3.0.

The following key explains the icons used to indicate browser support for the tags.

Key:    **HTML 2.0**   **HTML 3.2**   **Navigator**        **IE**

        **2.0**        **3.2**        **N**          **IE**

---

**<!-- -->**    **2.0**  **3.2**  **N**  **IE**

Allows authors to add comments to code.

**See page: 23**

**!DOCTYPE**    **2.0**  **3.2**  **N**  **IE**

Defines the document type. Required by all HTML documents.

**See page: 11**

**A**  | 2.0 | 3.2 | N | IE |

Used to insert an anchor, which can be either a local reference point or a hyperlink to another URL.

| Attributes | HTML 2.0 | HTML 3.2 | Navigator 3.0 | IE 3.0 |
|---|---|---|---|---|
| `HREF=url` | ✓ | ✓ | ✓ | ✓ |
| `NAME=name` | ✓ | ✓ | ✓ | ✓ |
| `TITLE=name` | x | ✓ | x | x |
| `TARGET=window` | x | x | ✓ | ✓ |

**Notes:** The **REL** and **REV** attributes are not well defined and should not be used.

See page: 64

**ADDRESS**  | 2.0 | 3.2 | N | IE |

Indicates an address. The address is typically displayed in italics.

See page: 45

**APPLET**  | 3.2 | N | IE |

Inserts an applet.

| Attributes | HTML 2.0 | HTML 3.2 | Navigator 3.0 | IE 3.0 |
|---|---|---|---|---|
| `ALIGN=left|right|top|` `texttop|middle|` `absmiddle|baseline|` `bottom|absbottom` | x | ✓ | ✓ | ✓ |
| `ALT=alternativetext` | x | ✓ | ✓ | ✓ |
| `CODE=appletname` | x | ✓ | ✓ | ✓ |
| `CODEBASE=url` | x | ✓ | ✓ | ✓ |
| `HEIGHT=n` | x | ✓ | ✓ | ✓ |

*Table continued on following page*

| Attributes | HTML 2.0 | HTML 3.2 | Navigator 3.0 | IE 3.0 |
|---|---|---|---|---|
| `HSPACE=n` | x | ✓ | x | ✓ |
| `NAME=name` | x | ✓ | x | ✓ |
| `VSPACE=n` | x | ✓ | x | ✓ |
| `WIDTH=n` | x | ✓ | ✓ | ✓ |

See page: 155

## *AREA*   `3.2`  `N`  `IE`

Defines a client-side imagemap area.

| Attributes | HTML 2.0 | HTML 3.2 | Navigator 3.0 | IE 3.0 |
|---|---|---|---|---|
| `ALT=alternativetext` | x | ✓ | ✓ | x |
| `COORDS=coords` | x | ✓ | ✓ | ✓ |
| `HREF=url` | x | ✓ | ✓ | ✓ |
| `NOHREF` | x | ✓ | ✓ | ✓ |
| `SHAPE=RECT\|CIRCLE\|POLY` | x | ✓ | ✓ | ✓ |
| `TARGET="window"\| _blank\|_parent\|_self\| _top` | x | x | ✓ | ✓ |

Notes: Internet Explorer also supports the values **RECTANGLE**, **CIRC**, and **POLYGON** for **SHAPE**.

See page: 78

## *B*   `2.0`  `3.2`  `N`  `IE`

Emboldens text.

See page: 44

### BASE  `2.0` `3.2` `N` `IE`

Base URL—defines the original location of the document. It is not normally necessary to include this tag. May be used only in **HEAD** section.

| Attributes | HTML 2.0 | HTML 3.2 | Navigator 3.0 | IE 3.0 |
|---|---|---|---|---|
| `HREF=url` | ✓ | ✓ | ✓ | ✓ |
| `TARGET="window"`\|`_blank`\|`_parent`\|`_self`\|`_top` | x | x | ✓ | ✓ |

See page: 13

### BASEFONT  `N` `IE`

Defines font size over a range of text.

| Attributes | HTML 2.0 | HTML 3.2 | Navigator 3.0 | IE 3.0 |
|---|---|---|---|---|
| `COLOR` | x | x | x | ✓ |
| `FACE` | x | x | x | ✓ |
| `SIZE=1`\|`2`\|`3`\|`4`\|`5`\|`6`\|`7` | x | x | ✓ | ✓ |

See page: 41

### BGSOUND  `IE`

Plays a background sound.

| Attributes | HTML 2.0 | HTML 3.2 | Navigator 3.0 | IE 3.0 |
|---|---|---|---|---|
| `LOOP` | x | x | x | ✓ |
| `SRC=url` | x | x | x | ✓ |

See page: 61

## BIG 　 3.2 　 N 　 IE

Changes the physical rendering of the font to one size larger.

See page: 45

## BLINK 　 N

Defines text that will blink on and off.

See page: 44

## BLOCKQUOTE 　 2.0 　 3.2 　 N 　 IE

Formats a quote—typically by indentation.

## BODY 　 2.0 　 3.2 　 N 　 IE

Contains the main part of the HTML document.

| Attributes | HTML 2.0 | HTML 3.2 | Navigator 3.0 | IE 3.0 |
|---|---|---|---|---|
| ALINK="#rrggbb" | x | ✓ | ✓ | x |
| BACKGROUND=url | x | ✓ | x | ✓ |
| BGCOLOR="#rrggbb" | x | ✓ | ✓ | ✓ |
| LINK="#rrggbb" | x | ✓ | ✓ | ✓ |
| TEXT="#rrggbb" | x | ✓ | ✓ | ✓ |
| VLINK="#rrggbb" | x | ✓ | ✓ | ✓ |
| BGPROPERTIES=fixed | x | x | x | ✓ |
| LEFTMARGIN=n | x | x | x | ✓ |
| TOPMARGIN=n | x | x | x | ✓ |

See page: 18

## BR  `2.0` `3.2` `N` `IE`

Line break.

| Attributes | HTML 2.0 | HTML 3.2 | Navigator 3.0 | IE 3.0 |
|---|---|---|---|---|
| CLEAR=left\|right\|all | x | ✓ | ✓ | ✓ |

See page: 29

## CAPTION  `3.2` `N` `IE`

Puts a title above a table.

| Attributes | HTML 2.0 | HTML 3.2 | Navigator 3.0 | IE 3.0 |
|---|---|---|---|---|
| ALIGN=top\|bottom\|left\|right | x | ✓ | ✓ | ✓ |

**Notes:** Netscape Navigator does not support the **left** and **right** values for the **ALIGN** attribute.

See page: 91

## CENTER  `3.2` `N` `IE`

Centers text or graphic.

See page: 29

## CITE  `2.0` `3.2` `N` `IE`

Indicates a citation, generally displaying the text in italics.

See page: 45

## CODE  `2.0` `3.2` `N` `IE`

Renders text in a font resembling computer code.

See page: 45

## COL    `3.2`   `IE`

Defines column width and properties for a table.

| Attributes | HTML 2.0 | HTML 3.2 | Navigator 3.0 | IE 3.0 |
|---|---|---|---|---|
| `ALIGN=left\|right\|center` | x | x | x | ✓ |
| `SPAN=n` | x | x | x | ✓ |

See page: 93

## COLGROUP    `3.2`   `IE`

Defines properties for a group of columns in a table.

| Attributes | HTML 2.0 | HTML 3.2 | Navigator 3.0 | IE 3.0 |
|---|---|---|---|---|
| `ALIGN=left\|right\|center` | x | x | x | ✓ |
| `SPAN=n` | x | x | x | ✓ |

See page: 94

## DD    `2.0`   `3.2`   `N`   `IE`

Definition description. Used in definition lists with **\<DT\>** to define the term.

See page: 34

## DFN    `3.2`   `N`   `IE`

Indicates the first instance of a term or important word.

See page: 44

## DIR    `2.0`   `3.2`   `N`   `IE`

Defines a directory list by indenting the text.

See page: 36

### DIV  `3.2`

Defines a block division of the <BODY>.

| Attributes | HTML 2.0 | HTML 3.2 | Navigator 3.0 | IE 3.0 |
|---|---|---|---|---|
| ALIGN=left\|right\|center | x | ✓ | ✓ | ✓ |
| NOWRAP | x | x | x | x |
| CLEAR=left\|right\|all | x | x | x | x |

### DL  `2.0`  `3.2`  `N`  `IE`

Defines a definition list.

See page: 34

### DT  `2.0`  `3.2`  `N`  `IE`

Defines a definition term. Used with definition lists.

See page: 34

### EM  `2.0`  `3.2`  `N`  `IE`

Emphasized text—usually italic.

See page: 45

### EMBED  `N`  `IE`

Defines an embedded object in an HTML document.

| Attributes | HTML 2.0 | HTML 3.2 | Navigator 3.0 | IE 3.0 |
|---|---|---|---|---|
| HEIGHT=n | x | x | ✓ | ✓ |
| NAME=name | x | x | ✓ | ✓ |

*Table continued on following page*

| Attributes | HTML 2.0 | HTML 3.2 | Navigator 3.0 | IE 3.0 |
|---|:---:|:---:|:---:|:---:|
| PALETTE=foreground\| background | x | x | x | ✓ |
| SRC=url | x | x | ✓ | ✓ |
| WIDTH=n | x | x | ✓ | ✓ |

See page: 139, 141

### FONT  `3.2`  `N`  `IE`

Changes font properties.

| Attributes | HTML 2.0 | HTML 3.2 | Navigator 3.0 | IE 3.0 |
|---|:---:|:---:|:---:|:---:|
| COLOR="#rrggbb" | x | ✓ | ✓ | ✓ |
| FACE=typeface | x | x | ✓ | ✓ |
| SIZE=1\|2\|3\|4\|5\|6\|7 | x | ✓ | ✓ | ✓ |

See page: 39

### FORM  `2.0`  `3.2`  `N`  `IE`

Defines part of the document as a user fill out form.

| Attributes | HTML 2.0 | HTML 3.2 | Navigator 3.0 | IE 3.0 |
|---|:---:|:---:|:---:|:---:|
| ACTION=url | ✓ | ✓ | ✓ | ✓ |
| ENCTYPE=enc_method | ✓ | ✓ | ✓ | ✓ |
| METHOD=get\|post | ✓ | ✓ | ✓ | ✓ |
| TARGET="window"\|_blank\| _parent\|_self\|_top | x | x | ✓ | ✓ |

See page: 120

## FRAME

Defines a single frame in a frameset.

| Attributes | HTML 2.0 | HTML 3.2 | Navigator 3.0 | IE 3.0 |
|---|---|---|---|---|
| ALIGN=top\|bottom\|left\|center\|right | x | x | ✓ | ✓ |
| FRAMEBORDER=0\|1 | x | x | x | ✓ |
| MARGINHEIGHT=n | x | x | ✓ | ✓ |
| MARGINWIDTH=n | x | x | ✓ | ✓ |
| NAME=name | x | x | ✓ | ✓ |
| NORESIZE | x | x | ✓ | ✓ |
| SCROLLING=yes\|no\|auto | x | x | ✓ | ✓ |
| SRC=url | x | x | ✓ | ✓ |

See page: 106

## FRAMESET

Defines the main container for a frame.

| Attributes | HTML 2.0 | HTML 3.2 | Navigator 3.0 | IE 3.0 |
|---|---|---|---|---|
| COLS=colswidth | x | x | ✓ | ✓ |
| FRAMEBORDER=1\|0 | x | x | ✓ | ✓ |
| FRAMESPACING=n | x | x | x | ✓ |
| ROWS=rowsheight | x | x | ✓ | ✓ |

See page: 105

### HEAD  `2.0` `3.2` `N` `IE`

Contains information about the document itself. Can include the following tags: TITLE, META, BASE, ISINDEX, LINK, SCRIPT, STYLE.

See page: 12

### Hn  `3.2` `N` `IE`

Defines a heading, can be one of `<H1>`,`<H2>`,`<H3>`,`<H4>`,`<H5>`, `<H6>` where `<H1>` is the largest and `<H6>` is the smallest.

| Attributes | HTML 2.0 | HTML 3.2 | Navigator 3.0 | IE 3.0 |
|---|---|---|---|---|
| ALIGN=left\|right\|center | x | ✓ | ✓ | ✓ |

See page: 27

### HR  `2.0` `3.2` `N` `IE`

Defines a horizontal rule.

| Attributes | HTML 2.0 | HTML 3.2 | Navigator 3.0 | IE 3.0 |
|---|---|---|---|---|
| ALIGN=left\|right\|center | x | ✓ | ✓ | ✓ |
| NOSHADE | x | ✓ | ✓ | ✓ |
| SIZE=n | x | ✓ | ✓ | ✓ |
| WIDTH=width | x | ✓ | ✓ | ✓ |
| COLOR="#rrggbb" | x | x | x | ✓ |

See page: 36

### HTML  2.0  3.2  N  IE

Signals the start and end of an HTML document.

See page: 12

### I  2.0  3.2  N  IE

Defines italic text.

See page: 44

### IFRAME  IE

Defines a 'floating' frame within a document.

| Attributes | HTML 2.0 | HTML 3.2 | Navigator 3.0 | IE 3.0 |
|---|---|---|---|---|
| ALIGN=top\|middle\|<br>bottom\|left\|right | x | x | x | ✓ |
| FRAMEBORDER=0\|1 | x | x | x | ✓ |
| HEIGHT=n | x | x | x | ✓ |
| MARGINHEIGHT=n | x | x | x | ✓ |
| MARGINWIDTH=n | x | x | x | ✓ |
| NAME=name | x | x | x | ✓ |
| NORESIZE | x | x | x | ✓ |
| SCROLLING=yes\|no\|auto | x | x | x | ✓ |
| SRC=url | x | x | x | ✓ |
| WIDTH | x | x | x | ✓ |

See page: 115

*IMG*  `2.0`  `3.2`  `N`  `IE`

Defines an inline image.

| Attributes | HTML 2.0 | HTML 3.2 | Navigator 3.0 | IE 3.0 |
|---|:---:|:---:|:---:|:---:|
| `ALIGN=top\|middle\| bottom\|left\|right` | ✓ | ✓ | ✓ | ✓ |
| `ALT=alternativetext` | ✓ | ✓ | ✓ | ✓ |
| `BORDER=n` | x | ✓ | ✓ | ✓ |
| `HEIGHT=n` | x | ✓ | ✓ | ✓ |
| `HSPACE=n` | x | ✓ | ✓ | ✓ |
| `ISMAP` | ✓ | ✓ | ✓ | ✓ |
| `SRC=url` | ✓ | ✓ | ✓ | ✓ |
| `USEMAP=mapname` | x | ✓ | ✓ | ✓ |
| `VSPACE=n` | x | ✓ | ✓ | ✓ |
| `WIDTH=n` | x | ✓ | ✓ | ✓ |
| `CONTROLS` | x | x | x | ✓ |
| `DYNSRC` | x | x | x | ✓ |
| `LOOP` | x | x | x | ✓ |
| `START` | x | x | x | ✓ |
| `LOWSRC` | x | x | ✓ | x |

See page: 51

## *INPUT*   `2.0`  `3.2`  `N`  `IE`

Defines a user input box.

| Attributes | HTML 2.0 | HTML 3.2 | Navigator 3.0 | IE 3.0 |
|---|---|---|---|---|
| `ALIGN=top\|middle\|bottom` | ✓ | ✓ | ✓ | ✓ |
| `CHECKED` | ✓ | ✓ | ✓ | ✓ |
| `MAXLENGTH=n` | ✓ | ✓ | ✓ | ✓ |
| `NAME=name` | ✓ | ✓ | ✓ | ✓ |
| `SIZE=n` | ✓ | ✓ | ✓ | ✓ |
| `SRC=url` | ✓ | ✓ | ✓ | ✓ |
| `TYPE=checkbox\|hidden\| image\|password\|radio\| reset\|submit\|text` | ✓ | ✓ | ✓ | ✓ |
| `VALUE=value` | ✓ | ✓ | ✓ | ✓ |

See page: 124

## *ISINDEX*   `3.2`  `N`  `IE`

Defines a text input field for entering a query.

| Attributes | HTML 2.0 | HTML 3.2 | Navigator 3.0 | IE 3.0 |
|---|---|---|---|---|
| `ACTION=url` | X | X | ✓ | ✓ |
| `PROMPT=message` | ✓ | ✓ | ✓ | ✓ |

See page: 13

## *KBD*   `2.0`  `3.2`  `N`  `IE`

Indicates typed text. Useful for instruction manuals, etc.

See page: 45

### LH

| 3.2 | N | IE |

Defines a list heading in any type of list.

### LI

| 3.2 | N | IE |

Defines a list item in any type of list other than a definition list.

| Attributes | HTML 2.0 | HTML 3.2 | Navigator 3.0 | IE 3.0 |
|---|---|---|---|---|
| TYPE=A\|a\|I\|i\|1 | ✓ | ✓ | ✓ | ✓ |
| VALUE=n | ✓ | ✓ | ✓ | ✓ |

Note: Netscape Navigator also supports
TYPE=disc\|square\|circle for use with unordered lists.

See page: 31

### LINK

| 3.2 | IE |

Defines the current document's relationship with other documents.

| Attributes | HTML 2.0 | HTML 3.2 | Navigator 3.0 | IE 3.0 |
|---|---|---|---|---|
| REL= | x | ✓ | ✓ | ✓ |
| HREF=url | x | ✓ | ✓ | ✓ |
| REV= | x | ✓ | ✓ | ✓ |
| TITLE= | x | ✓ | ✓ | ✓ |

See page: 14

### MAP

| 3.2 | N | IE |

Defines the different regions of a client-side imagemap.

| Attributes | HTML 2.0 | HTML 3.2 | Navigator 3.0 | IE 3.0 |
|---|---|---|---|---|
| NAME=mapname | x | ✓ | ✓ | ✓ |

See page: 78

**213**

## MARQUEE [IE]

Sets a scrolling marquee.

| Attributes | HTML 2.0 | HTML 3.2 | Navigator 3.0 | IE 3.0 |
|---|---|---|---|---|
| `ALIGN=top\|middle\|bottom` | x | x | x | ✓ |
| `BEHAVIOR=scroll\|`<br>`slide\|alternate` | x | x | x | ✓ |
| `BGCOLOR="#rrggbb"` | x | x | x | ✓ |
| `DIRECTION=left\|right` | x | x | x | ✓ |
| `HEIGHT=n` | x | x | x | ✓ |
| `HSPACE=n` | x | x | x | ✓ |
| `LOOP=n` | x | x | x | ✓ |
| `SCROLLAMOUNT=n` | x | x | x | ✓ |
| `SCROLLDELAY=n` | x | x | x | ✓ |
| `VSPACE=n` | x | x | x | ✓ |
| `WIDTH=n` | x | x | x | ✓ |

See page: 46

## MENU [2.0] [3.2]

Defines a menu list.

See page: 36

## META [2.0] [3.2] [N] [IE]

Describes the content of a document.

| Attributes | HTML 2.0 | HTML 3.2 | Navigator 3.0 | IE 3.0 |
|---|---|---|---|---|
| `CONTENT=` | ✓ | ✓ | ✓ | ✓ |

*Table continued on following page*

| Attributes | HTML 2.0 | HTML 3.2 | Navigator 3.0 | IE 3.0 |
|---|---|---|---|---|
| `HTTP-EQUIV` | x | ✓ | ✓ | ✓ |
| `NAME` | x | ✓ | ✓ | ✓ |
| `URL=document url` | x | x | x | ✓ |

See page: 15

### NOBR

Prevents a line of text breaking.

See page: 30

### NOFRAMES

Allows for backward compatibility with non-frame-compliant browsers.

See page: 103

### OBJECT

Inserts an object.

| Attributes | HTML 2.0 | HTML 3.2 | Navigator 3.0 | IE 3.0 |
|---|---|---|---|---|
| `ALIGN=baseline\|center\| left\|middle\|right\| textbottom\|textmiddle\| texttop` | x | x | x | ✓ |
| `BORDER=n` | x | x | x | ✓ |
| `CLASSID=url` | x | x | x | ✓ |
| `CODEBASE` | x | x | x | ✓ |
| `CODETYPE=codetype` | x | x | x | ✓ |

*Table continued on following page*

| Attributes | HTML 2.0 | HTML 3.2 | Navigator 3.0 | IE 3.0 |
|---|---|---|---|---|
| DATA=url | x | x | x | ✓ |
| DECLARE | x | x | x | ✓ |
| HEIGHT=n | x | x | x | ✓ |
| HSPACE=n | x | x | x | ✓ |
| NAME=url | x | x | x | ✓ |
| SHAPES | x | x | x | ✓ |
| STANDBY=message | x | x | x | ✓ |
| TYPE=type | x | x | x | ✓ |
| USEMAP=url | x | x | x | ✓ |
| VSPACE=n | x | x | x | ✓ |
| WIDTH=n | x | x | x | ✓ |

See page: 148

## OL    `2.0` `3.2` `N` `IE`

Defines an ordered list.

| Attributes | HTML 2.0 | HTML 3.2 | Navigator 3.0 | IE 3.0 |
|---|---|---|---|---|
| COMPACT | x | ✓ | ✓ | x |
| START=n | x | ✓ | ✓ | ✓ |
| TYPE=1\|A\|a\|I\|i | x | ✓ | ✓ | ✓ |

See page: 33

## OPTION    `3.2` `IE`

Used within the `<SELECT>` tag to present the user with a number of options.

| Attributes | HTML 2.0 | HTML 3.2 | Navigator 3.0 | IE 3.0 |
|---|---|---|---|---|
| SELECTED | x | ✓ | ✓ | ✓ |
| PLAIN | x | ✓ | ✓ | ✓ |
| VALUE | x | ✓ | ✓ | ✓ |
| DISABLED | x | ✓ | ✓ | ✓ |

See page: 131

## P    `2.0` `3.2` `N` `IE`

Defines a paragraph.

| Attributes | HTML 2.0 | HTML 3.2 | Navigator 3.0 | IE 3.0 |
|---|---|---|---|---|
| ALIGN=left\|right\|center | x | ✓ | ✓ | ✓ |

See page: 29

## PARAM    `3.2` `N` `IE`

Defines parameters for a Java applet.

| Attributes | HTML 2.0 | HTML 3.2 | Navigator 3.0 | IE 3.0 |
|---|---|---|---|---|
| NAME=name | x | ✓ | ✓ | ✓ |
| VALUE=value | x | ✓ | ✓ | ✓ |
| VALUETYPE=Data\|Ref\|Object | x | x | x | ✓ |
| TYPE=InternetMediaType | x | x | x | ✓ |

See page: 157

## *PRE*　`2.0`　`3.2`　`N`　`IE`

Pre-formatted text. Renders text exactly how it is typed, i.e. carriage returns, styles, etc., *will* be recognized.

| Attributes | HTML 2.0 | HTML 3.2 | Navigator 3.0 | IE 3.0 |
|---|---|---|---|---|
| WIDTH | x | ✓ | ✓ | x |

## *S*　`3.2`　`N`　`IE`

Strikethrough. Renders the text as deleted (crossed out).

**See page: 44**

## *SAMP*　`3.2`　`N`　`IE`

Sample output.

**See page: 45**

## *SCRIPT*　`3.2`　`N`　`IE`

Inserts a script.

| Attributes | HTML 2.0 | HTML 3.2 | Navigator 3.0 | IE 3.0 |
|---|---|---|---|---|
| LANGUAGE=VBScript\| JavaScript | x | ✓ | Note | ✓ |

**Note:** Netscape Navigator 3.0 only supports JavaScript.

**See page: 161**

## *SELECT*　`2.0`　`3.2`　`N`　`IE`

Defines the default selection in a list.

| Attributes | HTML 2.0 | HTML 3.2 | Navigator 3.0 | IE 3.0 |
|---|---|---|---|---|
| MULTIPLE | x | x | ✓ | ✓ |

*Table continued on following page*

| Attributes | HTML 2.0 | HTML 3.2 | Navigator 3.0 | IE 3.0 |
|---|---|---|---|---|
| NAME=name | ✓ | ✓ | ✓ | ✓ |
| SIZE=n | x | x | ✓ | ✓ |

See page: 128

### SMALL  `3.2` `N` `IE`

Changes the physical rendering of a font to one size smaller.

See page: 45

### SPAN  `IE`

Defines localized style information, e.g. margin width.

| Attributes | HTML 2.0 | HTML 3.2 | Navigator 3.0 | IE 3.0 |
|---|---|---|---|---|
| STYLE=Style | x | x | x | ✓ |

### STRIKE  `3.2` `N` `IE`

Strikethrough. Renders the text as deleted or crossed out.

### STRONG  `2.0` `3.2` `N` `IE`

Strong emphasis—usually bold.

See page: 45

### STYLE  `3.2` `IE`

Reserved for future use with style sheets.

See page: 180

## SUB $\quad$ 3.2 $\quad$ N $\quad$ IE

Subscript.

See page: 45

## SUP $\quad$ 3.2 $\quad$ N $\quad$ IE

Superscript.

See page: 45

## TABLE $\quad$ 3.2 $\quad$ N $\quad$ IE

Defines a series of columns and rows to form a table.

| Attributes | HTML 2.0 | HTML 3.2 | Navigator 3.0 | IE 3.0 |
|---|---|---|---|---|
| ALIGN= left\|right\| center | x | ✓ | ✓ | ✓ |
| VALIGN | x | ✓ | x | x |
| BORDER=n | x | ✓ | ✓ | ✓ |
| WIDTH=n | x | ✓ | ✓ | ✓ |
| CELLSPACING=n | x | ✓ | ✓ | ✓ |
| CELLPADDING=n | x | ✓ | ✓ | ✓ |
| FRAME=void\|above\| below\|hsides\|lhs\| rhs\|vsides\| box\|border | x | ✓ | x | ✓ |
| RULES=none\|groups\| rows\|cols\|all | x | ✓ | x | ✓ |
| BACKGROUND=url | x | x | x | ✓ |
| BGCOLOR="#rrggbb" | x | x | ✓ | ✓ |
| COLS=n | x | ✓ | x | ✓ |
| BORDERCOLOR="#rrggbb" | x | x | x | ✓ |
| BORDERCOLORDARK ="#rrggbb" | x | x | x | ✓ |

*Table continued on following page*

| Attributes | HTML 2.0 | HTML 3.2 | Navigator 3.0 | IE 3.0 |
|---|---|---|---|---|
| BORDERCOLORLIGHT ="#rrggbb" | x | x | x | ✓ |

Notes: **ALIGN**, **CHAR**, **CHAROFF**, and **VALIGN** are common to all cell alignments, and may be inherited from enclosing elements.

The **CENTER** value for the **ALIGN** attribute is not supported by Netscape Navigator 3.0 or Internet Explorer 3.0.

See page: 83

### TBODY  `3.2` `IE`

Defines the table body.

See page: 95

### TD  `3.2` `N` `IE`

Marks the start point for table data.

| Attributes | HTML 2.0 | HTML 3.2 | Navigator 3.0 | IE 3.0 |
|---|---|---|---|---|
| ALIGN=left\|right\|center | x | ✓ | ✓ | ✓ |
| ASIX | x | ✓ | x | x |
| AXES | x | ✓ | x | x |
| COLSPAN=n | x | ✓ | ✓ | ✓ |
| ROWSPAN=n | x | ✓ | ✓ | ✓ |
| NOWRAP | x | ✓ | ✓ | ✓ |
| WIDTH=n | x | Note | ✓ | x |
| BACKGROUND | x | x | x | ✓ |
| BGCOLOR="#rrggbb" | x | x | ✓ | ✓ |
| BORDERCOLOR="#rrggbb" | x | x | x | ✓ |

*Table continued on following page*

**221**

| Attributes | HTML 2.0 | HTML 3.2 | Navigator 3.0 | IE 3.0 |
|---|---|---|---|---|
| BORDERCOLORDARK ="#rrggbb" | x | x | x | ✓ |
| BORDERCOLORLIGHT ="#rrggbb" | x | x | x | ✓ |
| VALIGN=top\|middle\| bottom\|baseline | x | ✓ | ✓ | ✓ |

The **WIDTH** attribute is not in HTML 3.2, but support is recommended for backward compatibility. Use the **WIDTH** attribute for **COL** instead.

See page: 89

### TEXTFLOW `3.2`

Replacement for text in applet. May be inserted inside **<APPLET>** tag.

### TEXTAREA `2.0` `3.2` `N` `IE`

Defines a text area inside a **FORM** element.

| Attributes | HTML 2.0 | HTML 3.2 | Navigator 3.0 | IE 3.0 |
|---|---|---|---|---|
| NAME=name | ✓ | ✓ | ✓ | ✓ |
| ROWS=n | ✓ | ✓ | ✓ | ✓ |
| COLS=n | ✓ | ✓ | ✓ | ✓ |
| WRAP=off\|virtual\| physical | x | x | ✓ | x |

See page: 127

### TFOOT `3.2` `IE`

Defines a table footer.

See page: 95

*TH*  `3.2`  `N`  `IE`

Defines names for columns and rows.

| Attributes | HTML 2.0 | HTML 3.2 | Navigator 3.0 | IE 3.0 |
|---|---|---|---|---|
| ALIGN=left\|center\|right | x | ✓ | ✓ | ✓ |
| AXIS | x | ✓ | x | x |
| AXES | x | ✓ | x | x |
| COLSPAN | x | ✓ | ✓ | ✓ |
| ROWSPAN | x | ✓ | ✓ | ✓ |
| WIDTH=n | x | Note | ✓ | x |
| NOWRAP | x | ✓ | ✓ | ✓ |
| BACKGROUND | x | x | x | ✓ |
| BGCOLOR="#rrggbb" | x | x | ✓ | ✓ |
| BORDERCOLOR="#rrggbb" | x | x | x | ✓ |
| BORDERCOLORDARK ="#rrggbb" | x | x | x | ✓ |
| BORDERCOLORLIGHT ="#rrggbb" | x | x | x | ✓ |
| VALIGN=n | x | ✓ | ✓ | ✓ |

The **WIDTH** attribute is not in HTML 3.2, but support is
recommended for backward compatibility. Use the **WIDTH** attribute for
**COL** instead.

See page: 91

*THEAD*  `3.2`  `IE`

Defines a table header.

See page: 95

**TITLE**  `2.0`  `3.2`  `N`  `IE`

Defines the title of the document. Required by all HTML documents.

See page: 13

**TR**  `3.2`  `N`  `IE`

Defines the start of a table row.

| Attributes | HTML 2.0 | HTML 3.2 | Navigator 3.0 | IE 3.0 |
|---|---|---|---|---|
| `ALIGN=left\|right\|center` | x | ✓ | ✓ | ✓ |
| `CHAR` | x | ✓ | x | x |
| `CHAROFF` | x | ✓ | x | x |
| `BACKGROUND` | x | x | x | ✓ |
| `BGCOLOR="#rrggbb"` | x | x | ✓ | ✓ |
| `BORDERCOLOR="#rrggbb"` | x | x | x | ✓ |
| `BORDERCOLORDARK ="#rrggbb"` | x | x | x | ✓ |
| `BORDERCOLORLIGHT ="#rrggbb"` | x | x | x | ✓ |
| `VALIGN=top\|middle\| bottom\|baseline` | x | ✓ | ✓ | ✓ |

See page: 87

**TT**  `2.0`  `3.2`  `N`  `IE`

Renders text in fixed width, typewriter style font.

See page: 44

**U**  `3.2`  `N`  `IE`

Underlines text. Not widely supported at present, and not recommended, as could cause confusion with hyperlinks, which also normally appear underlined.

See page: 44

## UL

| 2.0 | 3.2 | N | IE |

Defines an unordered, usually bulleted list.

| Attributes | HTML 2.0 | HTML 3.2 | Navigator 3.0 | IE 3.0 |
|---|---|---|---|---|
| **COMPACT** | x | ✓ | ✓ | x |
| **TYPE=disc\|circle\|square** | x | ✓ | ✓ | x |

See page: 31

## VAR

| 3.2 |

Indicates a variable.

See page: 45

## WBR

Defines the word to break and wrap to the next line. Often used with **\<NOBR\>**

INSTANT

# HTML

# Appendix B - Commonly Used Tags by Category

Here, we have listed all the tags by category. When you know what you want to do, but you're not sure which tag will achieve the desired effect, use the reference tables below to put you on the right track.

## Document Structure

| Tag | Meaning |
|---|---|
| `<!DOCTYPE>` | Defines the document type. This is required by all HTML documents. |
| `<BASE>` | Base URL—defines the original location of the document. It's not normally necessary to include this tag. May only be used in **HEAD** section. |
| `<HEAD>` | Contains information about the document itself. |
| `<HTML>` | Signals the start and end of an HTML document. |
| `<BODY>` | Contains the main part of the HTML document. |
| `<DIV>` | Defines a block division of the `<BODY>`. |
| `<ISINDEX>` | Defines a text input field for entering a query. |
| `<LINK>` | Defines the current document's relationship with other documents. |
| `<META>` | Describes the content of a document. |
| `<!-- -->` | Allows authors to add comments to code. |

# Titles and Headings

| Tag | Meaning |
| --- | --- |
| `<H1>` | Heading level 1 |
| `<H2>` | Heading level 2 |
| `<H3>` | Heading level 3 |
| `<H4>` | Heading level 4 |
| `<H5>` | Heading level 5 |
| `<H6>` | Heading level 6 |
| `<TITLE>` | Defines the title of the document. Required by all HTML documents. |

## Paragraphs and Lines

| Tag | Meaning |
| --- | --- |
| `<P>` | Defines a paragraph. |
| `<HR>` | Defines a horizontal rule. |
| `<BR>` | Line break. |
| `<NOBR>` | Prevents a line of text breaking. |
| `<WBR>` | Defines the word to break and wrap to the next line. Often used with `<NOBR>`. |

## Text Styles

| Tag | Meaning |
| --- | --- |
| `<FONT>` | Changes font properties. |
| `<BASEFONT>` | Defines font size over a range of text. |
| `<BIG>` | Changes the physical rendering of the font to one size larger. |
| `<SMALL>` | Changes the physical rendering of a font to one size smaller. |
| `<B>` | Emboldens text. |
| `<I>` | Defines italic text. |

*Table continued on following page*

| Tag | Meaning |
|---|---|
| **\<U\>** | Underlines text. Not widely supported at present, and not recommended, as could cause confusion with hyperlinks, which also normally appear underlined. |
| **\<STRONG\>** | Strong emphasis—usually bold. |
| **\<EM\>** | Emphasized text—usually italic. |
| **\<S\> \<STRIKE\>** | Strike through. Renders the text as 'deleted' (crossed out). |
| **\<SUB\>** | Subscript. |
| **\<SUP\>** | Superscript. |
| **\<SAMP\>** | Sample output. |
| **\<CODE\>** | Renders text in a font resembling computer code. |
| **\<TT\>** | Renders text in fixed width, typewriter style font. |
| **\<CITE\>** | Indicates a citation, generally displaying the text in italics. |
| **\<DFN\>** | Indicates the first instance of a term or important word. |
| **\<VAR\>** | Indicates a variable. |
| **\<ADDRESS\>** | Indicates an address. The address is typically displayed in italics. |
| **\<BLOCKQUOTE\>** | Formats a quote—typically by indentation |
| **\<KBD\>** | Indicates typed text. Useful for instruction manuals, etc. |
| **\<PRE\>** | Pre-formatted text. Renders text exactly how it is typed, i.e. carriage returns, styles, etc., *will* be recognized. |

## Lists

| Tag | Meaning |
|---|---|
| **\<OL\>** | Defines an ordered (numbered) list. |
| **\<UL\>** | Defines an unordered (bulleted) list. |

*Table continued on following page*

| Tag | Meaning |
|---|---|
| <LI> | Defines a list item in any type of list other than a definition list. |
| <LH> | Defines a list heading in any type of list. |
| <DL> | Defines a definition list. |
| <DT> | Defines a definition term. Used with definition lists. |
| <DD> | Definition description. Used in definition lists with <DT> to define the term. |
| <DIR> | Defines a directory list by indenting the text. |
| <MENU> | Defines a menu list. |

## Tables

| Tag | Meaning |
|---|---|
| <TABLE> | Defines a series of columns and rows to form a table. |
| <CAPTION> | Puts a title above a table. |
| <TR> | Defines the start of a table row. |
| <TD> | Marks the start point for table data. |
| <TH> | Defines names for columns and rows. |
| <TBODY> | Defines the table body. |
| <THEAD> | Defines a table header. |
| <TFOOT> | Defines a table footer. |
| <COL> | Defines column width and properties for a table. |
| <COLGROUP> | Defines properties for a group of columns in a table. |

## Links

| Tag | Meaning |
|---|---|
| <A> | Used to insert an anchor, which can be both a local reference point or a hyperlink to another URL. |

*Table continued on following page*

**230**

| Tag | Meaning |
|---|---|
| `<A HREF="url">` | Hyperlink to another document. |
| `<A NAME="name">` | Link to a local reference point. |

## Graphics and Multimedia

| Tag | Meaning |
|---|---|
| `<IMG>` | Defines an inline image. |
| `<AREA>` | Defines a client-side imagemap area. |
| `<MAP>` | Defines the different regions of a client-side imagemap. |
| `<APPLET>` | Inserts an applet. |
| `<PARAM>` | Defines parameters for a Java applet. |
| `<TEXTFLOW>` | Replacement for text in applet. May be inserted inside `<APPLET>` tag. |
| `<BGSOUND>` | Plays a background sound. |
| `<OBJECT>` | Inserts an object.. |
| `<SCRIPT>` | Inserts a script. |
| `<MARQUEE>` | Sets a scrolling marquee. |
| `<EMBED>` | Defines an embedded object in an HTML document. |

## Forms

| Tag | Meaning |
|---|---|
| `<FORM>` | Defines part of the document as a user fill-out form. |
| `<INPUT>` | Defines a user input box. |
| `<OPTION>` | Used within the `SELECT` tag to present the user with a number of options. |
| `<SELECT>` | Defines the default selection in a list. |
| `<TEXTAREA>` | Defines a text area inside a `FORM` element. |

# Frames

| Tag | Meaning |
|---|---|
| `<FRAME>` | Defines a single frame in a frameset. |
| `<FRAMESET>` | Defines the main container for a frame. |
| `<NOFRAMES>` | Allows for backward compatibility with non-frame compliant browsers. |
| `<IFRAME>` | Defines a 'floating' frame within a document. |

# HTML

# Appendix C - Special Characters

The following table gives you the codes you need to insert special characters into your HTML documents. Some characters have their own mnemonic names—for example, the registered trademark character can be written in HTML as &reg. Where there is no mnemonic name, you can insert the character simply by including its decimal code.

| Character | Decimal Code | HTML | Description |
|---|---|---|---|
| " | &#34; | &quot; | Quotation mark |
| & | &#38; | &amp; | Ampersand |
| < | &#60; | &lt; | Less than |
| > | &#62; | &gt; | Greater than |
| |   |   | Non-breaking space |
| ¡ | &#161; | &iexcl | Inverted exclamation |
| ¢ | &#162; | &cent | Cent sign |
| £ | &#163; | &pound | Pound sterling |
| ¤ | &#164; | &curren | General currency sign |
| ¥ | &#165; | &yen | Yen sign |
| ¦ | &#166; | &brvbar | Broken vertical bar |
| § | &#167; | &sect | Section sign |
| ¨ | &#168; | &uml | Diæresis /umlaut |
| © | &#169; | &copy | Copyright |
| ª | &#170; | &ordf | Feminine ordinal |

*Table continued on following pages*

| Character | Decimal Code | HTML | Description |
|---|---|---|---|
| « | &#171; | &laquo | Left angle quote, |
| ¬ | &#172; | &not | Not sign |
| - | &#173; | &shy; | Soft hyphen |
| ® | &#174; | &reg | Registered trademark |
| ¯ | &#175; | &macr | Macron accent |
| ° | &#176; | &deg | Degree sign |
| ± | &#177; | &plusmn | Plus or minus |
| 2 | &#178; | &sup2 | Superscript two |
| 3 | &#179; | &sup3 | Superscript three |
| ´ | &#180; | &acute | Acute accent |
| µ | &#181; | &micro | Micro sign |
| ¶ | &#182; | &para | Paragraph sign |
| · | &#183; | &middot | Middle dot |
| ¸ | &#184; | &cedil | Cedilla |
| 1 | &#185; | &sup1 | Superscript one |
| º | &#186; | &ordm | Masculine ordinal |
| » | &#187; | &raquo | Right angle quote |
| ¼ | &#188; | &frac14 | Fraction one quarter |
| ½ | &#189; | &frac12 | Fraction one half |
| ¾ | &#190; | &frac34 | Fraction three-quarters |
| ¿ | &#191; | &iquest | Inverted question mark |
| À | &#192; | &Agrave; | Capital A, grave accent |
| Á | &#193; | &Aacute; | Capital A, acute accent |
| Â | &#194; | &Acirc; | Capital A, circumflex |
| Ã | &#195; | &Atilde; | Capital A, tilde |
| Ä | &#196; | &Auml; | Capital A, diæresis/umlaut |
| Å | &#197; | &Aring; | Capital A, ring |
| Æ | &#198; | &AElig; | Capital AE ligature |
| Ç | &#199; | &Ccedil; | Capital C, cedilla |
| È | &#200; | &Egrave; | Capital E, grave accent |
| É | &#201; | &Eacute; | Capital E, acute accent |
| Ê | &#202; | &Ecirc; | Capital E, circumflex |

| Character | Decimal Code | HTML | Description |
|---|---|---|---|
| Ë | &#203; | &Euml; | Capital E, diæresis/umlaut |
| Ì | &#204; | &Igrave; | Capital I, grave accent |
| Í | &#205; | &Iacute; | Capital I, acute accent |
| Î | &#206; | &Icirc; | Capital I, circumflex |
| Ï | &#207; | &Iuml; | Capital I, diæresis/umlaut |
| Ð | &#208; | &ETH; | Capital Eth, Icelandic |
| Ñ | &#209; | &Ntilde; | Capital N, tilde |
| Ò | &#210; | &Ograve; | Capital O, grave accent |
| Ó | &#211; | &Oacute; | Capital O, acute accent |
| Ô | &#212; | &Ocirc; | Capital O, circumflex |
| Õ | &#213; | &Otilde; | Capital O, tilde |
| Ö | &#214; | &Ouml; | Capital O, diæresis/umlaut |
| × | &#215; | &times | Multiplication sign |
| Ø | &#216; | &Oslash; | Capital O, slash |
| Ù | &#217; | &Ugrave; | Capital U, grave accent |
| Ú | &#218; | &Uacute; | Capital U, acute accent |
| Û | &#219; | &Ucirc; | Capital U, circumflex |
| Ü | &#220; | &Uuml; | Capital U, diæresis/umlaut |
| Ý | &#221; | &Yacute; | Capital Y, acute accent |
| Þ | &#222; | &THORN; | Capital Thorn, Icelandic |
| ß | &#223; | &szlig; | German sz |
| à | &#224; | &agrave; | Small a, grave accent |
| á | &#225; | &aacute; | Small a, acute accent |
| â | &#226; | &acirc; | Small a, circumflex |
| ã | &#227; | &atilde; | Small a, tilde |
| ä | &#228; | &auml; | Small a, diæresis/umlaut |
| å | &#229; | &aring; | Small a, ring |
| æ | &#230; | &aelig; | Small ae ligature |
| ç | &#231; | &ccedil; | Small c, cedilla |
| è | &#232; | &egrave; | Small e, grave accent |

| Character | Decimal Code | HTML | Description |
|---|---|---|---|
| é | &#233; | &eacute; | Small e, acute accent |
| ê | &#234; | &ecirc; | Small e, circumflex |
| ë | &#235; | &euml; | Small e, diæresis/umlaut |
| ì | &#236; | &igrave; | Small i, grave accent |
| í | &#237; | &iacute; | Small i, acute accent |
| î | &#238; | &icirc; | Small i, circumflex |
| ï | &#239; | &iuml; | Small i, diæresis/umlaut |
| ð | &#240; | &eth; | Small eth, Icelandic |
| ñ | &#241; | &ntilde; | Small n, tilde |
| ò | &#242; | &ograve; | Small o, grave accent |
| ó | &#243; | &oacute; | Small o, acute accent |
| ô | &#244; | &ocirc; | Small o, circumflex |
| õ | &#245; | &otilde; | Small o, tilde |
| ö | &#246; | &ouml; | Small o, diæresis/umlaut |
| ÷ | &#247; | &divide | Division sign |
| ø | &#248; | &oslash; | Small o, slash |
| ù | &#249; | &ugrave; | Small u, grave accent |
| ú | &#250; | &uacute; | Small u, acute accent |
| û | &#251; | &ucirc; | Small u, circumflex |
| ü | &#252; | &uuml; | Small u, diæresis/umlaut |
| ý | &#253; | &yacute; | Small y, acute accent |
| þ | &#254; | &thorn; | Small thorn, Icelandic |
| ÿ | &#255; | &yuml; | Small y, diæresis/umlaut |

Remember, if you want to show HTML code in a browser, you have to use the special character codes for the angled brackets in order to avoid the browser interpreting them as start and end of tags.

# Appendix D - Color Names

Both Internet Explore and Netscape Navigator support the use of color names in the place of hexadecimal numbers.

At the time of writing, Internet Explorer supports 16 standard color names:

| | | | |
|---|---|---|---|
| AQUA | BLACK | BLUE | FUCHSIA |
| GRAY | GREEN | LIME | MAROON |
| NAVY | OLIVE | PURPLE | RED |
| SILVER | TEAL | WHITE | YELLOW |

Netscape, on the other hand, supports over a hundred color names in addition to the above, as defined by the X-Windows system. These are listed below.

| | | |
|---|---|---|
| ALICEBLUE | CORNFLOWERBLUE | DARKSLATEGRAY |
| ANTIQUEWHITE | CYAN | DARKTORQUOISE |
| AQUAMARINE | DARKBLUE | DARKVIOLET |
| AZURE | DARKCYAN | DEEPPINK |
| BEIGE | DARKGOLDENROD | DEEPSKYBLUE |
| BISQUE | DARKGRAY | DIMGRAY |
| BLACK | DARKGREEN | DODGERBLUE |
| BLANCHEDALMOND | DARKKHAKI | FIREBRICK |
| BLUE | DARKMAGENTA | FLORALWHITE |
| BLUEVIOLET | DARKOLIVEGREEN | FORESTGREEN |
| BROWN | DARKORANGE | GAINSBORO |
| BURLYWOOD | DARKORCHID | GHOSTWHITE |
| CADETBLUE | DARKRED | GOLD |
| CHARTEUSE | DARKSALMON | GOLDENROD |
| CHOCOLATE | DARKSEAGREEN | GRAY |
| CORAL | DARKSLATEBLUE | GREEN |

GREENYELLOW
HONEYDEW
INDIANRED
IVORY
KHAKI
LAVENDER
LAVENDERBLUSH
LAWNGREEN
LEMONCHIFFON
LIGHTBLUE
LIGHTCORAL
LIGHTCYAN
LIGHTGOLDENROD
LIGHTGOLDENRODYELLOW
LIGHTGRAY
LIGHTGREEN
LIGHTPINK
LIGHTSALMON
LIGHTSEAGREEN
LIGHTSKYBLUE
LIGHTSLATEBLUE
LIGHTSLATEGRAY
LIGHTSTEELBLUE
LIGHTYELLOW
LIMEGREEN
LINEN
MAGENTA
MAROON
MEDIUMAQUAMARINE

MEDIUMBLUE
MEDIUMORCHID
MEDIUMPURPLE
MEDIUMSEAGREEN
MEDIUMSLATEBLUE
MEDIUMSPRINGGREEN
MEDIUMVIOLETRED
MIDNIGHTBLUE
MINTCREAM
MISTYROSE
MOCCASIN
NAVAJOWHITE
NAVY

NAVYBLUE
OLDLACE
OLIVEDRAB
ORANGE
ORANGRED
ORCHID
PALEGOLDENROD
PALEGREEN
PALETURQUOISE
PALEVIOLETRED
PAPAYAWHIP
PEACHPUFF
PERU
PINK
PLUM

POWDERBLUE
PURPLE
RED
ROSYBROWN
ROYALBLUE
SADDLEBROWN
SALMON
SANDYBROWN
SEAGREEN
SEASHELL
SIENNA
SLATEBLUE
SLATEGRAY
SNOW
SPRINGGREEN
STEELBLUE
TAN
THISTLE
TOMATO
TURQUOISE
VIOLET
VIOLETRED
WHEAT
WHITE
WHITESMOKE
YELLOW
YELLOWGREEN

INSTANT

# HTML

# Appendix E - VBScript Reference

## Array Handling

**Dim**—declares an array variable. This can be static, with a defined number of elements, or dynamic, with up to 60 dimensions.

**ReDim**—used to change the size of an array variable which has been declared as dynamic.

**Preserve**—keyword used to preserve the contents of an array being resized. If you need to use this then you can only re-dimension the rightmost index of the array.

```
Dim strEmployees ()
ReDim strEmployees (9,1)

strEmployees (9,1) = "Phil"

ReDim strEmployees (9,2)    'loses the contents of element
                                            (9,1)
strEmployees (9,2) = "Paul"

ReDim Preserve strEmployees (9,3) 'preserves the contents
                                            of (9,2)
strEmployees (9,3) = "Smith"
```

**LBound**—returns the smallest subscript for the dimension of an array. Note that arrays always start from the subscript zero, so this function will always return the value zero.

**UBound**—used to determine the size of an array.

```
Dim strCustomers (10, 5)
intSizeFirst = UBound (strCustomers, 1)    'returns
                                            SizeFirst = 10
intSizeSecond = UBound (strCustomers, 2)   'returns
                                            SizeSecond = 5
```

> The actual number of elements is always one greater than
> the value returned by UBound, because the array starts
> from zero.

# Assignments

**Let**—used to assign values to variables (optional).
**Set**—used to assign an object reference to a variable.

```
Let intNumberOfDays = 365

Set txtMyTextBox = txtcontrol
txtMyTextBox.Value = "Hello World"
```

# Constants

**Empty**—an empty variable is one that has been created but not yet
assigned a value.
**Nothing**—used to remove an object reference.

```
Set txtMyTextBox = txtATextBox    'assigns object reference
Set txtMyTextBox = Nothing        'removes object reference
```

**Null**—indicates that a variable is not valid. Note that this isn't the
same as **Empty**.
**True**—indicates that an expression is true. Has numerical value -1.
**False**—indicates that an expression is false. Has numerical value 0.

# Control Flow

**For...Next**—executes a block of code a specified number of times.

```
Dim intSalary (10)
For intCounter = 0 to 10
    intSalary (intCounter) = 20000
Next
```

**Do...Loop**—executes a block of code while a condition is true or until a condition becomes true.

```
Do While strDayOfWeek <> "Saturday" And strDayOfWeek <>
                                            "Sunday"
    MsgBox ("Get Up! Time for work")
    ...
Loop
```

```
Do
    MsgBox ("Get Up! Time for work")
    ...
Loop Until strDayOfWeek = "Saturday" Or strDayOfWeek =
                                            "Sunday"
```

**If...Then...Else**—used to run various blocks of code depending on conditions.

```
If intAge < 20 Then
    MsgBox ("You're just a slip of a thing!")
ElseIf intAge < 40 Then
    MsgBox ("You're in your prime!")
Else
    MsgBox ("You're older and wiser")
End If
```

**Select Case**—used to replace **If...Then...Else** statements where there are many conditions.

```
Select Case intAge
Case 21,22,23,24,25,26
    MsgBox ("You're in your prime")
Case 40
    MsgBox ("You're fulfilling your dreams")
Case 65
    MsgBox ("Time for a new challenge")
End Select
```

Note that **Select Case** can only be used with precise conditions and not with a range of conditions.

**While...Wend**—executes a block of code while a condition is true.

```
While strDayOfWeek <> "Saturday" AND strDayOfWeek <>
                                            "Sunday"
    MsgBox ("Get Up! Time for work")
    ...
Wend
```

**241**

# Functions

| Conversion Functions |
| --- |
| Asc |
| AscB |
| AscW |
| Chr |
| ChrB |
| ChrW |
| CBool |
| CByte |
| CDate |
| CDbl |
| CInt |
| CLng |
| CSng |
| CStr |
| Hex |
| Oct |
| Fix |
| Int |
| Sgn |

| Date/Time Functions |
| --- |
| Date |
| Time |
| DateSerial |
| DateValue |
| TimeSerial |
| TimeValue |
| Day |
| Month |
| Weekday |
| Year |
| Hour |
| Minute |
| Second |
| Now |

| Math Functions |
| --- |
| Atn |
| Cos |
| Sin |
| Tan |
| Exp |
| Log |
| Sqr |
| Randomize |
| Rnd |

| String Functions |
| --- |
| Instr |
| InStrB |
| Len |
| LenB |
| Lcase |
| Ucase |
| Left |
| LeftB |
| Mid |
| MidB |
| Right |
| RightB |
| Space |
| StrComp |
| String |
| Ltrim |
| Rtrim |
| Trim |

| Variable Testing Functions |
| --- |
| IsArray |
| IsDate |
| IsEmpty |
| IsNull |
| IsNumeric |
| IsObject |
| VarType |

# Variable Declarations

**Dim**—declares a variable.

# Error Handling

**On Error Resume Next**—indicates that if an error occurs, control should continue at the next statement.
**Err**—this is the error object which provides information about run-time errors.

Error handling is very limited in VB Script, and the **Err** object must be tested explicitly to determine if an error has occurred.

# Input/Output

This consists of the MsgBox for output, and the Input box for input:

## MsgBox

This displays a message and can return a value indicating which button was clicked.

```
MsgBox "Hello There",20,"Hello Message",
                    "c:\windows\MyHelp.hlp",123
```

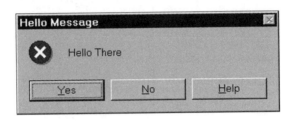

The 5 parameters are explained below:

**"Hello There"**—this contains the text of the message and is obligatory.

**20**—this determines which icon and buttons appear on the message box.

**"Hello There Message"**—this contains the text that will appear as the title of the message box.

**"c:\windows\MyHelp.hlp"**—this adds a Help button to the message box and determines the help file that is opened if the button is clicked.

**123**—this is a reference to the particular help topic that will be displayed if the Help button is clicked.

The value of the icon and buttons parameter is determined using the following tables:

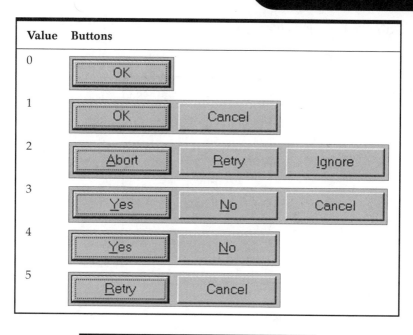

| Value | Buttons |
|-------|---------|
| 0 | OK |
| 1 | OK · Cancel |
| 2 | Abort · Retry · Ignore |
| 3 | Yes · No · Cancel |
| 4 | Yes · No |
| 5 | Retry · Cancel |

| Value | Description | Icon |
|-------|-------------|------|
| 16 | Critical Message | |
| 32 | Questioning Message | |
| 48 | Warning Message | |
| 64 | Informational Message | |

To specify which buttons and icon are displayed, you simply add the relevant values together. So, in our example, we add together 4 + 16 to display the Yes and No buttons with the Critical icon.

You can determine which button was clicked by the user by assigning the return code of the **MsgBox** function to a variable:

```
intButtonClicked = MsgBox ("Hello There",35,
                                  "Hello Message")
```

**245**

Notice that the **MsgBox** parameters are enclosed by brackets when used in this format. The value assigned to the variable **ButtonClicked** is determined by the following table:

| Value | Button Clicked |
|-------|----------------|
| 1 | OK |
| 2 | Cancel |
| 3 | Abort |
| 4 | Retry |
| 5 | Ignore |
| 6 | Yes |
| 7 | No |

# InputBox

This accepts text entry from the user and returns it as a string.

```
strTextEntered = InputBox ("Please enter your
                name","Login","John Smith",500,500)
```

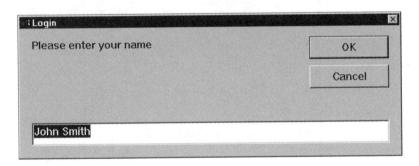

**"Please enter your name"**—this is the prompt displayed in the input box.
**"Login"**—this is the text displayed as the title of the input box.
**"John Smith"**—this is the default value displayed in the input box.
**500**—specifies the x position of the input box.
**500**—specifies the y position of the input box.

As with the **MsgBox** function, you can also specify a help file and topic to add a Help button to the input box.

# Procedures

**Call**—optional method of calling a subroutine.
**Function**—used to declare a function.
**Sub**—used to declare a subroutine.

# Other Keywords

**Rem**—old style method of adding comments to code.
**Option Explicit**—forces you to declare a variable before it can be used.

# Visual Basic Run-time Error Codes

The following error codes also apply to VBA code, and many will not be appropriate to an application built completely around VBScript. However, if you have built your own components, then these error codes may well be brought up when such components are used.

| Code | Description |
|------|-------------|
| 3 | Return without GoSub |
| 5 | Invalid procedure call |
| 6 | Overflow |
| 7 | Out of memory |
| 9 | Subscript out of range |
| 10 | This array is fixed or temporarily locked |
| 11 | Division by zero |
| 13 | Type mismatch |
| 14 | Out of string space |
| 16 | Expression too complex |
| 17 | Can't perform requested operation |
| 18 | User interrupt occurred |
| 20 | Resume without error |
| 28 | Out of stack space |
| 35 | Sub or Function not defined |

*Table continued on following page*

| Code | Description |
|------|-------------|
| 47 | Too many DLL application clients |
| 48 | Error in loading DLL |
| 49 | Bad DLL calling convention |
| 51 | Internal error |
| 52 | Bad file name or number |
| 53 | File not found |
| 54 | Bad file mode |
| 55 | File already open |
| 57 | Device I/O error |
| 58 | File already exists |
| 59 | Bad record length |
| 61 | Disk full |
| 62 | Input past end of file |
| 63 | Bad record number |
| 67 | Too many files |
| 68 | Device unavailable |
| 70 | Permission denied |
| 71 | Disk not ready |
| 74 | Can't rename with different drive |
| 75 | Path/File access error |
| 76 | Path not found |
| 322 | Can't create necessary temporary file |
| 325 | Invalid format in resource file |
| 380 | Invalid property value |
| 423 | Property or method not found |
| 424 | Object required |
| 429 | OLE Automation server can't create object |
| 430 | Class doesn't support OLE Automation |
| 432 | File name or class name not found during OLE Automation operation |
| 438 | Object doesn't support this property or method |
| 440 | OLE Automation error |

*Table continued on following page*

| Code | Description |
|------|-------------|
| 442 | Connection to type library or object library for remote process has been lost. Press OK for dialog to remove reference |
| 443 | OLE Automation object does not have a default value |
| 445 | Object doesn't support this action |
| 446 | Object doesn't support named arguments |
| 447 | Object doesn't support current locale setting |
| 448 | Named argument not found |
| 449 | Argument not optional |
| 450 | Wrong number of arguments or invalid property assignment |
| 451 | Object not a collection |
| 452 | Invalid ordinal |
| 453 | Specified DLL function not found |
| 454 | Code resource not found |
| 455 | Code resource lock error |
| 457 | This key is already associated with an element of this collection |
| 458 | Variable uses an OLE Automation type not supported in Visual Basic |
| 481 | Invalid picture |
| 500 | Variable is undefined |
| 501 | Cannot assign to variable |
| 1001 | Out of memory |
| 1002 | Syntax error |
| 1003 | Expected ':' |
| 1004 | Expected ';' |
| 1005 | Expected '(' |
| 1006 | Expected ')' |
| 1007 | Expected ']' |
| 1008 | Expected '{' |
| 1009 | Expected '}' |
| 1010 | Expected identifier |
| 1011 | Expected '=' |
| 1012 | Expected 'If' |

*Table continued on following page*

| Code | Description |
|------|-------------|
| 1013 | Expected 'To' |
| 1014 | Expected 'End' |
| 1015 | Expected 'Function' |
| 1016 | Expected 'Sub' |
| 1017 | Expected 'Then' |
| 1018 | Expected 'Wend' |
| 1019 | Expected 'Loop' |
| 1020 | Expected 'Next' |
| 1021 | Expected 'Case' |
| 1022 | Expected 'Select' |
| 1023 | Expected expression |
| 1024 | Expected statement |
| 1025 | Expected end of statement |
| 1026 | Expected integer constant |
| 1027 | Expected 'While' or 'Until' |
| 1028 | Expected 'While', 'Until' or end of statement |
| 1029 | Too many locals or arguments |
| 1030 | Identifier too long |
| 1031 | Invalid number |
| 1032 | Invalid character |
| 1033 | Unterminated string constant |
| 1034 | Unterminated comment |
| 1035 | Nested comment |
| 1036 | 'Me' cannot be used outside of a procedure |
| 1037 | Invalid use of 'Me' keyword |
| 1038 | 'loop' without 'do' |
| 1039 | Invalid 'exit' statement |
| 1040 | Invalid 'for' loop control variable |
| 1041 | Variable redefinition |
| 1042 | Must be first statement on the line |
| 1043 | Cannot assign to non-ByVal argument |

INSTANT

# HTML

# Appendix F - JavaScript Reference

## General Information

JavaScript is included in an HTML document with the **&lt;SCRIPT&gt;** tag. Here's an example:

```
<HTML>
<HEAD>

<!-- wrap script in comments
<SCRIPT LANGUAGE = "JavaScript">
script code would be here
</SCRIPT>
<!-- End of Script>

</HEAD>
<BODY>
 HTML document would be here
</BODY>
</HTML>
```

The following points should be kept in mind:

All JavaScript code should be put in the **&lt;HEAD&gt;** section of the document. This ensures that all the code has been loaded before an attempt is made to execute it.

The script code should be wrapped in a comment, as this stops older (non-JavaScript) browsers from trying to read the code.

JavaScript is case-sensitive.

# Values

JavaScript recognizes the following data types:

- Strings—"Hello World"
- Numbers—both integers(86) and decimal values(86.235)
- Boolean—true or false

A null (or nil) value is assigned with the keyword **null**.

JavaScript also makes use of 'special characters' similar to other programming languages:

| Character | Function |
|-----------|----------|
| \n | Newline |
| \t | Tab |
| \f | Form feed |
| \b | Backspace |
| \r | Carriage return |

You may escape other characters by preceding them with a backslash (\). This is most commonly used for quotes and backslashes.

```
document.write("I want to \"quote\" this without
terminating my string.");
document.write("The following is a backslash: \\");
```

# Variables

JavaScript is a *loosely typed language*. This means that variables do not have an explicitly defined variable type. Instead, every variable can hold values of various types. Conversions between types are done automatically when needed, as this example demonstrates:

```
x = 55;      // x is assigned to be the integer 55;
y = "55";    // y is assigned to be the string "55";

z = 1 + y;
<!-- even though y is a string, it will be automatically
converted to the appropriate integer value so that 1 may be
added to it. -->
```

```
<!-- the number 55 will be written to the screen. Even
though x is an integer and not a string, Javascript will
make the  necessary conversion for you. -->
document.write(x);
```

Variable names must start with either a letter or an underscore.
Beyond the first letter, variables may contain any combination of
letters, underscores, and digits. JavaScript is case-sensitive, so
**this_variable** is not the same as **This_Variable**.

Variables do not need to be declared before they are used. However,
you may use the **Var** keyword to explicitly define a variable. This is
especially useful when there is the possibility of conflicting variable
names. When in doubt, use **Var**.

```
Var x = "55";
```

# Arrays

Currently, JavaScript has no explicit array structure. However,
JavaScript's object mechanisms allow for easy creation of arrays.

The following is the standard 'array-creation' code taken from
Netscape's documentation:

```
function MakeArray(n) {
    this.length = n;
    for (var i = 1; i <= n; i++) {
       this[i] = 0 }
       return this
}
```

Once this code is included in your script, you may create arrays by
doing the following:

```
cats = new MakeArray(20);
```

You can then populate the array like this:

```
cats[1] = "Boo Boo"
cats[2] = "Purrcila"
cats[3] = "Sam"
cats[4] = "Lucky"
```

# Assignment Operators

The following operators are used to make assignments in JavaScript:

| Operator | Example | Result |
|----------|---------|--------|
| = | x=y | x equals y |
| += | x+=y | x equals x +y |
| -= | x-=y | x equals x-y |
| *= | x*=y | x equals x multiplied by y |
| /= | x/=y | x equals x divided by y |
| %= | x%=y | x equals x modulus y |

Each operator assigns the value on the right to the variable on the left.

```
x = 100;
y = 10;

x += y;
// x now is equal to 110
```

# Equality Operators

| Operator | Result |
|----------|--------|
| == | Equal |
| != | Not equal |
| > | Greater than |
| >= | Greater than or equal to |
| < | Less than |
| <= | Less than or equal to |

# Other Operators

| Operator | Result |
|----------|--------|
| + | Addition |
| - | Subtraction |
| * | Multiplication |

*Table continued on following page*

| Operator | Result |
|----------|--------|
| / | Division |
| % | Modulus |
| ++ | Increment |
| -- | Decrement |
| - | Unary Negation |
| & | Bitwise AND |
| \| | Bitwise OR |
| ^ | Bitwise XOR |
| << | Bitwise Left Shift |
| >> | Bitwise Right Shift |
| >>> | Zero-fill Right Shift |
| && | Logical AND |
| \|\| | Logical OR |
| ! | Not |

# Comments

| Operator | Result |
|----------|--------|
| // | A single line comment |
| /* ... */ | A multiline comment; the comment text replaces the ... |

# Control Flow

There are two ways of controlling the flow of a program in JavaScript. The first way involves conditional statements, which follow either one branch of the program or another. The second way is to use a repeated iteration of a set of statements.

## Conditional Statements

JavaScript has one conditional statement:

**if...then...else**—used to run various blocks of code—depending on conditions. **if...then...else** statements have the following general form in JavaScript:

```
if (condition) {
 code to be executed if condition is true;
}
else {
 code to be executed if condition is false;
}
```

In addition:

- The **else** portion is optional
- **if** statements may be nested
- Multiple statements must be enclosed by braces

Here is an example:

```
person_type = prompt("what are ya?", "");
if (person_type == "cat") {
  alert("Here, have some cat food");
  }
    else {
    if (person_type == "dog") {
      alert("Here, have some dog food");
      }
      else {
        if (person_type == "human") {
        alert("Here have some, er, human food!");
        }
      }
}
```

# Loop Statements

**for**—executes a block of code a specified number of times.

```
for (i = 0; i = 10; i++) {
        document.write(i);
        }
```

**while**—executes a block of code while a condition is true.

```
while (condition) {
    statements...
}
```

**break**—will cause an exit from a loop regardless of the condition statement.

```
x = 0;
while (x != 10) {
   x = prompt("Enter a number or q to quit", "");
   if (x == "q") {
      alert("See ya");
      break;
      }
   }
```

**continue**—will cause the loop to jump immediately back to the condition statement.

```
x = 0;
while (x != 1) {

  if (!(confirm("Should I add 1 to x?"))) {
      continue;
      // the following x++ is never executed
      x++;
      }
  x++;
  }

alert("Bye");
```

# Input/Output

In JavaScript, there are three different methods of providing information to the user, and getting a response back.

## Alert

This displays a message with an OK button.

```
alert("Hello World!");
```

# Confirm

Displays a message with both an OK and a Cancel button. True is
returned if the OK button is pressed, and false is returned if the
Cancel button is pressed.

```
confirm("Are you sure you want to quit?");
```

# Prompt

Displays a message and a text box for user input. The first string
argument forms the text that is to be displayed above the text box.
The second argument is a string, integer, or property of an existing
object, which represents the default value to display inside the box. If
the second argument is not specified, "**&lt;undefined&gt;**" is displayed
inside the text box.

The string typed into the box is returned if the OK button is pressed.
False is returned if the Cancel button is pressed

```
prompt("What is your name?", "");
```

# JavaScript Events

| Event | Event Handler | Description |
|-------|---------------|-------------|
| blur | onBlur | Focus is removed from a form |
| click | onClick | Click on form or link |
| change | onChange | User changes value of text, textarea, or select |
| focus | onFocus | Focus is moved to a form |
| load | onLoad | Page is loaded |
| mouseover | onMouseOver | Mouse focus is on link or anchor |
| select | onSelect | User selects form element's input field |
| submit | onSubmit | A form is submitted |
| unload | onUnload | User exits the page |

# Built-in Objects

Both Internet Explorer and Netscape Navigator provide a set of built-in objects with their own set of properties, events, and methods, which can be accessed with JavaScript code. Here is a list of the most significant objects, along with their properties, events, and methods.

# Date Object

JavaScript does not have a date type, so the Date object provides a set of methods for date and time manipulation.

| Methods | Description |
|---------|-------------|
| `getDate()` | Returns the day of the month for the specified date |
| `GetDay()` | Returns the day of the week for the specified date |
| `getHours()` | Returns the hour for the specified date |

*Table continued on following page*

| Methods | Description |
|---------|-------------|
| getMinutes() | Returns the minutes for the specified date |
| getMonth() | Returns the month for the specified date |
| GetSeconds() | Returns the seconds in the current time |
| GetTime() | Returns a numeric value corresponding to the time for the specified date |
| GetTimeZoneoffset() | Returns the time zone offset, in minutes, for the current locale |
| GetYear() | Returns the year in the specified date |
| parse(dateString) | Returns the number of milliseconds in a date string, since Jan. 1, 1970 00:00:00 local time |
| SetDate(dayValue) | Sets the day of the month for a specified date |
| setHours(hoursValue) | Sets the hours for a specified date |
| setMinutes(minutesValue) | Sets the minutes for a specified date |
| setMonth(monthValue) | Sets the month for a specified date |
| setSeconds(secondsValue) | Sets the seconds for a specified date |
| setTime(timevalue) | Sets the value of a date object |
| setYear(yearValue) | Sets the year for a specified date |
| ToGMTString() | Converts a date to a string, using Internet GMT conventions |
| ToLocaleString() | Converts a string, using the current locale's conventions |
| UTC(year, month, day [, hrs] [, min] [, sec]) | Returns the number of milliseconds in a date object, since Jan. 1, 1970 00:00:00 Universal Coordinated Time (GMT) |

# Math Object

Provides a set of methods for mathematical constants and functions.

| Methods | Description |
| --- | --- |
| abs(number) | Returns the absolute value |
| acos(number) | Returns the arc cosine (in radians) |
| asin(number) | Returns the arc sine (in radians) |
| atan(number) | Returns the arc tangent (in radians) |
| ceil(number) | Returns the least integer greater than or equal to a number |
| cos(number) | Returns the cosine of a number |
| exp(number) | Returns the Euler's constant to number |
| floor(number) | Returns the greatest integer less than or equal to a number |
| log(number) | Returns the natural logarithm (base e) of a number |
| max(number1, number2) | Returns the greater of two numbers |
| min(number1, number2) | Returns the lesser of two numbers |
| pow(base, exponent) | Returns the base to the exponent power |
| random() | Returns a pseudo-random number between zero and one |
| round(number) | Returns the value of a number rounded to the nearest integer |
| sin(number) | Returns the sine of a number |
| sqrt(number) | Returns the square root of a number |
| tan(number) | Returns the tangent of a number |

# Navigator Object

Provides properties which hold information about the browser. Note that there are no methods.

| Properties | Description |
|---|---|
| appCodeName | Browser code name |
| appName | Browser name |
| appVersion | Browser version |
| userAgent | User agent header |

# String object

Provides a set of methods for text manipulation.

| Methods | Description |
|---|---|
| anchor(nameattribute) | Creates an HTML anchor to be used as a hypertext target |
| big() | Adds **\<BIG>** attribute to text |
| blink() | Adds **\<BLINK>** attribute to text |
| bold() | Adds **\<BOLD>** attribute to text |
| charAt(index) | Returns the character in the string at index |
| Fixed() | Adds **\<tt>** attribute to text |
| fontcolor(color) | Changes text to specified color |
| fontsize(size) | Changes font to specified size |
| indexOf(searchValue [, fromIndex]) | Returns first occurrence of **searchValue**, starting from **fromIndex** |
| italics() | Adds **\<i>** attribute to text |
| LastIndexOf (searchValue [, fromIndex]) | Returns last occurrence of **searchValue**, starting from **fromIndex** |
| link(hrefAttribute) | Creates a hypertext link to **hrefAttribute** |
| small() | Adds **\<small>** attribute to text |
| strike() | Adds **\<strike>** attribute to text |
| sub() | Adds **\<sub>** attribute to text |

*Table continued on following page*

| Methods | Description |
|---------|-------------|
| `substring(indexA, indexB)` | Returns substring from **indexA** to **indexB** |
| `sup()` | Adds **<sup>** tag to text |
| `ToLowerCase()` | Returns the string in lowercase |
| `ToUpperCase()` | Returns the string in uppercase |

| Properties | Description |
|------------|-------------|
| `length` | The length of the string. |

# Window Object

This is the top-level object, which contains properties that apply to the entire window.

| Methods | Description |
|---------|-------------|
| `alert("message")` | Displays a dialog box with an OK button |
| `close()` | Closes the specified window |
| `confirm("message")` | Displays a dialog box with OK and Cancel buttons |
| `open("URL", "windowName", "windowFeatures")` | Opens a new window with the specified attributes |
| `prompt(message, [inputDefault])` | Displays a dialog box with a message and an input field |
| `SetTimeout(expression, msec)` | Evaluates expression, after the specified number of milliseconds have elapsed. Returns a timeoutID. |
| `ClearTimeout(timeoutID)` | Cancels a timeout that was set with **setTimeout** |

| Properties | Description |
|---|---|
| `defaultStatus` | Default message displayed in the status bar |
| `Frames` | An array reflecting all the frames in the window |
| `Length` | The number of frames in the parent window |
| `Name` | The window name |
| `Parent` | Refers to the parent window |
| `Self` | Refers to the window itself |
| `Status` | Specifies a priority message in status bar |
| `Top` | Refers to the topmost Navigator window |
| `Window` | The current window |

| Event Handlers |
|---|
| `onLoad` |
| `onUnload` |

# Other Objects

Here is a list of the other objects which can be used in JavaScript and have their own properties, methods, and events:

- *Anchors* array—an array containing information about hyperlink targets.

- Button—a button on a form.

- Checkbox—a box on a form that can be selected/deselected by the user.

- Document—an object that is created when a page is loaded.

- *Elements* array—an array of elements in a form.

- Form (*forms* array)—an object representing a form.

- Frame (*frames* array)—a set of windows on the same page that can be referred to as separate documents.

- Hidden—a text object that isn't visible on the form.

- History—a list of previous URLs, in order of visitation.

Link—a hypertext link defined either as text or as an image.

Location—the URL information of the current document.

Password—an element that accepts a password in a form (letters are asterisked out).

Radio—a button which, when selected, deselects the other radio buttons in that group.

Reset—a button which resets a form to its original values.

Select (*options* array)—a list of options on a form.

Submit—a submit button on a form.

Text—an input field on a form.

Textarea—an input field with multiple lines.

# Reserved Words

The following are reserved words which can't be used for function, method, variable, or object names. Note that while some words in this list are not currently used as JavaScript keywords, they have been reserved for future use.

| | | | |
|---|---|---|---|
| abstract | extends | int | super |
| boolean | false | interface | switch |
| break | final | long | synchronized |
| byte | finally | native | this |
| case | float | new | throw |
| catch | for | null | throws |
| char | function | package | transient |
| class | goto | private | true |
| const | if | protected | try |
| continue | implements | public | var |
| default | import | return | void |
| do | in | short | while |
| double | instanceof | static | with |
| else | | | |

# Additional Information

Complete JavaScript documentation can be found at:

```
http://home.netscape.com/eng/mozilla/3.0/
handbook/javascript/index.html
```

# Index

## Symbols

%0D%0A  127
&, name-value pairs in forms
    121
.htm, web pages  8
.html, web pages  8
.js, JavaScript file  163
<!--comment-->
    adding to HTML document  23
<!DOCTYPE>
    declaring HTML version  11
    HTML 3.2 and frames  102
    syntax  12
@import, style sheets  181
    drawbacks  181

## A

<A>  64, 108
    attributes  64
    HREF  21, 65
        example  68
        imagemap, HTML code  75
        Netscape Navigator, relative
            links  72

sound, adding to your web
    pages  61
style sheets, pointing to  180
TARGET  108, 109
    implicit names  109
    named frames  109
    window values  66
<APP>  139
<APPLET>  139, 155
    <PARAM>, passing parameters
        to Java applet  157
    attributes  155
    HTML, incorporating tag into
        157
<AREA>
    attributes  78
    imagemaps, creating  77, 78
absolute URLs  64
ActiveMovie (AM)  142
    uses  154
ActiveX  148
    controls
        adding to web pages  153
        introduction to  153
AIFF
    ActiveMovie  154
    LiveAudio  139

alignment. *see* individual tag attributes

ALT, with <IMG>  52, 74

anchors

  anchor tag, <A>  64, 108

    *see also* HTML tags, <A>  64

    attributes  65

    images, as hyperlinks  68, 69

    text as a hyperlink  67

  hypertext links  63

    creating hypertext links  63

animation  137

  ActiveX  153

    ActiveX movie (AM)  154

  client pull  146

  GIF animation  137

  Java animation  155

    Animator applet  157, 158

  server push

    advantages/disadvantages 147

  vendor-specific tags  139

Animator applet, Java  157-158

  <APPLET>

    incorporating tag into HTML 157

Apache server, imagemap file formats  75

Arena browser, CLASS attribute support  24

array handling, VBScript. *see* Appendix E

arrays, JavaScript. *see* Appendix F

assignment operators, JavaScript. *see* Appendix F

assignments, VBScript. *see* Appendix E

attributes, tags  9

  listed. *see* Appendix A

  syntax  10

AU

  ActiveMovie  154

  LiveAudio  139

audio

  <A>, adding sound to your web pages  61

  <BGSOUND>, adding sound to your web pages  61

  ActiveMovie  142

  RealAudio (RA)  60

  TrueSpeech, adding sound to your web pages  60

  WAVs, converting to TrueSpeech  60

audio support, HTML  139

authoring tags, Netscape  141

AVI

  ActiveMovie  154

  embedding video-clips, <IMG> DYNSRC attribute  143

**B**

<B>  9

<BASE>  13

  bookmarks  13

  browser support for  13

<BASEFONT>

  attributes  42

  syntax  41

<BGSOUND>

  sound, adding to web pages  61

<BODY>  18, 102

  attributes  18

<BR>  29

  attributes  29

  CLEAR=value, text flow round tables  83

_blank, TARGET  66

body, tables 95
  TBODY 95
    attributes 95
body, web pages 7, 18
  *see also* <BODY>
bookmarks, <BASE> 13
borders, tables 83, 84, 98
browser
  default settings, viewing the
    HTML document 10
  frames 101, 118
    aligning frame and text
    106, 117
    borders, defining 3D 105, 107
    columns, defining
    105, 112, 114
      <FRAMESET> 103
    contents frame 102
    creating frames 101
      <FRAME>, distinguishing
    from <FRAMESET> 101
      <FRAMESET>, distinguish-
    ing from <FRAME> 101
    example 102
    floating frames 115
      <IFRAME> 115
    graphics in frames
      <IMG> 115
    hyperlinks 109
      TARGET 109
    implicit names 109
    layout, of frames 112
    margins, in frames 107, 117
    name of frame, specifying 108
    named frames 109
    navigation frame 102
    nested frames 113
    no frame support
      <NOFRAMES> 103
    preventing resizing 108
    reload, problems with 104

rows, defining 106, 112, 114
  <FRAMESET> 103
scrollbars, specifying 108
source file, specifying 108
space, between edges and
  contents of frames 107
space, between frames, adding
  105
uses of frames 101
built-in objects, JavaScript. *see*
  Appendix F
button values, VBScript. *see*
  Appendix E

**C**

<CAPTION> 91
<CENTER>
  text layout 29
<COL>
  attributes 93
<COLGROUP>
  attributes 93
carriage returns, text layout 28
CERN, imagemaps
  file formats 75
  htimage, default server script 77
CGI (Common Gateway Inter-
    face)
  CGI scripts 77
  imagemaps, creating 74, 77
  processing forms 135
CLASS, universal attribute 24
classes, style sheets 184
client pull, animation 146
client-server connection
  how the World Wide Web works
  2

client-side imagemaps 77
  advantages 77
  creating, steps involved
    <AREA> 78
    <IMG>, USEMAP attribute 77
    <MAP> 77, 78
  simple map example 79
color names. *see* Appendix D
colors, web pages 20
  *see also* Appendix D
  example 21
  fonts 40
  horizontal rules 37
  scrolling text, background 47
  tables 86, 93, 98
COM (Microsoft Component
  Object Model) 148
comments, adding to document
  23
comments, JavaScript. *see*
  Appendix F
conditional statements,
  JavaScript. *see* Appendix F
constants, VBScript. *see*
  Appendix E
container tags
  *see* end tags
contents frame 102
contextual selectors, style sheets
  184
control flow, JavaScript. *see*
  Appendix F
control flow, VBScript. *see*
  Appendix E
conversion functions, VBScript.
  *see* Appendix E
CSS1 (Cascading Style
  Semantics and Specification
  Language)
  @import, implementing style
    sheets 181

declaration format 182
declarations 183
inheritance 183
properties
  188, 190, 191, 193, 195, 197
shortcomings 185
style sheets 177


**D**

<DD>
  definition list entries 31
  syntax 34
<DIR>
  lists, text layout 36
<DL>
  definition lists 30
<DT>
  definition list entries 31
  syntax 34
data types, JavaScript. *see*
  Appendix F
date object, JavaScript. *see*
  Appendix F
date/time functions, VBScript.
  *see* Appendix E
default file, index.html 64
default, imagemaps 75
default settings, browser 10
DocObjects, ActiveX 148
DSSSL (Document Style Semantics
  and Specification Language)
  177
DSSSL-Online, style sheets 177
DTD (Document Type Definition)
  3, 12
  introduction to 5
DYNSRC attribute, <IMG> 139,
  143
  controlling attributes 144
  using, example 145

## E

\<EM>
logical tags, example  43
\<EMBED>, Microsoft-specific
141
attributes  141
using  142
\<EMBED>, Netscape-specific
139
attributes  140
using  141
elements, HTML document  8
end tags  7
error handling, VBScript. *see*
Appendix E
events, JavaScript. *see* Appendix
F
events, script  163

## F

\<FONT>  28
attributes  39
text formatting  39
\<FORM>  119
attributes
METHOD, GET and POST  120
name-value pairs  121
\<FRAME>  101
attributes  106
\<FRAMESET>  101
attributes  105
setting frame borders and
spacing  106
setting rows and columns  103
favorites. *see* bookmarks
files
hypertext links, linking to other
files  63
anchor tag, \<A>  64

creating links  63
images, as hyperlinks  68
imagemaps  73
imagemaps, text-based links
74
relative links  72
text as a hyperlink  67
text-based links, imagemaps
74
URLs  63
floating frames  115
\<IFRAME>  115
fonts, text formatting  39
\<BASEFONT>  41
\<FONT>  39
embedding in documents  39
logical tags  43
physical tags  43
which to use?  40
foot, tables  95
TFOOT  95
forms  119
\<FORM>  119
attributes  120
\<INPUT>  119, 123
attributes  124
\<SELECT>  124, 128
attributes  128
default list entry  129
example  129
searches  14
\<TEXTAREA>  124
attributes  127
creating a form  119
entering data  124
example  121
processing  135
CGI (Common Gateway
Interface)  135
pull-down menu  124
\<SELECT>, default list entry
129
radio buttons  124

Submit button  124
tables, using to align text input
    boxes  133
    Netscape bug  134
testing your forms, NCSA  134
frames  101
    aligning frame and text  106, 117
    borders, defining 3D  105, 107
    columns, defining  105, 112, 114
    contents frame  102
    creating frames  101
        <FRAME>  101
        <FRAMESET>  101
        example  102
    floating frames  115
        <IFRAME>  115
    graphics in frames
        <IMG>  115
    hyperlinks  109
        TARGET  109
    implicit names  109
    layout, of frames  112
    margins, in frames  107, 117
    name of frame, specifying  108
    named frames  109
    navigation frame  102
    nested frames  113
    no frame support
        <NOFRAMES> tag  103
    preventing resizing  108
    reload, problems with  104
    rows, defining  106, 112, 114
        <FRAMESET>  103
    scrollbars, specifying  108
    source file, specifying  108
    space, between edges and
        contents of frames  107
    space, between frames, adding
        105
    target names, specifying  118
    uses of frames  101

## G

GET, sending form data to
    server  121
GIF (Graphics Interchange
    Format), image format  55
    animated GIF  137
    GIF87  55
    GIF89a  55
    interlaced images  56
    single-pixel GIF trick  57
GIF (Graphics Interchange
    Format), animation,  137
    <IMG>
        DYNSRC attribute
            controlling  144
            using  145
        LOWSRC and SRC, using
        together  143
            two-frame example  143
    controlling  144
    delay, between images  138
    example  138
    GIF format  138
    GIF89a  137
    HTML, incorporating animated
        GIF into  139
    images, adding  138
    loop, how many times  138
    LOWSRC (low resolution
        graphic), Netscape  143
    PhotoImpact GIF Animator  138
    support, browser  137
    video clips, embedding
        <IMG>, DYNSRC attribute
        143
    VRML Worlds (virtual reality
        worlds), embedding
        <IMG>, DYNSRC attribute
        143

graphics
  animation 137
    ActiveX 153
    ActiveX movie (AM) 154
    editor, obtaining 138
    GIF animation 137
    graphics tool, obtaining 138
    Java 155
  frames 115
  images 51
    <IMG>, attributes 51
    formats 55
    interlaced images 56
  vendor-specific tags 139

**H**

<HEAD> 12
  tags <HEAD> encloses 13
<Hn> 27
  <FONT> 28
  attributes 9, 27
<HR>
  attributes 36
<HTML> 12
head, tables 95
  <TFOOT> 95
    attributes 95
  <THEAD> 95
    attributes 95
head, web pages 7, 12
  see also <HEAD>
headings, page layout 27
  <Hn> 27
horizontal rules, text layout
  <HR> 36
  example 38
HREF, <A> attribute 65
  imagemap, HTML code 75
  Netscape Navigator, relative links 72

style sheet, pointing to 180
text as a hyperlink, example 68
HTML, creating a document 7
  .html, .htm 8
  as a markup language 4, 10
  body 7
  colors 20, 37, 40, 47
  comments, adding to document 23
  creating document skeleton 11
  elements 8
  head 7
  revision numbers, adding to document 23
  tags 7
HTML, general introduction to 1
HTML tags 53
  see Appendix A, tags and attributes listing
  <!--comment-->
    adding comments to your document 23
  <!DOCTYPE>
    declaring HTML version 11
    syntax 12
  <A> 64
    adding sound to your web pages 61
    attributes 65
      HREF example 68
      NAME example 69
    images, as hyperlinks 69
    text as a hyperlink, example 68
  <APP> 139
  <APPLET> 139
    <PARAM>, parameter passing 157
    attributes 155
    HTML, incorporating tag into 157

<AREA> 78
  attributes 78
  imagemaps 78
<B> 9
<BASE> 13
  bookmarks 13
  browser support for 13
<BASEFONT>
  attributes 42
<BGSOUND>
  adding sound to your web
  pages 61
<BODY> 18
  attributes 18
<BR> 29
  attributes 29
  line breaks 29
<DD>
  definition list entries 31
  syntax 34
<DIR>
  lists 36
<DL>
  definition lists 30
<DT>
  definition list entries 31
  syntax 34
<EM>
  logical tags, example 43
<EMBED>, Microsoft-specific
  141
  attributes 141
  using 142
<EMBED>, Netscape-specific
  139
  using 141
<FONT> 28, 39
  attributes 39
<FORM> 119
  attributes 120
  form example 121
  name-value pairs 121

<FRAME>
  attributes 106
  creating frames 101
<FRAMESET> 101
  attributes 105
  creating frames 101
<HEAD> 12
  tags <HEAD> encloses 13
<Hn> 9, 27
  attributes 27
  page layout 27
<HR>
  attributes 36
<HTML> 12
<I> 9
<IFRAME>, floating frames 115
  attributes 116
<IMG> 51, 139
  attributes 51
      DYNSRC, Microsoft-specific
  143
    image size 54
    LOWSRC Netscape-specific
  143
  images, as hyperlinks 68, 69
  incorporating animated GIF
  into HTML 139
  file format 55-57
<INPUT> 119, 123
  attributes 124
<INSERT>. see <OBJECT>
<ISINDEX>
  searches 13
<LH> list headers 31
<LI>
  numbered and bulleted list
  entries 31
<LINK> 14, 180
  <A> HREF attribute, pointing
  to style sheet 180
  attributes 14
<MAP> 78
  attributes 78
  imagemaps 78

<MARQUEE> 46
  attributes 46
<MENU>
  lists 36
<META> 15
  attributes 15
  browser access 15
  client pull 146
  using 16
<NOFRAMES> 103
<OBJECT> 141, 148
  <PARAM> 154
  ActiveX, using with 153
  attributes 149
  future developments 148
  plug-in support, Netscape 148
  uses 148
<OL>
  attributes 33
  list example 33
  numbered lists 30
  syntax 33
<P> 29
  <CENTER> 29
  attributes 29
<PARAM>
  passing parameters to Java
  applet 157
<SCRIPT> 161
  attributes 162
  hiding the script 162
  IE extensions 163
  JavaScript 164
  JavaScript
    form validation example
  167
    SRC attribute 166
  language, specifying 162
  support, browser 162
  syntax 161
  URL, specifying 163
  VBScript 169
    dialog box example 170

  flow control example 171
  form validation example
  173
<SELECT> 124, 128
  attributes 128
  example 129
<STYLE> 15, 180-181
<TABLE> 81
  IE extensions 86
  text flow round table, <BR
  CLEAR=value> 83
<TBODY> 95
  attributes 95
<TD> 82
  Microsoft extensions 90
<TEXTAREA> 124, 128
  attributes 127
<TFOOT> 95
  attributes 95
<THEAD> 95
  attributes 95
<TITLE> 13
<TR> 82
<UL>
  attributes 32
  bulleted lists 30
  list example 32
  syntax 31
animation tags
  <APP> 139
  <APPLET> 139, 155, 157
  <EMBED>, Microsoft-specific
  141
  <EMBED>, Netscape-specific
  139
  <IMG> 139
  <META> 146
    URL attribute 147
  <OBJECT> 141, 148
attributes 9
  see also Appendix A, listing
  values 10

audio 60
   \<A> 61
   \<BGSOUND> 61
   RealAudio (RA) 60
   TrueSpeech 60
commonly used tags by category,
   Appendix B 225
document formatting 67
executable code
   \<APP>, \<APPLET> 139
forms 119
   \<FORM> 119
   \<INPUT> 119, 123
   \<SELECT> 124, 128
   \<SELECT>, example 129
   \<TEXTAREA> 124, 127
   entering data 124
   example 121
   processing 135
      CGI 135
   pull-down menu 124
   radio buttons 124
   Submit button 124
   tables, using to align text input
   boxes 133
   testing your forms, NCSA 134
graphics
   images 51
images 51
   \<IMG> 51
   formats
      GIF 55
      JPEG 55
      PNG 57
   interlaced images, GIF 56
logical tags 39, 43
   \<EM> example 43
   examples 45
media objects 137
physical tags 39, 43
   examples 44
scripting
   \<SCRIPT> 162

style sheets
   \<LINK> 180
tables 81
   \<BR CLEAR=value>, text flow
   round tables 83
   \<CAPTION> 91
   \<COL>
      attributes 93
   \<COLGROUP>
      attributes 93
   \<TD> 89
   \<TH> 91
   \<TH>, alignment and
   \<COLGROUP> 95
   \<TR> 87
   adding a caption 91
   borders 83, 84, 98
   colors 98
      example 93
   creating 81
   enhancing the look of, IE
   extensions 86
   forms, using tables to align
   text input boxes 133
   head, foot and body elements
   95
   including other elements 96
   nesting tables 96
   row and column headings 91
   text flow round tables,
   \<BRCLEAR=value> 83
   using, example 91
  tags and attributes, listing. *see*
   Appendix A
HTTP (HyperText Transfer
   Protocol) 3, 64
World Wide Web, how it works 2
hyperlink targets, JavaScript 109
hypertext links 63
   \<A> tag HREF attribute example
   68
   creating the links 63
      anchor tag, \<A> 64
      anchor tag, \<A>, attributes 65

anchors 63
images as hyperlinks, anchor
tag, <A> 64
internal hypertext links,
NAME attribute 65
URLs 63
example 67
frames 109, 118
images, as hyperlinks 64, 68
<IMG> 68
images, as hyperlinks,
imagemaps, text-based links
74
lists, <A> NAME attribute 69
relative links 68
Netscape Navigator, HREF 72
targets 109
implicit names 109
named frames 109
window values 66
text, using as a hyperlink 67
text-based links, imagemaps 74


**I**

<I> 9
<IFRAME> 115
attributes 116
<IMG> 51, 68, 115, 139
ALT attribute 52, 74
attributes 51
DYNSRC, Microsoft-specific
attribute 143
controlling 144
image size 54
using 145
LOWSRC, Netscape-specific
attribute 143
SRC, using with 143
two-frame example 143
vertical alignment, Netscape
53

incorporating animated GIF into
HTML 139
ISMAP attribute
imagemaps 75
USEMAP attribute
client-side imagemaps,
creating 78
<INPUT> 119, 123
attributes 124
<INSERT>. see <OBJECT>
<ISINDEX>
searches 13
icon values, VBScript. see
Appendix E
ID, universal attribute 24
IE, CLASS attribute support 24
IE extensions, <SCRIPT> 163
IE extensions, <TABLE> 86
imagemaps 73
client-side imagemaps 77
<AREA> 77
<MAP> 77
advantages 77
creating, steps involved
<AREA> 77, 78
<IMG>, USEMAP 78
<MAP> 77, 78
simple map example 79
server-side imagemaps
CGI map program permissions
73
creating, steps involved 74
CGI scripts 77
creating the image 74
imagemap files 75
imagemap HTML code 75
disadvantages 73
files for 73
processing the imagemap 73
text-based hyperlinks, providing 74

images  51
  <IMG>
    attributes  51
      image size  54
    formats
      GIF  55
        single-pixel GIF trick  57
      JPEG  55
      PNG  57
    interlaced images, GIF  56
images, as hyperlinks  68
  <IMG>  69
  anchor tag, <A>  64
  imagemaps  73, 74
    client-side imagemaps  73, 77
      <AREA>  77, 78
      <IMG>, USEMAP attribute 78
      <MAP>  77, 78
      advantages  77
      simple example  79
    server-side imagemaps  73
      CGI map program
    permissions  73
      creating, steps involved  74
      disadvantages  73
      processing the imagemap 73
implicit names, frames  109
important flag, style sheets  187
inheritance, style sheets  183
  contextual selectors  184
input/output, JavaScript. *see* Appendix F
input/output, VBScript. *see* Appendix E
interactive web pages. *see* scripting
interlaced images, GIF image format  56

internal hypertext links
  NAME, <A> attribute  65
Internet Explorer
  color names. *see* Appendix D
  floating frame  115
Internet Media Type. *see* MIME
ISMAP, <IMG> attribute
  imagemap, HTML code  75


**J**

Java, animation  155
  <APPLET>  155
    <PARAM>, passing parameters to an applet  157
    attributes  155
    incorporating tag into HTML 157
  Animator applet  157, 158
JavaScript  161
  *see also* Appendix F
  .js  163
  <SCRIPT>  164
  Alert, button click example  164
  assignment expression, (=)  167
  dialog box  169
  equality expression, (==)  167
  form validation, example  167
  information, more sources  175
  purpose  164
  security  175
  SRC example  166
  support, browser  175
JPEG (Joint Photographic Experts Group)  57
  image format  55
    photographic images  55
    lossy compression technique  57

## L

<LH> 31
  list headers 31
<LI>
  numbered and bulleted list
    entries 31
<LINK> 14
  attributes 14
  style sheets
    <A> HREF attribute, pointing
      to style sheet 180
    implementing 180
labels, frames 108
layout, frames 112
line breaks, text layout
  <BR> 29
link type, <LINK> 14
links, files
  hypertext links 63
    anchor tag, <A> 64
      URLs 63
    example 67
    images, as hyperlinks 64, 68
      <IMG> 68
      imagemaps 73
      imagemaps, text-based links
        74
    relative links 68
    text, using as a hyperlink 67
    text-based links, imagemaps
      74
lists, text layout 30
  <DD>
    definition list entries 31
    syntax 34
  <DIR> 36
  <DL> 30
  <DT>
    definition list entries 31
    syntax 34
<LH>
  list headers 31
<LI>
  numbered and bulleted list
    entries 31
<MENU> 36
<OL> 30
  attributes 33
  list example 33
  syntax 33
<UL> 30
  attributes 32
  list example 32
  syntax 31
  nested lists, example 35
lists, using <A> NAME attribute
  70
LiveAudio 140
  AIFF 140
  AU 140
  MIDI 140
  WAV 140
LiveVideo (AVI) 140
logical tags, text formatting
  39, 43
loop statements, JavaScript. see
  Appendix F
loops, GIF animation 138
lossy compression technique 57

## M

<MAP>
  attributes 78
  imagemaps, creating 77, 78
  NAME 78
<MARQUEE>
  attributes 46
<MENU>
  lists, text layout 36

<META> 15-17, 146
  attributes 15
  browser access 15
  client pull 146
  URL attribute, updating 147
  using 16
    example 16
MapThis!
  imagemaps, generating the files
    77
margins, frames 107, 117
math functions, VBScript. *see*
    Appendix E
math object, JavaScript. *see*
    Appendix F
media objects
  *see* <OBJECT>
meta-information
  *see also* <META>
  client pull, web site animation
    146
meta-languages
  *see also* SGML
Microsoft Component Object
    Model (COM) 148
MIDI
  ActiveMovie 154
  LiveAudio 139
MIME (Multimedia Internet
    Mail Extensions) 2, 152
MOV, QuickTime MOVies 139
  ActiveMovie 154
MPEG Audio and Video (.mpg)
    155
  ActiveMovie 154
MsgBox, VBScript dialog box
    example 171
multimedia 137
  *see also* animation

**N**

<NOFRAMES> 103-104
NAME, <A> attribute 65
  example 69
  internal hypertext links 65
name-value pairs, <FORM> 121
named frames 109
navigation frame 102
navigator object, JavaScript. *see*
    Appendix F
NCompass Labs
  plug-in for ActiveX 148
NCSA, imagemaps
  file formats 75
  htimage, default server script 77
nested frames 113
nested lists, example 35
nested tags 9
nesting tables, example 96
Netscape Navigator
  color names. *see* Appendix D
  HREF, relative links 72

**O**

<OBJECT> 141, 148
  <PARAM> 154
  ActiveX, using with 153
  attributes 149
  future developments 148
  plug-in support, Netscape 148
  uses 148
<OL>
  attributes 33
  list example 33
  numbered lists 30
  syntax 33
objects, built-in, JavaScript. *see*
    Appendix F

objects, media
    see also <OBJECT>
OCX, Visual Basic  153
operators, JavaScript. see
    Appendix F

## P

<P> 29
    <CENTER>  29
    attributes  29
<PARAM>  154
    passing parameters to Java applet
    157
Paint Shop Pro 4.1, GIF anima-
    tion  138
paragraphs, text layout
    <P>, </P>  29
parameters
    <PARAM>, passing to Java
        applets  157
    passing with Microsoft's <EM-
        BED>  142
    passing with Netscape's <EM-
        BED>  141
_parent, TARGET  66
photographic images
    JPEG image format  55
PhotoImpact GIF Animator 1.0,
    GIF animation  138
physical tags, text formatting
    39, 43
    examples  44
PICS  17
pixel_clear.gif  57-60
plug-ins
    QuickTime  141
    RealAudio (RA)
        sound, adding to web pages
        60

TrueSpeech
    sound, ading to your web
        pages  60
PNG, image format  57
POST, sending form data to
    server  121
precedence, style sheets  186
procedures, VBScript. see
    Appendix E
protocols  63
    FTP (File Transfer Protocol)  64
    Gopher  64
    HTTP (HyperText Transfer
        Protocol)  64
    Telnet  64
pseudo-elements, style sheets
    185
pull-down menu, forms  124
    <SELECT>, default list entry  129

## Q

QuickTime MOVies  139, 141
    ActiveMovie  154

## R

radio buttons, forms  124
ratings  17
RealAudio
    adding sound to your web pages
        60
relative links
    see also hypertext links
    Netscape Navigator, HREF  72
reload, problems with frames
    104
reserved words, JavaScript. see
    Appendix F

resizing, frames 108, 118
revision numbers, HTML
    document 23
  syntax 23
RFC (Request for Comments) 3
run-time error codes, VBScript.
    *see* Appendix E


# S

<SCRIPT>
  attributes 162
  hiding the script 162
  JavaScript 164-169
    Alert, button click example
    164
    form validation example 167
    SRC attribute example 166
  support, browser 162
  syntax 161
  URL, specifying 163
  VBScript 169-174
    flow control example 171
    form validation example 173
<SELECT> 124, 128
  attributes 128
  example 129
<STYLE> 15
  style sheets
    implementing 180
    problems with using <STYLE>
    181
  with individual tags 182
scripting 161
  <SCRIPT> 162
    attributes 162
    form validation example 167
    hiding the script 162
    IE extensions 163
    JavaScript, SRC attribute 166
    language, specifying 162

support, browser 162
  syntax 161
compatibility, between browsers
  175
information, more sources 175
JavaScript 164-169
scripting events 163
scripting language 161
  JavaScript 161
  VBScript 161
scripts 161
security 175
uses 161
VBScript 169-174
  dialog box, example 169
  flow control example 171
  form validation example 173
scrolling, frames 108, 118
scrolling text, producing
  <MARQUEE> 46
security, scripting 175
selectors. *see* CSS1, declaration
  format
_self, TARGET 66
server push, animation 147
server-side imagemaps
  CGI map program permissions
  73
  creating, steps involved 74
    CGI scripts 77
    creating the image 74
    imagemap files 75
    imagemap HTML code 75
  disadvantages 73
  files for 73, 75
  processing the imagemap 73
  text-based hyperlinks, providing
  74
servers
  URLs, specifying the server 64
SGML (Standard General
  Markup Language) 3
  introduction to 4

specifier. *see* URL
start tags 7
string functions, VBScript. *see* Appendix E
string object, JavaScript. *see* Appendix F
style sheets 177
  alternative sheets, referencing 180
  cascading style sheets 186
  classes 184
    syntax 185
  creating 182
    syntax 182
    syntax, CCS1 declaration format 182
  example 178
  implementing 180
    <LINK> 180
    <STYLE> 180
    <STYLE>, problems with using 181
    <STYLE>, using with indivdual tags 182
    @import 181
  important flag 187
  importing styles 181
  inheritance 183
    contextual selectors 184
    example 183
  precedence 186
    details 187
  pseudo-classes 185
  pseudo-elements 185
    advantages 186
  syntax
    example 183
  using 177
    advantages 178
    CSS1 177
    CSS1, shortcomings 185
    DSSSL 177
Submit button, forms 124

**T**
<TABLE> 81
  attributes 83
  IE extensions 86
  text flow round table, <BR CLEAR=value> 83
<TD> 82, 89
  attributes 89
  Microsoft extensions 90
<TEXTAREA> 124, 128
  attributes 127
<TH> 91
  alignment and <COLGROUP> 95
<TITLE> 13
<TR> 82, 87
  attributes 87
  Microsoft extensions 88
tables 81
  <CAPTION> 91
  <COL>
    attributes 93
    using column groups 94
  <COLGROUP>
    attributes 93
    using column groups 94
  <TABLE> 81
    attributes 83
    IE extensions 86
  <TD> 82, 89
    attributes 89
    Microsoft extensions 90
  <TH> 91
    alignment and <COLGROUP> 95
  <TR> 82, 87
    Microsoft extensions 88
  adding a caption 91
  borders 83, 84, 98
  colors 93
  creating 81

enhancing the look of,
   IE extensions  86
forms, using tables to align text
   input boxes  133
   Netscape bug  134
head, foot and body elements  95
   <TBODY>  95
   <TFOOT>  95
   <THEAD>  95
including other elements
   example  96
nesting tables
   example  96
row and column headings  91
using, example  91
tags
   *see also* HTML tags and listings,
     Appendices A and B
   attributes  9
   container tags  31
   creating an HTML document  7
   end tags  7
   inheritance  183
     contextual selectors  184
   logical tags  39, 43
   nested tags  9
   physical tags  39, 43
   start tags  7
   universal attributes
     CLASS  24
     ID  24
   universal tags  24
tags and attributes, listing. *see*
   Appendix A
TARGET, <A> attribute  66
   window values  66
TBODY  95
   attributes  95
terminology, how the World
   Wide Web works  3
text, as a hyperlink  67, 109

text, formatting  27
   <FONT>  28
   text emphasis and style  39
     fonts  39
   text layout
     breaking up text  28
     headings  27
       <Hn>  27
     horizontal rules  36
       example  38
     lists  30
text-based browsers
   <IMG> tag, ALT attribute
     informing browser that image
     is imagemap  74
TFOOT  95
   attributes  95
THEAD  95
   attributes  95
_top, TARGET  66
top, <A> NAME attribute
   lists in a document  71
TrueSpeech
   adding sound to your web pages
     60
   WAVs, converting to TrueSpeech
     60

## U

<UL>
   attributes  32
   bulleted lists  30
   list example  32
   syntax  31
universal attributes
   CLASS  24
   ID  24
universal tags  24

URL (Uniform Resource
     Locator) 3
  absolute URLs 64
  format of 63
  how the World Wide Web works
     2
  hypertext links
     creating hypertext links 63
  specifying servers 64
USEMAP, <IMG> attribute
  client-side imagemaps, creating
     78


**V**

values, attributes 10
variable assignments, VBScript.
     *see* Appendix E
variable testing functions,
     VBScript. *see* Appendix E
variables, JavaScript. *see* Appen-
     dix F
VBScript 161, 169-174
  *see also* Appendix E, VBScript
     reference
  advantages 169
  dialog box, example 169
  example
     button click 170
     form validation, example 173
  information, more sources 175
  support, browser 169, 175
  Visual Basic, relation to 169
video support, HTML 139
video-clips, embedding
  <IMG>, DYNSRC attribute 143
VRML worlds (virtual reality
     worlds), embedding
  <IMG>, DYNSRC attribute 143


**W**

W3C 1, 12
WAVs
  ActiveMovie 154
  converting to TrueSpeech 60
  LiveAudio 139
web pages
  *see also* HTML tags, frames,
     forms, images, graphics,
     animation, style sheets and
     tables
  HTML, creating the pages
     body 7, 18
     colors 20, 37, 40, 47
     comments, adding to your
        document 23
     head 7, 12
     revision numbers, adding to
        document 23
     text, formatting 27
web pages, interactive. *see*
     scripting
web site
  web pages
     *see also* HTML tags, frames,
        forms, images, graphics,
        animation, style sheets, and
        tables
     HTML, creating the pages 7
window object, JavaScript. *see*
     Appendix F
window, TARGET 66
World Wide Web, how it works
     2


**X**

x,y coordinates, imagemap files
     76, 79

# Tell Us What You Think

We've worked hard on this book to make it useful. We've tried to understand what you are willing to exchange your hard earned money for, and tried to make the book live up to your expectations.

Please let us know what you think about this book. Tell us what we did wrong, and what we did right. This isn't just marketing flannel—we really do all huddle around the e-mail to find out what you think. If you don't believe it, then send us a note. We'll answer, and we'll take whatever you say on board for future editions. The easiest way is to use e-mail:

**feedback@wrox.com**
**Compuserve 100063,2152**

You can also find more details about Wrox Press on our web site. Here you'll find the code from our latest books, sneak previews of forthcoming titles, and information about the authors and editors. You can order Wrox titles directly from the site, or find out where your nearest local bookstore with Wrox titles is located. The address of our site is:

**http://www.wrox.com**

## Beginning Linux Programming

Authors: Neil Matthew, Richard Stones
ISBN: 187441680
Price: $36.95  C$51.95  £33.99

The book is unique in that it teaches UNIX programming in a simple and structured way, using Linux and its associated and freely available development tools as the main platform. Assuming familiarity with the UNIX environment and a basic knowledge of C, the book teaches you how to put together UNIX applications that make the most of your time, your OS and your machine's capabilities.

Having introduced the programming environment and basic tools, the authors turn their attention initially on shell programming. The chapters then concentrate on programming UNIX with C, showing you how to work with files, access the UNIX environment, input and output data using terminals and curses, and manage data. After another round with development and debugging tools, the book discusses processes and signals, pipes and other IPC mechanisms, culminating with a chapter on sockets. Programming the X-Window system is introduced with Tcl/Tk and Java. Finally, the book covers programming for the Internet using HTML and CGI.

The book aims to discuss UNIX programming as described in the relevant POSIX and X/Open specifications, so the code is tested with that in mind. All the source code from the book is available under the terms of the Gnu Public License from the Wrox web site.

## Professional SQL Server 6.5 Server

Authors: Various    ISBN: 1874416494
Price: $44.95  C$62.95  £41.49

This book is not a tutorial in the complete product, but is for those who need to become either professionally competent in preparation for Microsoft exams or those DBAs needing real-world advice to do their job better. It assumes knowledge of databases and wastes no time on getting novices up to speed on the basics of data structure and using a database server in a Client-Server arena.

The book covers everything from installation and configuration right through to the actual managing of the server. There are whole chapters devoted to essential administrative issues such as transaction management and locking, replication, security, monitoring of the system and database backup and recovery. We've used proven techniques to bring robust code and script that will increase your ability to troubleshoot your database structure and improve its performance. Finally, we have looked very carefully at the new features in 6.5, such as the Web Assistant and Distributed Transaction Controller (DTC) and provided you with key practical examples. Where possible, throughout the book we have described a DBA solution in Transact SQL, Visual Basic and the Enterprise Manager.

## Instant VBScript

Authors: Alex Homer, Darren Gill
ISBN: 1861000448
Price: $25.00  C$34.95  £22.99

This is the guide for programmers who already know
HTML and another programming language and want
to waste no time getting up to speed. This book
takes developers right into the code, straight from
the beginning of Chapter 1. The first object is to get
the programmer to create their own 'reactive' web pages as quickly as
possible while introducing the most important HTML and ActiveX controls. This new
knowledge is quickly incorporated into more complex examples with a complete sample
site built early in the book.

As Internet Explorer is the browser that introduced VBScript, we also take a detailed
look at how to use VBScript to access different objects within the browser. We create
our own tools to help us with the development of applications, in particular a debugging
tool to aid error-trapping. Information is provided on how to build your own controls and
sign them to secure Internet download. Finally we take a look at server side scripting
and how with VBScript you can get the clients and server communicating freely. The
book is supported by our web site which contains all of the examples in the book in an
easily executable form.

## Beginning Visual C++

Author: Ivor Horton
ISBN: 1874416591
Price: $36.95  C$51.95  £34.49

The book starts by teaching the reader the basics
of C++ programming, covering such things as
using variables and the different variable types
available, how to perform loops and branches in
the code, using pointers and how to write structured programs
with functions. It then goes on to describe how to use C++ to write
object-oriented programs. This is used as an introduction to Windows
programming using Visual C++ and, in particular, how to use the Microsoft
Foundation Classes (MFC). The main parts of the MFC are divided into logical
sections, detailing such things as how to create and react to menus, drawing
to the window, displaying text, using dialog boxes, using files, how to write
your own DLL and finally how to write your own OCX.

**Wrox Press**
http://www.wrox.com/

## Instant SQL Programming

Author: Joe Celko
ISBN: 1874416508
Price: $29.95 C$41.95 £27.99

This is the fastest guide for developers to the most common database management language. If you want to get the most out of your database design, you will need to master Structured Query Language. SQL is the standard database language supported by almost every database management system on the market. This book takes you into the concepts and implementation of this key language quickly and painlessly, covering the complete ANSI standard SQL '92 from basic database design through to some of the more complex topics such as NULLS and 3-valued logic. We take you through the theory step-by-step, as you put into practice what you learn at each stage, gradually building up an example database while mastering essential techniques.

## Visual C++ MasterClass

Authors: Various   ISBN: 1874416443
Price: $49.95 C$69.95 £46.99

The book starts by covering software design issues related to programming with MFC, providing tips and techniques for creating great MFC extensions. This is followed by an analysis of porting issues when moving your applications from 16 to 32 bits.

The next section shows how you can use COM/OLE in the real world. This begins with an examination of COM technologies and the foundations of OLE (aggregation, uniform data transfer, drag and drop and so on) and is followed by a look at extending standard MFC OLE Document clients and servers to make use of database storage.

The third section of the book concentrates on making use of, and extending, the features that Windows 95 first brought to the public, including the 32-bit common controls, and the new style shell. You'll see how to make use of all the new features including appbars, file viewers, shortcuts, and property sheets.

The fourth section of the book provides a detailed look at multimedia and games programming, making use of Windows multimedia services and the facilities provided by the Game SDK (DirectX).

The final section covers 'net programming, whether it's for the Internet or the intranet. You'll see how to make the most of named pipes, mailslots, NetBIOS and WinSock before seeing how to create the corporate intranet system of your dreams using WinINet and ActiveX technology.

## Beginning WordBasic Programming

Author: Alex Homer
ISBN: 1874416869
Price: $39.95  C$55.95  £37.49

Starting with an introduction to WordBasic, macros and templates, the first section of the book goes on to look at the language elements of WordBasic. We cover everything from statements, functions and control structures to communicating with your users using dialog boxes. There are clear  discussions on the complex issues of the dynamic dialog!

In the second section of the book we look at Word in the workplace covering topics such as creating wizards and add-ins for using Word in a business environment. We show you how to manage large documents and how to automate some of the tasks faced by publishing companies such as controlling changes to documents, creating indexes and tables of contents and improving Word's printing options. We then go into detail on creating Help systems and HTML pages for the Internet. The book takes time out to look at Word Macro viruses and the complexities of DDE with Excel and Access.

All the source code from the book is included on the disk.

## Revolutionary Guide to Visual Basic 4 Professional

Author: Larry Roof
ISBN: 1874416370
Price: $44.95  C$62.95  £49.99

This book focuses on the four key areas for developers using VB4: the Win32 API, Objects and OLE, Databases and the VB development cycle. Each of the areas receives in-depth coverage, and techniques are illustrated using rich and complex example projects that bring out the real issues involved in commercial VB development. It examines the Win32 API from a VB perspective and gives a complete run-down of developing multimedia apps. The OLE section includes a help file creator that uses the Word OLE object, and we OLE automate Netscape Navigator 2. The database section offers complete coverage of DAO, SQL and ODBC, finishing with a detailed analysis of client/server database systems. The final section shows how to design, code, optimize and distribute a complete application. The book has a CD including all source code and a hypertext version of the book.

# Professional Java Fundamentals

Authors: Shy Cohen, Tom Mitchell, Andres Gonzalez, Larry Rodrigues, Kerry Hammil
ISBN: 1861000383     Price: $35.00  C$49.00  £32.49

Professional Java Fundamentals is a high-level, developer's book that gives you the detailed information and extended coverage you need to program Java for real, making the most of Java's potential.

It starts by thoroughly recapping the basics of Java, providing a language reference, looking at object-oriented programming issues and then at Java's fundamental classes. The book then details advanced language features, such as multithreading, networking, file I/O and native methods. There are five Abstract Windowing Toolkit chapters which provide in-depth coverage of event handling, graphics and animation, GUI building blocks and layout managers. Lastly, the book shows you how to design and implement class libraries in Java.

The book is supported by the Wrox web site, from which the complete source code is available.

# Professional ISAPI Programming in C++

Author: Michael Tracy    ISBN: 1861000664    Price: $40.00  C$56.00  £36.99

This is a working developer's guide to customizing Microsoft's Internet Information Server, which is now an integrated and free addition to the NT4.0 platform. This is essential reading for real-world web site development and expects readers to already be competent C++ and C programmers. Although all techniques in the book are workable under various C++ compilers, users of Visual C++ 4.1 will benefit from the ISAPI extensions supplied in its AppWizard.

This book covers extension and filter programming in depth. There is a walk through the API structure but not a reference to endless calls. Instead, we illustrate the key specifications with example programs.

HTTP and HTML instructions are issued as an appendix. We introduce extensions by mimicking popular CGI scripts and there's a specific chapter on controlling cookies. With filters we are not just re-running generic web code - these are leading-edge filter methods specifically designed for the IIS API.

## Professional NT Internet Information Server 2 Admin

Authors: Christian Gross et al
ISBN: 1861000480    Price: $40.00  C$56.00  £36.99

This book is a guide for real world, working Administrators who are about to, or have already installed the Microsoft Internet Information Server 2.0 on their NT 3.51/4.0 system.

Rather than regurgitate the install procedure, we take you through the essentials of setting up and configuring your Server for actual robust usage.

Once you're up and running you'll need access to proven techniques for performance analysis, troubleshooting and security - which we cover in dedicated chapters. For super-fine tuning and trimming we walk you through IIS within the NT registry and cover, in extensive detail, how to interpret and respond to the broad logging capabilities within NT & IIS.

Finally, we tackle the black art of multi-homing and load balancing. The Author has applied his experience from the first IIS 1.0 betas thru 2.0 to help you master this function of Inter/Intranet Servers. This book will enable you to run, and expand, a professional Web Site with absolute minimum downtime...and minimum user complaints.

## Professional Web Optimization

Author: Scott Ware et al   ISBN: 186100074x  Price: $40.00  C$56.00  £36.99

OK, you've installed your web server, and it's working fine and you've even got people interested in visiting your site - too many people, in fact. The real challenge is just starting you need to make it run faster, better and more flexibly.

This is the book for every webmaster who needs to improve site performance. You could just buy that new T-1 you've had your eye on, but what if the problem is really in your disk controller?  Or maybe it's the way you've designed your pages or the ISP you're using.

The book covers web server optimization for all major platforms and includes coverage of LAN performance, ISP performance, basic limits imposed by the nature of HTTP, IP and TCP. We also cover field-proven methods to improve static & dynamic page content from database access and the mysteries of graphic file manipulation and tuning.

If you've got the choice between spending fifteen thousand on a new line, or two hundred dollars in new hardware plus the cost of this book, which decision would your boss prefer?

## WROX

### WROX PRESS INC.

Wrox writes books for you. Any suggestions, or ideas
about how you want information given in your
ideal book will be studied by our team.
Your comments are always valued at Wrox.

Free phone in USA 800-USE-WROX          UK Tel. (0121) 706 6826   Fax   (0121) 706 2967
Fax (312) 397 8990

**NB.** If you post the bounce back card below in the UK, please send it to:
Wrox Press Ltd. 30 Lincoln Road, Birmingham, B27 6PA

---

## Instant HTML - Programmer's Reference

Name

Address

City ——————— State/Region

Country ——————— Postcode/Zip

E-mail

Occupation

How did you hear about this book?

☐ Book review (name)

☐ Advertisement (name)

☐ Recommendation

☐ Catalog

☐ Other

Where did you buy this book?

☐ Bookstore (name) ——————— City

☐ Computer Store (name)

☐ Mail Order

☐ Other

What influenced you in the
purchase of this book?

☐ Cover Design
☐ Contents
☐ Other (please specify)

How did you rate the overall
contents of this book?

☐ Excellent      ☐ Good
☐ Average        ☐ Poor

What did you find most useful about this book?

What did you find least useful about this book?

Please add any additional comments.

What other subjects will you buy a computer
book on soon?

What is the best computer book you have used this year?

*Note: This information will only be used to keep you updated
about new Wrox Press titles and will not be used for any other
purpose or passed to any other third party.*

0766

0766   Check here if you don't want a subscription to The Developer's Journal or to receive further support for this book.

**WROX**

**NB.** If you post the bounce back card below in the UK, please send it to:
Wrox Press Ltd. 30 Lincoln Road, Birmingham, B27 6PA

NO POSTAGE
NECESSARY
IF MAILED
IN THE
UNITED STATES

# BUSINESS REPLY MAIL

FIRST CLASS MAIL   PERMIT#64   LA VERGNE, TN

POSTAGE WILL BE PAID BY ADDRESSEE

WROX PRESS
1512 NORTH FREMONT
SUITE 103
CHICAGO IL 60622-2567